PREHISTORIC INDIA TO 1000 B.C

MAVEN BOOKS

PREHISTORIC INDIA TO 1000 B.C

Stuart Piggott

Professor of Prehistoric Archaeology

Edinburgh University

MAVEN BOOKS

Chennai   **Trichy**   **Tirunelveli**   **New Delhi**

MAVEN BOOKS

An Imprint of **MJP Publishers**

ISBN 978-93-88694-49-0 **Maven Books**

All rights reserved   No. 44, Nallathambi Street,
Printed and bound in India Triplicane, Chennai 600 005

MJP 778   © Publishers, 2020

Publisher : C. Janarthanan

Publisher's Note

The legacy of a country is in its varied cultural heritage, historical literature, developments in the field of economy and science. The top nations in the world are competing in the field of science, economy and literature. This vast legacy has to be conserved and documented so that it can be bestowed to the future generation. The knowledge of this legacy is slowly getting perished in the present generation due to lack of documentation.

Keeping this in mind, the concern with retrospective acquiring of rare books has been accented recently by the burgeoning reprint industry. Maven Books is gratified to retrieve the rare collections with a view to bring back those books that were landmarks in their time.

In this effort, a series of rare books would be republished under the banner, "Maven Books". The books in the reprint series have been carefully selected for their contemporary usefulness as well as their historical importance within the intellectual. We reconstruct the book with slight enhancements made for better presentation, without affecting the contents of the original edition.

Most of the works selected for republishing covers a huge range of subjects, from history to anthropology. We believe this reprint edition will be a service to the numerous researchers and practitioners active in this fascinating field. We allow readers to experience the wonder of peering into a scholarly work of the highest order and seminal significance.

Maven Books

CONTENTS

LIST OF PLATES

(Between pages 128 and 129)

LIST OF FIGURES IN TEXT

CHRONOLOGICAL TABLES

PREFACE

THIS book renders an account of our knowledge of Indian prehistory from the earliest times to the settlement of the Aryans in the north-west in the second half of the second millennium B.C. It does not pretend to be more than a stock-taking of our incomplete evidence and interpretation, as a preliminary and incentive to further work in the field. Some form of working hypothesis is essential, however drastically it may have to be revised, and I have therefore attempted to indicate what seem to me to be the nature and succession of the various human cultures making up the pattern of the earliest India.

Much of the material presented in the book is either new and hitherto unpublished or is a synthesis made for the first time. It is therefore inevitable that a great deal of technical detail has to be included, and much of the argument addressed to the specialist in oriental archaeology. But despite this, it is hoped that a coherent story of the general course of events in prehistoric India has been presented to the non-specialist reader.

The original work on which Chapters IV to VI are based was carried out in Indian museums (and to a very limited extent in the field) between 1942 and 1945 in the intervals of military intelligence duties. My gratitude is due to my friends on the Archaeological Survey of India who helped and encouraged me, notably the late Rao Bahadur Dikshit, formerly Director-General of the Survey, and Dr K. N. Puri. In 1944 Dr (now Professor) R. E. Mortimer Wheeler was appointed Director-General, and while we were both in India and since my return to Britain he has spared neither time nor trouble in giving me every assistance. It is a pleasant duty to record my gratitude here.

. In my own university, my colleagues Mr H. J. H. Drummond and Professor Myles Dillon (now of the Institute for Advanced Studies in Dublin) have been kind enough to read and criticize in draft Chapters II and VI respectively. In my discussion of the Aryan chariot I have been materially helped by Miss H. L. Lorimer, who most generously allowed me to read in typescript portions of her forthcoming book, *Homer and the Monuments*. I have been particularly fortunate in having had the opportunity of discussing the final drafts of Chapters III to VI with Dr Donald McCown of the Oriental Institute of the University of Chicago. Dr Claude Schaeffer's great work on the comparative chronology of west Asiatic sites in the period 2500 to 1100 B.C. appeared after my book had been written, but I have been able to incorporate certain revised dates bearing on the Indian problems. On the whole our conclusions, independently reached, were in relatively close agreement. The illustrations include much material published for the first time and are mainly based on original drawings by the author. Figs. 1, 3, 13–23 and 25 are by Mr L. F. Venables, and Figs. 4–10 and 12 by Miss E. M. Howard. The half-tone plates are from photographs supplied by the Archaeological Survey of India with the sanction of the Director-General.

To the Editor of this series, Professor M. E. L. Mallowan, I owe a debt of gratitude for his help in the construction and detail of the book, as well as for the initial invitation to attempt the synthesis which is here presented.

University of Edinburgh   STUART PIGGOTT
      1949

CHAPTER I

The Discovery of Prehistoric India

A mere man of letters, retired from the world, and allotting his whole time to philosophical or literary purposes, is a character unknown among European residents in India.

Asiatick Researches, 1 (1788).

THE distinction between 'history' and 'prehistory' in India is a peculiarly elusive one: one can say, with Henri Berr, 'India has had some episodes, but no history', and indeed this unfair generalization does come home when one is attempting to work out any sort of coherent chronological framework in periods allegedly within the realm of recorded Indian history; but nevertheless there are certain phases of ancient Indian culture which lie distinctly beyond any possible form of literary record. Western Asiatic prehistory in general ends with the appearance of the arts of writing in Mesopotamia, the adjacent parts of Iran, and in Egypt in the centuries immediately after 3000 B.C. With the art of writing there comes the record of dynasties, king-lists and the like, which, however controversial in details, yet can be interpreted to form the outline of a fairly reliable chronology in terms of actual years before the Christian era.

But in India, though writing was known and employed in the third and second millennia B.C., the peculiar script is still undeciphered, and the civilization which produced it is as prehistoric as Minoan Crete, also formally literate but with an unread script. This Indian script may have been used up to about 1500 B.C., but after this there is a complete gap in any known written documents on stone or clay or metal until we come to the inscriptions of Asoka set up about the middle of the third century B.C. For contemporary records of the intervening periods we have to depend on occasional contact with the Western world, where recorded history was an established discipline, or on the information to be extracted from the legendary or liturgical literature of India, orally transmitted for centuries.

So prehistoric India may in its widest sense embrace all human communities in the sub-continent, from the Old Stone Age to somewhere near the Christian era, or in many regions well beyond this limit. The discovery and interpretation of Indian prehistory must therefore rely on the same methods as have been used in Europe to study the course of human development before the advent of written history (which as a rule begins with the incorporation of the region in question into the Roman Empire). These methods, the techniques of archaeology, are, in their distinctively scientific forms of the present day, of comparatively modern growth, though many aspects have been familiar to Englishmen since the eighteenth century.

The introduction to India of European habits of thought, including the concept of history and of historical research, was brought about by men whose primary interests were not academic, though their education was sufficiently broadly based in the humanities for them to appreciate the value of such studies, and even to undertake them themselves in the intervals of busy professional lives in an exacting climate. The great contributions made to the knowledge of oriental linguistics and comparative philology by such figures as Sir William Jones or Carey of Serampore in the late eighteenth century were in themselves partly practical – the translation of the Bible, or an understanding of Hindu law were the immediate aims – though the purely academic issue was never forgotten. The foundation of the Asiatic Society of Bengal marks the establishment of antiquarian interests in India, as well as of the other aspects of research which, in the phrase of the time, would be classed as 'philosophical', and this antiquarianism would be prepared to concern itself with any period of India's past, historic or prehistoric, that it encountered.

But the fact that the earlier British settlements were in Bengal, a region still almost wholly unknown from the viewpoint of prehistoric antiquities, and where the natural luxuriance of vegetation renders any ruins invisible within a decade, gave little impetus to the study of field monuments of Indian antiquity. The great contribution of the Bengal School of antiquaries must always be their immense linguistic studies. And although field archaeology and the observation and record of monuments of antiquity, whether prehistoric earthworks or medieval abbeys, had become by the early nineteenth century a recognized English pastime among the educated squirearchy, India was not England. The Western Ghats were something very different from the mild pastoral slopes of Wiltshire: travel was difficult and dangerous; the country unmapped; distances were immense. It is therefore not surprising that archaeological field-work had to wait for altered circumstances, even were the men interested in such pursuits to be found in the services of the Company or the army.

Curiously enough, the discovery of the great prehistoric civilization of north-western India, with which this book largely deals, was the accidental result of Victorian enterprise in that most characteristic engineering activity of the age, railway construction. By accident, too, we know the circumstances in some detail, and they are worth recounting. In 1856 two brothers, John and William Brunton, were engaged in laying out and building the East Indian Railway from Karachi to Lahore – John was in charge of the southern section, his brother of that in the Punjab, from Multan northwards. John, in retirement, wrote a very delightful book of memoirs for his grandchildren, covering the years 1812 to 1899, and in this he tells how he had heard of a

ruined ancient city, Brahminabad, not very far from the line
of the railway he was building – 'I had been much exercised in my mind', he writes, 'how we were to get *ballast* for
the line of the Railway. If all I heard were true, this ruined
city, built of bricks, would form a grand quarry for ballast.'
Brahminabad (a medieval city) was therefore effectually
plundered by this uncompromising English engineer, and
the line laid.

Now the Multan–Lahore line ran not far from another
ancient city, by then a shapeless heap of huge, dusty mounds,
part of which had been robbed of bricks to build the modern
village of Harappā on the site. John must have told William
of his brilliant scheme for obtaining ballast for the track: a
prehistoric capital of the Punjab, Harappā, was plundered
as ruthlessly as Brahminabad had been, and today the trains
rumble over a hundred miles of line laid on a secure foundation of third-millennium brick-bats. During the brick-robbing antiquities of various kinds were found, and some of
the more curious kept by the workmen and the engineers.

The Brunton connexion with archaeology does not, however, end here. At Karachi, John Brunton was captain of the
Corps of Volunteers, and, himself an excellent shot, he had
trained a most efficient rifle team, which competed with the
regular Line Regiments stationed there. The general com-
manding 'was much annoyed at the repeated victories of the
Volunteer Rifle teams': his name was Cunningham, and
when he retired from active service in 1861 he was appointed
Director-General of an Archaeological Survey of Northern
India. General Cunningham is one of the greatest figures of
nineteenth-century Indian archaeology, and he had visited
Harappā in 1856, when the Brunton depredation was in progress. He obtained various antiquities from the workmen,
including engraved steatite seals of a type which we now
know to be characteristic of the prehistoric Indus and Punjab civilization, with the symbols of an unknown script upon

them, and the figure of a bull. Cunningham realized that these seals were something quite outside the range of Indian antiquities known to him: he felt they were extremely ancient and important. It was not until seventy years later that their true significance was recognized and the civilization now named from the site of Harappā was identified and defined.

Three years after Cunningham's visit to Harappā, in 1859, Darwin's *Origin of Species* was published, and in the same year Sir John Evans, with Falconer and Prestwich the geologists, made the famous visit to Abbeville where they were convinced of the geological antiquity of man-made flint implements associated with extinct species of mammals. In 1863 Lyell published his *Geological Evidence of the Antiquity of Man*: in Europe at least Palaeolithic Man was being recognized. But in this same year the geologist Bruce Foote found the first Indian palaeolithic implement near Madras, and the first step in the conception of the essential unity of the earlier Stone Age cultures throughout the Old World had been taken. Further discoveries were soon to be made, and recognized for what they were within the limits of the geological and archaeological knowledge of the day. Today we can with some show of probability refer these earliest stone tools from India to a date somewhere around four hundred thousand years ago.

After these initial recognitions of prehistoric India – Foote in the south establishing the existence of the Old Stone Age, Cunningham in the north showing the probable presence of ancient civilizations outside the range of recorded history – nineteenth-century antiquarian investigation in India turned more to the elucidation of the very complex problems of the allegedly historic eras. Although by the beginning of the present century communications within India had become very good and the political situation peaceful, archaeological field-work declined rather than increased,

and men of the calibre and range of interests of Sir William
Jones or General Cunningham were not to be found among
the British in India. It was as if the archaeological pursuits
of the pioneers of a century or more before had become as
outmoded and reprehensible as an Englishman smoking a
hookah or keeping a native mistress. Archaeological activity
was canalized into an inadequately-financed State depart-
ment, in which workers were comparatively few and their
technique was out of touch with European developments.

Though the Archaeological Survey of India did, within
its limited powers, achieve a considerable body of research in
Indian antiquities in the first quarter-century of its life, yet
it was not until the nineteen-twenties that attention was
directed to those prehistoric sites whose existence had been
half-suspected by Cunningham on the Harappā evidence.
It is to the credit of an Indian officer of the Survey, the late
Mr R. D. Banerji, that Harappā's great twin city, Mohenjo-
daro in Sind, was recognized in 1922 and excavations started
in that year. Work at Harappā had begun two years earlier
under the direction of Daya Ram Sahni, the work at the two
sites being co-ordinated by the then Director-General of
Archaeology in India, Sir John Marshall.

The Mohenjo-daro and Harappā excavations continued,
with interruptions, for several seasons – at the Sind site
from 1922 to 1931, and on the more northern site in the
Punjab from 1920 to 1921 and again from 1933 to 1934.
Concurrently with this large-scale excavation work, that
great explorer of Western Asia, the late Sir Aurel Stein,
undertook to survey the little-known areas of Baluchistan
on the extreme western edge of British India and to search
for prehistoric sites: his two journeys, in North Baluchistan
in 1926–27 and in South Baluchistan in 1927–28, brought to
light a vast amount of material of first-rate importance for
linking the prehistory of north-western India with the other
areas of ancient civilization in Iran and Mesopotamia.

Stein's campaigns were essentially those of reconnaissance: he made few excavations beyond trenching sites here and there, and collected mainly surface indications of ancient habitation in the form of the all-important potsherds which contribute so much to the archaeologist's knowledge of the ancient Orient. But Hargreaves partially excavated a cemetery and a settlement in Baluchistan in 1925, and produced important evidence which amplified Stein's own remarkable results.

Archaeological field-work, however, was not wanting in India itself, and the brilliant young Indian archaeologist N. G. Majumdar carried out a comprehensive survey of Sind and the Indus plain between 1927 and 1931, defining the extent of the minor prehistoric settlements within the area dominated by the cities of Harappā and Mohenjo-daro, and making certain very important excavations. He was undertaking fresh field-work in 1938 when he was killed by bandits in the Kirthar Hills.

One other major excavation was undertaken in a north-west Indian prehistoric site – that of the town of Chanhu-daro in Sind, which was dug by the late Ernest Mackay, who had been in charge of the later excavations at Mohenjo-daro in 1935–36. Here extremely important evidence was available for the final phases of the Harappā Civilization, as it was now beginning to be called.

Such, then, was the state of knowledge of prehistoric north-west India by the late 1930's. There were extensive excavations at two major cities and one smaller town in the Punjab and Sind, trial trenches dug in several sites in Sind and Baluchistan, and a fair idea of the geographical extent of the various prehistoric cultures as the result of Majumdar's and Stein's explorations. Stein made further discoveries in Rajputana and in Las Bela state in the early years of the 1939–45 war, again adding to our knowledge of the extent of the various types of regional cultures.

For the achievements of this field-work, under arduous conditions and in difficult terrain, one can have nothing but praise, but unfortunately the same cannot be said of much of the excavation which should provide us with the essential background for our study. Criticism is here inevitable, and also necessary if the Indian material is to be evaluated correctly. Of the broad facts of town-planning, streets, houses, drains, and so forth at Mohenjo-daro we have abundant evidence, even if its detail is sketchy, and the recognition of the great urban civilization of the Indus Valley would hardly have been possible without the wholesale methods of exploration which were in fact employed. But the reports on Harappā, Mohenjo-daro and Chanhu-daro published in eight impressive quarto volumes between 1931 and 1943 cannot, in all fairness, be said to approach the archaeological standards set in European archaeology by the 1890's, and in common employment since the 1920's.

That there is no inherent impossibility in applying these standards and methods to Indian excavations has been happily, but all too briefly, shown by the recent work carried out in India by an archaeologist trained in, and an outstanding exponent of, the highest standards in European techniques. Professor R. E. Mortimer Wheeler's excavations on Indian sites between 1945 and 1948 have cut ruthlessly across the old traditions whereby stratification was ignored and 'levels' were fixed by measurement from a datum. By this 'incredible system', in Wheeler's words, 'the so-called "stratification" of the Indus Valley civilization is dominated, not by local observation, but at long range by the sea-level at Karachi. ... It is a survival of an obsolete device evolved in the alluvial plains of the great river-valleys of Egypt and Mesopotamia as a rough substitute for exact observation in ill-controlled "mass-excavations". It has no place whatsoever in the technique of modern field-archaeology.' The 1946 excavations of the hitherto unrecognized defences of the citadel of Harappā have given a new significance to the city, and have established the first sure facts in the stratigraphy of the site.

An example of what can be done has at least been set for Pakistan and India, and it is hoped that the tradition may be carried on by future workers who have received some training in the methods new to India, if familiar to us in England. Only by the frequent interchange of persons and ideas in European and Oriental archaeology can these standards be preserved and kept up to date. It is largely the British who have been to blame in the past for inadequate financial support of the Archaeological Survey of India, and for the failure to keep it abreast of developments in excavation technique.

Side by side with the collection of material in India and Baluchistan, new work was being carried out in other countries of Western Asia. Iran in particular was yielding up the secrets of her prehistory to the excavations of the French and Americans in the 1930's, and the indefatigable Sir Aurel Stein made a noteworthy series of explorations from Fars to Lake Urmia which filled in the geographical background for the distribution of the cultures found in stratified contexts in the excavations. Already in 1933 Professor Gordon Childe had made a penetrating synthesis of the North-west Indian material in its relation to the other cultures of the most ancient East; ten years later the accidents of war brought me to New Delhi and enabled me to start on a revision of Childe's basic work in the light of the accumulated new knowledge of the intervening decade, and this has been continued since the war by Dr. Donald McCown of the Oriental Institute of Chicago.

Investigation of the Indian Stone Age was neglected, after the pioneer work of Bruce Foote, until the 1930's, when Mr Miles Burkitt turned to the interpretation of certain South Indian material at much the same time as other

workers were investigating ancient stone industries and geological phenomena in the north-west. This culminated in a
joint expedition by the Universities of Yale and Cambridge
in 1935, led by de Terra and Patterson, and their work has
been supplemented by that of Movius and Krishnaswami.
The studies of these investigators have made us acquainted
with an extremely important series of Old Stone Age human
industries associated with geological deposits which, in the
river-terraces of the Himalayan region at all events, seem to
offer promising correlations with the known sequence in
Northern Europe.

But there are still enormous gaps in our knowledge of
Indian prehistory, and that just mentioned between the
Old Stone Age and the earliest settlements in Baluchistan is
outstanding in immensity and obscurity. Hardly less obscure
are the happenings after the collapse of the Harappā Civilization in the middle of the second millennium B.C. – a period
traditionally associated with the arrival from the west of the
Indo-European-speaking tribes who called themselves the
Aryans, but scarcely attested by direct archaeological evidence. Nevertheless the time is ripe for a stocktaking and an
attempt to assess our present knowledge of prehistoric India
before new work and up-to-date techniques once again
advance the horizon of our knowledge.

Notes to Chapter I

For a general account of archaeological work in India, see *Revealing
India's Past* (ed. J. Cumming, 1939); earlier work on the Palaeo-
lithic period is commented on by Krishnaswami in *Ancient India*,
no. 3 (1947), 13. *John Brunton's Book* was edited by Professor J. H.
Clapham and published in 1939. In addition to the special reports
on excavations referred to later in this book, the Archaeological
Survey of India has published a long series of *Memoirs* and *Annual
Reports*. The latter series is now in abeyance, and a publication,
Ancient India, was started in 1946, four parts of which have
appeared. Since the formation of the Dominions of India and of

Pakistan there has been no announcement on future archaeological publications.

Detailed criticism of the standard of the previous excavations in India is to be found in *Ancient India*, no. 3 (1947), 143–149, by Professor R. E. M. Wheeler, then Director-General of Archaeology in India, with a comment on Chanhu-daro by myself.

CHAPTER II

Prelude – The Indian Stone Age

> They think these finished specimens of skill in the art of chip-
> ping prove that the human race is of greater antiquity than has
> been previously supposed; and the fact that there is no other
> relic to prove the position they consider of no moment what-
> ever.
>
> T. L. Peacock, *Gryll Grange* (1860).

THE archaeological record of prehistoric human settlement
in India goes back to a period of geological remoteness
whose immensity leaves it without very much meaning to the
ordinary person. The vast periods of time involved in geological reckoning, even in those final phases of the natural
sequence where traces of man first appear, though they can
be expressed in terms of solar years, still leave the mind
bewildered. Such reckoning, however, has been attempted,
and the results have met with some measure of agreement;
the methods employed involve a correlation between the
geological phenomena of the Pleistocene period and the
fluctuating curve of solar radiation with which those happenings seem to be closely connected, and the result has
been to place the beginning of the period somewhere about
600,000 years ago. To this fantastically remote time seem to
belong the earliest tools made of chipped stone which attest
the existence of man as a tool-using being in the Old
World – a hundred thousand years later there is no doubt
about the relatively competent technique that has developed
in making stone tools to certain recognizable patterns, dis-
tinguishable at least in Europe and probably in Africa. To
this time too may belong the skull from Modjokerto in Java,
claimed by some geologists as the earliest representative

of the *Pithecanthropus* race of primitive man. From this
time onwards tools and fossils carry on the story of man's
earlier evolution across the millennia to the coming of
'modern' times, which from the geological standpoint is a
mere fifteen or twenty thousand years ago.

The whole of this epoch constitutes the major geological
division of the Quaternary Period and the sub-division
known as the Pleistocene phase. Archaeologically the human
remains and tools from Pleistocene deposits are classed together as the Palaeolithic or Old Stone Age phase of man's
development, and both the Pleistocene and the Palaeolithic
are further divided into two major subdivisions, Lower and
Upper. But there are other important subdivisions of the
Pleistocene geological sequence, linked to those fluctuations
in solar radiation already mentioned.

Throughout the Pleistocene there occurred certain enormous rhythmic climatic changes, spread over many thousand years but constituting alternate phases of comparative
heat and cold in the northern regions of the Old World, and
probably corresponding phases of wet or dry climate farther
south. The cold phases, during which the limit of what is
now the North Polar ice-sheet spread south in Europe to
form a continuous ice mass to the River Thames in England
and in the Himalayas of North India reached the foothills,
are the familiar Ice Ages or glacial periods, separated by
interglacial phases, both of varying periods of duration.
Four main glacial periods have been recognized, separated
by three interglacials, and the study of Palaeolithic man is
closely linked to these great changes, which were directly
responsible for the limits of land available for human occupation or settlement, and for the climate beyond the fringes
of the zone of permanent, uninhabitable ice.

The Palaeolithic period is one of immense, monumental
inanition over millennia, with human progress, as deduced
from the tangible remains of man's handiwork that have

survived, making but the slowest imaginable moves. During
the 'Great Interglacial' period, probably lasting for nearly
200,000 years, the changes in the type of tool manufactured
are matters of archaeological minutiae which reveal a slow
increase in mastery of the technique of fracturing and
flaking stones to the required shape; if in the later Pleistocene there appears some acceleration in modifying tools and
weapons, this is only on the geological time-scale in which
fifty thousand years may become a significant period of
change.

And as in time so in space the Palaeolithic cultures have
an enormous duration. At a given period in the Pleistocene
one can take, almost without selection, tools from South
India, Africa and South England which show identical techniques of manufacture and form, and in all three areas essentially the same evolution can be traced leading up to and
developing from these forms and methods of manufacture.
Tool-making traditions in the Palaeolithic have trans-con-
tinental distributions: what happens at one end of the area
seems to be happening more or less simultaneously at the
other.

Throughout the Palaeolithic period the basis of subsist-
ence was hunting and food-gathering in one form or another,
and the evidence permits us to visualize a small population
living in tiny groups of families or small tribes, following the
animals they killed for food over great tracts of country.
Life was impermanent, precarious and isolated, and ideas
could not readily be transmitted from group to group. Did
psychologists permit us to believe in a group mind, we might
well see it as responsible, at an early stage of the evolution
of the human consciousness, for the slow changes in tool
techniques over vast regions of the earth's habitable surface.

The surviving elements of Palaeolithic material culture
are confined to tools made of imperishable stone, and until
Upper Palaeolithic times we hardly have even the certain

traces of any human settlement, if only a hunters' camping-place. Discarded stone tools lying in river-gravels, an occasional human fossil, and frequently those of the animals hunted, are almost all we have to rely on for our study of Lower Palaeolithic man and his achievements. All archaeological study suffers from the accident of survival – the least perishable substances will survive alone out of a people's material culture – but of no period of prehistory is our knowledge so imperfect as of the Palaeolithic. The study of these remote periods must always have a certain inhumanity and lack relationship to anything we know or can visualize within the comprehensible bounds of human history. It is, I think, impossible to do more in describing the earlier phases of the Indian Stone Age than to show how the known stone industries fit into our knowledge of the general pattern of human evolution in the Old World, and their relationship in time and space. Within these limits it is possible to indicate India's place in the Palaeolithic so far as we have the evidence available: to treat the enormous period of the most ancient hunting peoples as a prelude to the periods which follow the introduction of agriculture in the fourth or fifth millennium B.C., and from which the bulk of our information on prehistoric India comes.

In the geological deposits of the lower slopes of the Himalayas of the Kashmir and Punjab region it has been possible to trace a succession of glacial periods, each indicated by typical products of glacial action. These in turn can be related to the structure of the river valleys in the Rawalpindi area, where terraces have been formed by the flow of the river cutting into the detritus brought down in an earlier phase. These problems of glacial geology are complex, and here, without involving the reader in a discussion of its difficulties, one can do no more than stress this complexity. But the combined evidence from glacial phenomena and river-terraces in Northern India suggests that there were in

Pleistocene times five glacial periods ('Ice Ages') separated
by interglacials in that area.

The importance of this sequence is that it appears to run
more or less parallel with that long ago determined first in
the Alps and later in Northern Europe. The Indian glaciations would appear to correspond to the main Ice Ages of
Europe (excluding the first), and the last glaciations in India
seem equivalent to the three periods of maximum intensity
in the last European glaciation. As, both in Europe and in
India, man-made tools have been found in many of the
river terraces associated with this sequence of climatic
changes, one would expect that the long-distance correlation
established between the natural phenomena would be repeated in the tool types – and this is indeed the case, with
parallel evolution in techniques taking place in both areas.
It is probable that the North-west Indian climatic sequence
can also be extended to take in Upper Burma and North
China, and there is reason to think that the natural forces
(probably mainly changes in solar radiation) responsible
for the glacial and interglacial periods of the more northerly
areas may also have produced the alternating periods of
comparatively wet or dry climate (pluvial and interpluvial
periods) implied by geology and the remains of fossil
animals in South India and in East Asia.

Against this natural background of changing climatic
phases in Asia and Europe we can trace certain important
major groupings of tool types, which presumably represent
a similar grouping of human traditions or techniques. While
the process of fracturing or flaking stone into the shape
required for a specific purpose – cutting or cleaving, for
instance – has certain basic principles in common wherever
such manufacture is carried out, yet nevertheless there is
some indication that within certain large geographical areas
there was a preference, if nothing more, for characteristic
techniques throughout the Lower Palaeolithic. The primary

division of techniques, suggested by archaeologists when the possibility of making these major groupings was first envisaged, was into *core* and *flake* tools. In the former group, a tool is made by flaking or chipping away from a parent block until the resultant form is satisfactory – a principle broadly analogous to sculpture. In flake tools, however, the first process is to detach a large flake from a block of stone and then to work this into the finished tool. The production of core tools naturally produced flakes in the very process of manufacture, and these were in turn often made into tools, but there is always a very high preponderance of tools made from the core. In the flake industries, on the other hand, the core technique appears only when contact with true core-tool cultures can be traced.

This original simple division has by some authorities been modified by the introduction of a third major group, allied to the flake industries but considered worthy of separate distinction, and comprising tools presumed to be used as choppers. This *chopper-chopping tool* group (as it has been called, very clumsily) is of particular importance to Asia, since it includes certain distinctive North Indian Lower Palaeolithic industries which are regarded by other archaeologists as within the flake cultures, without the necessity of further distinction. In South and Central India, however, there is abundant evidence of core cultures about which there is no dispute, and in certain regions fusion in techniques between the two main Indian groups can be seen.

In India itself, unfortunately, no remains of the skeletons of Palaeolithic man have been discovered, though Asia has produced some of the most important evidence of man's early evolution. In the Upper Miocene deposits of the Siwalik Hills (within the Tertiary geological period, and separated from the Pleistocene by the intervening Pliocene phase, and many million years) have been discovered important remains of fossil apes which seem to have occupied a place

in the evolution of the common stock from which man and
the contemporary anthropoids eventually sprung. The evidence of these apes, and of others from Africa, probably
equally ancient, suggests that certain elements in the skull of
modern man (the structure of the lower jaw, for instance)
are extremely ancient, and are foreshadowed in these fossils,
and that the process of divergent specialization, which
has gone on over the millennia, is partly one in which
the skulls of contemporary apes are more specialized,
and more remote from the common ancestral form, than
our own.

By the Middle Pleistocene it is possible to distinguish two
main groups of fossil men, the Neoanthropic and Palaeoanthropic stems, and as they have already by this time reached
a considerable degree of divergence, the period in which the
undifferentiated common ancestors lived must be very remote. In Europe at least there is evidence that the Neoanthropic group, whose skulls differ little from that of modern
man, is associated with the type of tools within the core cultures, and that the Palaeoanthropic stem, whose skulls bear
greater resemblances to the common man-ape stock, may
possibly be associated with the chopper-tool culture in East
Asia; certainly by later Palaeolithic times the descendants of
this particular group are essentially makers of flake-tools.
The East Asian representative of the Palaeoanthropidae is
the famous *Pithecanthropus* of Java, and his relatives from
Choukoutien in China. In the latter site rough quartzite
implements associated with the human fossils have been considered as comparable to others from North India and other
Asiatic localities, as we shall see later.

To sum up, the background of the Old Stone Age in India
is the presence of climatic phases during the Pleistocene
which can be correlated with similar phases in Europe, and
probably with others in South India and Africa, where
pluvial conditions replace glaciations. Against this natural

setting can be set two main traditions in implement manufacture – one in the north of India related to other similar
flake or chopper industries known from several East Asiatic
sites; the other, in the south, belonging to the core-tool family whose distribution includes Africa and Western Europe.
While no human fossils have been found, the evidence from
elsewhere in the Old World suggests the tentative conclusion
that tools of the flake or chopper tradition may be the products
of the 'Ancient' or Palaeoanthropic stem in human evolution
(such as *Pithecanthropus*), and that those of the core technique
were made by the earliest representatives of *Homo sapiens* in
the 'Modern' or Neoanthropic family. With this outline in
our minds, we can turn to consider the Indian evidence in
slightly more detail.

The earliest indication of tool-making men in Pleistocene
India appears to be in the last phase of the Second Glaciation or at the beginning of the Second (Great) Interglacial.
In deposits of this geological age in Northern India, in the
Potwar (Rawalpindi) region, and perhaps again in Central
India, in the Upper Narbada valley (Hoshangabad, Jubbul-
pore, district) large rough flake-tools have been found, and
should belong to the very end of the Lower Pleistocene
phase and be contemporary with the earlier Pithecanthro-
poids in Java. In West and Central Europe at this time both
core and flake industries are recognizable in distinctive
forms. The Indian flake-industry is known as the *Pre-Soan*
industry, to indicate its chronological position before the
main series of Lower Palaeolithic cultures in the valley of
the Soan River, a tributary of the Indus in the Potwar region
of the Punjab. These early flake-tools have no close relatives
in other Asiatic industries, as far as these are known at
present.

In the Second Interglacial Period of the Himalayas, however, well-defined human industries belonging to the two
main groups already referred to can be traced in river

terraces and other deposits in North-West India. It will be
convenient to deal first with those tools which come within the
flake (or chopper) family, which in India, as far as is known
at present, are confined to a series of localities in the valley
of the Soan, and the Indus, in Poonch, near Jhelum and in
the Salt Range. This industry, which can be divided into
three phases, has been called the *Soan Culture*.

The Early Soan industry contains two main types of im·
plements, one series made from rounded pebbles, which of
course exercise some control over the form of the implement
as only the minimum flaking necessary to obtain a choppe
shape is found. Such massive pebble-tools have been foun
in approximately contemporary (or rather earlier) Palaeo
lithic deposits in South and East Africa, but the simplicity of
the form, so greatly dictated by the raw material, makes i
dangerous to insist on such comparisons. The other type.
within the Early Soan comprise thick, heavy flakes and th
equally crude parent cores from which they were detached
These flake-implements have been compared to the earliest
flake-tools of Europe in the Clactonian industries, and some
archaeologists would therefore include this aspect of the
Soan within a general 'Clactonian' family of flake-tools
distributed over most of the Old World. But recently it has
been suggested by the American archaeologist Movius that
a new group of chopper-tools must be recognized, allied to
the Clactonian flake-tools but not part of it. In this chopper·
tool group Movius would group the Soan industry as well as
other similar industries in Burma (the Anyathian), Malaya
(Tampanian), and Java (Pajitanian), and probably also the
rough quartzite and limestone tools found with *Pithecan·
thropus* at Choukoutien. If this last correlation were correct,
it would afford a very valuable link between tool-groups and
types of fossil man, and give more reality to the East Asiatic
chopper-tool group of the Middle Pleistocene as the products of the Palaeoanthropic branch of the human family.

But at least we can say that the Soan industry is East Asiatic in affinities. Intervening sites between Northern India and Burma should appear if field-work is undertaken.

The Soan industry develops in technique as the geological context becomes later – the Early Soan is mainly of early Middle Pleistocene date, within the Second Interglacial period and, dated by the solar radiation method, between about 400,000 and 200,000 years ago. By the end of this period, however, technical developments in stone-flaking can be seen dividing into two the industries which become distinct in the Late Soan industries, apparently beginning in Third Glacial times, but surviving later. In one of these the pebble element is retained in a pronounced form, but in the other this primitive feature is discarded and use is made of a technique of preparing the core before detaching the flake similar to that which appears more or less contemporaneously in South Africa, Palestine, and Western Europe. It is generally felt, however, that the appearance of this particular technique need indicate no more than parallel evolution in flake production in the various regions in which it occurs. These final phases of the Soan industries persist into the Last Interglacial period and beyond, and are distributed far afield in North-West India.

The core-tool family of Lower Palaeolithic stone implements is represented by a large number of finds, centred in South-East India but also coming from Central and Western India and even represented in the area of the Soan Culture itself. To this Indian representative of the core-tool group the name *Madras Industry* (or *Madras-Acheul*) has been given from its area of apparent main concentration.

The appearance of a few tools of this type from four sites of Second Interglacial date in the river-terrace system of the Soan and Indus enables us to correlate the industry with the glacial sequence and so with a general chronological scheme, and the persistence there of the cultural tradition

the type of tool represents is shown by the occurrence of
evolved forms of core-tools with Late Soan types in one site
in the same region (Chauntra). In South and Central India,
where evidence of pluvial periods replaces that of glaciation,
core-tools have been found in a pluvial period which may
equate in part with the Second Interglacial phase, but which
goes on into Third Interglacial times or even later.

The tool-type of the Madras Industry is essentially pear-
shaped or oval, flaked on both faces in such a way as to produce a continuous cutting edge – the so-called 'hand-axe'.
There is constant interaction between the Madras and Soan
industries, and, as one would expect, the core-tool element
is strongest in the south and south-east, while the flake or
chopper types dominate when one comes farther north –
e.g. in the Kurnool area. A development in technique can
be traced over the long range of finds from Early Middle to
Early Upper Pleistocene times, in which this greater skill is
acquired in the process of flaking, with the consequent production of more elaborately finished – and smaller – tools.
There is some evidence that suggests that the primary flaking
in the Madras industry was done (as in the Soan) with a
hammer-stone, and the finer work of the later phases with a
bar of wood or horn, which alone will reproduce the characteristic flat flake-scars. (This has been shown experimentally
in the study of the European Palaeolithic industries.) But
many of the hand-axes of the Madras in the Kurnool area,
where Soan influence was strong, are more or less manufactured by Soan techniques of stone-flaking. In addition to
the regions mentioned, tools of the Madras Industry have
been found in India as far south as the Rivers Cauvery and
Vaigai, in the west round Bombay and north of the Narbada, and north-east as far as the upper reaches of the Son,
a tributary of the Ganges.

The Madras Industry is almost exactly similar, in its tool
techniques and their evolution, to the Lower Palaeolithic

industries of South Africa of the Stellenbosch group – recently re-named, in terms of the analogous French sequence of core-tools, 'Chelles-Acheul'. This use of French terminology reminds us that the core-tool province stretches north-westwards to include Europe and Southern England, and that in all areas – India, South Africa, Western Europe – strong similarities, sometimes amounting to identity, can be seen in the hand-axes and their techniques of manufacture. To this vast Eurafrican province, then, the South Indian Palaeolithic cultures belong, and, as far as is known at present, represent its farthest eastward extension. Probably the nearest core-tool area geographically is that of Arabia, where traces of similar industries exist. If the evidence from Swanscombe, in England, is accepted as representative of the whole province, we could attribute the core-tools to *Homo sapiens*, a skull almost indistinguishable from contemporary types having been found associated with a core-tool industry of the Acheul (or Madras) type at this site.

It must be confessed that the evidence of stone tools in the Lower Palaeolithic of India takes us a very small way in visualizing anything of the life of their makers, but other areas of the world have contributed practically nothing more. We seem to have the imperishable remnant of the material culture of nomadic hunting groups, who may have been well equipped with other objects made of such impermanent substances as wood, fibre, grass, leaves or other organic materials such as skin and leather. The use to which the Soan choppers or the Madras hand-axes were put is unknown: we can guess, more or less unprofitably, at many uses to which a simple cutting or hacking tool might be turned, from chopping at meat or wood to grubbing for roots. The most striking feature of the Lower Palaeolithic industries is their immense duration – from about 400,000 to the end of the last glaciation, perhaps 10,000 years ago –

and the slowness of human progress in technological achievement in that time.

The final phases of the Palaeolithic period in India are still obscure. There seems to have been some continuance of the later Soan tradition in flake-tools with the characteristic technique of core preparation (the so-called Levallois technique) surviving in more than one area (the Punjab, the Narbada, and in South India) into the last Glacial period and possibly beyond, and it has been claimed that certain stone industries from Kurnool in the Dekkan and near Bombay represent a new type of tool based not on the massive flake but on the slender blade detached from a core.

Now such industries are characteristic of the final phases of the Palaeolithic in Europe and in certain parts of Western Asia, during the Last Glacial Period. Comparative study of these industries has shown that they are likely to be divisible into three main early groups, all of which originate outside Europe and probably in Western Asia. Of these groups, which in European stratified sites can be shown as representing successive waves of folk-movement westwards, the second is the Aurignacian (formerly known as Middle Aurignacian), and is not known to occur farther east than Palestine and Transcaucasia; but it has been suggested that its point of origin should lie at least as far away as the Iranian plateau, and some of the Chinese industries of the Shuitungkou River suggest that Aurignacian forms may exist there. The third of these early Upper Palaeolithic industries, the Gravettian, is in fact known from sites as far east as Kurdistan, in Northern Iraq, and it is clear that the identification of true blade industries in India, whether or not related to the groups already known, would throw a very considerable light on Upper Palaeolithic problems.

For the present there is not enough material to form a basis for discussion, and the most hopeful line of research would seem to be the excavation of caves and rock-shelters

in India such as were so often inhabited as winter retreats by
Upper Palaeolithic man in Europe and West Asia. Bone implements, described as similar to the Upper Palaeolithic
Magdalenian forms, were found in 1884 in a cave near Kurnool with bones of extinct mammals, but they have been
lost and nothing further is known about them; it is inci-
dently most improbable that they were Magdalenian in
type, since this culture is one restricted almost entirely to
France. It will be seen however (p.237 below) that certain
metal harpoons from the Ganges Valley, of mid second
millennium B.C. date, are copies of barbed bone or antler
points in the Upper Palaeolithic or Mesolithic tradition.

In passing, mention must be made of the paintings found
in certain Central Indian rock-shelters, as in those at Singan-
pur. These paintings have been claimed as Upper Palaeolithic and compared with the well-known series in the caves
of Western France and Spain, but Gordon's recent work has
shown that not only is there no evidence of a Palaeolithic
date, but that inferential evidence makes it difficult to date
any of the paintings before the fifth century B.C. at the earliest. Conclusive evidence for the existence in India of any
Upper Palaeolithic cultures comparable to those of Europe
or the Near East is, therefore, still to be found. It may not be
without significance that the Anyathian industry of Burma
(a chopper-tool culture comparable to Soan) appears to have
continued uninterrupted by outside influences until the local
Neolithic, which may well have been a very recent event.

In Europe and North and East Africa, and again in Palestine, it has been shown that in immediately post-glacial
times, when the ice was making its final retreat to within its
present bounds, various regional industries or cultures grew
up, based on Upper Palaeolithic traditions of blade-tools
but showing a marked tendency to reduce these blades to
often absurdly small dimensions, presumably as the arma-
ment of composite tools made largely of wood or bone. In a

large number of regions in South or Central India, south of
a line joining the Upper Ganges to the Rann of Cutch, and
sporadically elsewhere (in Sind and in North-West Punjab)
there occur stone industries consisting of such dimunitive
implements, which are comparable to the Capsian group of
post-glacial, Mesolithic industries of Europe and North
Africa. The Capsian industry is represented in Kenya, and
it has been claimed that certain skeletons from Gujerat,
allegedly of the same date as a local microlithic industry,
show Hamitic or Negroid characteristics. Whatever weight
we give to this evidence, there is nevertheless a likelihood
that the Indian microlithic industries are not unconnected
with those moves from North Africa eastwards which can be
traced in other regions.

The Indian microlithic industries have not been found at
any site in a geological deposit of known age, nor in such
stratigraphical relationship to earlier human industries that
a connexion with the final phases of Palaeolithic cultures can
be shown. But there is evidence that the industries survived
in certain areas at least down to early historic times. They
may truly represent a transition from Palaeolithic industries
to those of a more advanced or specialized type, but this
transition need not have taken place at a period as remote as
the parallel phenomenon in countries farther west, since the
Palaeolithic cultures themselves may have a very long post-
glacial survival.

The fact that the microlithic industries of India seem to
represent the arrival of new peoples, probably from the west,
rather than the fact that they are an evolution out of a more
or less non-existent Upper Palaeolithic blade industry, re-
lates them more to those cultures which follow them than to
those they supersede. It is not known whether the Indian
communities which made the microliths were (as their counterparts in Europe were) hunters and food-gatherers in the
Palaeolithic tradition or whether they were agriculturalists;

still less is it known whether it can be shown that in India, as in certain other regions of the Old World, there existed a stage of human progress in which the arts of agriculture and stock-breeding were practised, but metal was not known – a so-called Neolithic stage of development.

There certainly exist a vast quantity of ground stone axes of the type known in 'Neolithic' contexts elsewhere, from many sites scattered over the country, not infrequently associated with microliths, but so far no distinctive habitation site has been found which places allegedly 'Neolithic' material in stratigraphical relationship to the earliest known agricultural communities in Baluchistan or Sind. Typology or colour-staining of the surface of an axe is a very untrustworthy guide to antiquity, and claims for a high dating for surface finds on these grounds can be ignored. On the other hand, certain stratified sites have produced ground stone axes and pottery in a distinct cultural layer, and these need to be considered.

The South Indian stone-axe cultures have been put on a new footing by Wheeler's recent work in Mysore State. His earlier work on the Coromandel coast in 1945 had provided the first fixed date in the sequence of indigenous cultures in that region, by establishing their relationship to imported coins and pottery of the first century A.D. in a Roman trading-post at Arikamedu near Pondicherry. With dated types of native pottery now identified it was possible to use this evidence in Mysore in conjunction with finds of Roman coins of the same period, and in the Chitaldrug region a sequence was established as follows:

I. *Stone Axe Culture*. This was characterized by polished, pointed-butt axes of local rock and a crude microlithic industry in jasper, flint, agate, and crystal. Two small copper objects show that metal was known but extremely scarce. Pottery was hand-made, rarely painted or incised.

The beginnings of this phase may go back to early in the
first millennium B.C., and it was followed about 200 B.C.
by a

II. *Megalithic Culture*. This was an intrusive iron-using
culture, making wheel-turned pottery and building elaborate megalithic tombs. It continued into the first century A.D., overlapping with

III. The historical *Andhra Culture* dated in its earlier
phases by Roman coins of the early first century A.D. and
pottery of Arikamedu types, and continuing to the third
century A.D.

This evidence, then, shows that in certain areas of South
India at least the 'Neolithic' cultures are of relatively late
date, surviving almost to the dawn of recorded history.
Wheeler has published a map showing the known distribution of stone axes and microliths in India; they appear to
occur almost exclusively to the south and east of a line from
the Gulf of Cambay to Lucknow, with a few microlithic
sites between Cambay and Karachi.

Extravagant claims have been made for a very early Neolithic culture in Kashmir. The excavations at Burzahom,
between Srinagar and Gandarbal, do not seem to have been
very satisfactory, and the report upon them is certainly most
inadequate. A sequence was found as follows:

Layer A – Buddhist, fourth century A.D.

Layer B – Sherds of highly polished black ware and
others with incised patterns.

Layer C – Unweathered post-glacial loess, 9 feet in
thickness, at the base of which, on virgin
soil, was a hearth with polished axes, bone
awls, and pottery.

In interpreting this sequence the excavators compared the
pottery from Layer B with the Jhangar Ware described in

Chapter.V, which is itself undated but is certainly later than
the middle of the second millennium B.C. On the other hand
the polished ware sounds as though it might be Wheeler's
'Northern Black Polished Ware', known for instance from
Taxila, dated between the fifth and second centuries B.C.,
and spread widely over the Mauryan kingdom. But, whatever the date of Layer B, it is obviously highly dangerous to
regard the 9 feet of loess as implying such a passage of time
that the Neolithic material at its base would be of an antiquity 'far beyond' the earliest Mesopotamian agricultural
cultures of the fifth or sixth millennia B.C., as has been done
by the excavators. There is really no valid reason for regarding the Kashmir Neolithic culture as of any proven antiquity
beyond perhaps the first millennium B.C., followed locally
by a relatively rapid accumulation of wind-deposited soil.

In Sind, at Rohri and Sukkur, and again near Karachi at
Drigh Road, a characteristic industry made from chert or
flint from the Sukkur limestone has been known for many
years. Some long thin blades and the conical cores from
which they have been struck are precisely comparable to
those from the Harappā Culture of c. 2500–1500 B.C., and
the rather earlier cultures such as Amri in Sind or those in
the Zhob Valley, which again produce a similar flint industry. But other implements suggest an independent and
probably early tradition, while the presence of archaic survivals, such as Levallois flaking and oval hand-axes, in addition to the cores and blades, does suggest that the Rohri
industry may be of relatively great antiquity. Of the date
of the apparently comparable industry from Raichur in
Hyderabad (Dekkan) State one can say nothing.

Our evidence, therefore, shows that Lower Palaeolithic
cultures within the core and flake (or chopper) groups were
both present in India at the beginning of Middle Pleistocene
times and that they survived in archaic forms long after the
close of the last Glacial Period in a way rather comparable

to that of the Palaeolithic industries of Burma. The micro-lithic flint industries may be contemporary with those of fairly early post-glacial date in Europe and the Near East, or they may be later; in any event they seem likely, in the absence of the Upper Palaeolithic blade industries which might be considered ancestral to them in India, to represent a new cultural, and perhaps ethnic, element. These micro-lithic cultures again had a long survival, side by side with communities making pottery and ground stone axes in the Neolithic tradition. The origin of these Neolithic cultures is unknown, though they are more likely to be the result of folk-movements from the west than of independent invention within India. Neither in Central India nor in Kashmir can such cultures be dated satisfactorily much before 500 B.C. on the evidence at present available.

The blade industries in Sind, while certainly in part re-lated to their counterparts in the Amri or later cultures, nevertheless have some claims to a Palaeolithic ancestry and a relatively ancient date. Other aspects of the flint industry are presumably introductions to the region from farther west with the earliest agriculturalists.

To understand the subsequent prehistory of India we must look beyond its present frontiers to the other lands of West-ern Asia. A knowledge of the sequence of prehistoric cultures in Persia and Mesopotamia is necessary for an under-standing of the Indian material, which has to be compared and equated with that of the more westerly lands, our knowledge of which is greater. So in the next chapter we turn to the story of the early agricultural communities in Western Asia between the fifth or sixth and the second millennium B.C.

Notes to Chapter II

Pleistocene cultures and chronology in the Orient as well as else-where are discussed by Professor F. E. Zeuner in *Dating the Past* (1946), and the Indian material is conveniently summarized by

V. D. Krishnaswami in *Ancient India*, no. 3 (1947), 11–57. The most important special studies are H. H. De Terra and T. T. Paterson, *Studies on the Ice Age in India and Associated Human Cultures* (Carnegie Institution of Washington, 1939), and H. L. Movius, *Early Man and Pleistocene Stratigraphy in Southern and Eastern Asia* (Papers of the Peabody Museum, Harvard, 1944). Accessible summaries of the main points in this latter book and of the current views on *Pithecanthropus* are given by Professor W. E. Le Gros Clark in *Antiquity*, XIX (1945), 1–5; *ibid.*, XX (1946), 9–12. For a general summary of our knowledge of fossil men in Asia and elsewhere, see the same writer's *History of the Primates* (1949).

The Upper Palaeolithic in Western Asia and in Europe is treated by Professor Dorothy Garrod in *Proc. Prehist. Soc.*, IV (1938), 1–26. For the cave-paintings in India, see Krishnaswami's paper referred to above, and Col. D. H. Gordon's paper on those of the Mahadeo Hills in *Indian Art and Letters*, X, 35–41. For the stone axe culture in Mysore, Professor Wheeler's excavation report is in *Ancient India*, no. 4 (1948), 181–310. He has described the 'Northern Black Polished Ware', referred to in connexion with the Burzahom site, in *Ancient India*, no. 1 (1946), 55–58.

CHAPTER III

The Background – Early Agricultural Communities in Western Asia

> The Earth has her hill-sides and her uplands, hers is the wide plain, she is the bearer of plants of many uses: may she stretch out her hand and be bountiful to us!
>
> *Atharvaveda*, XII, i.

WITH an economy based on hunting and some gathering of fruits or other edible vegetable products, little development of the arts of living was possible, in either Western Asia or Northern Europe; and with the final withdrawal of the ice sheet large tracts of the Old World were sparsely populated by small hunting groups, on whom the changing climatic conditions imposed successive problems, generation after generation, as the herds of animals migrated or died out. It was a decisive moment in the history of mankind – a 'moment' spread over several thousand years – when man, instead of following the animals in search of climates and regions where he could continue his ancient way of life unchanged, elected to adapt himself to his changed environment and find new methods of obtaining food.

This process of adaptation to environment can be seen taking place over much of Europe and in North Africa from about 10,000 B.C. onwards, in the so-called Mesolithic stage. The axe seems to be invented to attack the trees of the encroaching forests in the north, and with the smaller game now available for the chase, the dog is domesticated to help in hunting. But this Mesolithic stage was only an ingenious prolongation of the Palaeolithic way of life with but little modification, and the insecurity of the food supply was still there to render the formation of large or permanent settlements impossible. The essential still lacking was the discovery of a technique of food production over which a large degree of human control could be exercised, and it is this revolutionary concept – the change-over from hunter to farmer and stockbreeder – that lay behind the ancient civilizations of the Old World. With the formation of agricultural communities, it was possible for man to live within a framework of comparative economic security, to accumulate some surplus material resources, and thereby to increase his leisure and stimulate the activities of other craftsmen on his behalf.

We cannot trace this process in India itself, and on the whole it seems improbable that this essential transition from food gathering to food production was made independently in India as early as it was farther west. Agriculture begins in the archaeological record, as we shall see, with the growing of grains of the wheat and barley types. The prehistory of the cultivation of rice, the other staple Asiatic crop, is at present very obscure. It seems probable that rice cultivation began earlier in India than it did in China, and that the knowledge reached the latter country by way of the Yangtze, to make its appearance in the Chinese Bronze Age about 2000 B.C., the Neolithic crop in North China having been millet. But by 2000 B.C. agriculture had been established for at least three thousand years in Persia and Mesopotamia, and for a thousand in Western India, and it is to the region stretching between Persia and Egypt that we must look for evidence of the transition from hunting to farming.

It is not only archaeology that points the way to this area, but the evidence of botany and zoology. The wild grasses ancestral to the present cultivated types of wheat and barley have their natural habitat over just this area, where postglacial climatic conditions were suitable for their growth. Wild barley is distributed from Asia Minor through

Transcaucasia to Persia, Turkestan, and Afghanistan, and probably also in Arabia and Abyssinia. The primitive variety of wheat known as *Emmer* (*Triticum diococcum*) extends from Syria and Palestine through Mesopotamia to West Persia, and probably again also in Abyssinia (though the acceptance of this region as an ancient centre of wild cereals depends on certain botanical assumptions not universally accepted); another primitive form, *Triticum monococcum*, is known wild from the Balkans through Asia Minor to North Syria and the borders of Kurdistan and Persia. It is clear that the appreciation of the possibilities of grass seeds as a foodstuff which might be gathered, even if not cultivated at first, would be likely to be gained by the ancient hunting groups who inhabited these areas, and that communities, assured of a grain crop at least, could be formed once the potentialities of deliberate sowing and harvesting were grasped. Grain crops can have more than one use: man cannot live by bread alone, and fermented beer can be made from most cereals, and is likely to be as old as agriculture. To the mind of primitive man, it may be as important as the food crop – tribes in Northern Rhodesia were found, when Europeans first visited them, to endure an annual food shortage rather than encroach upon the grain set aside for beer!

We do not know whether the most ancient agriculture went side by side with domestication of animals: the two elements in mixed farming may have two different origins, grain-growing from the food gatherers (perhaps mainly the women of the tribe), and domestication from the hunters, who had already tamed the dog – and indeed grain might have been grown first of all to provide food to induce wild animals to come under subjection. But in just the same regions as those in which the 'noble' grasses grow wild, can the wild ancestors of sheep, goats, and cattle be identified. With the wild sheep this is particularly clear, with the Mouflon distributed from the Mediterranean through Asia Minor to Persia, the Urial from Persia, Turkestan and Afghanistan to the Punjab and Baluchistan, and the Argal eastwards of this again. It cannot have been long before grain-growing and stock-breeding, even if differing in origins, became combined in one distinctive economy; and man had become a mixed farmer.

This need not in itself have entailed wholly settled communities – pastoralism may involve complete mobility, and even primitive hoe-cultivation soon exhausts the land. If there is no river-inundation to provide fresh mud each year, the settlement must seek new fields every few seasons. But camping sites may be re-visited regularly, and some of the tribe may remain more or less permanently to guard the crops. The increased and more assured food supply of a farming community allows for larger families, and children can be put to more uses in herding, weeding or hoeing than the limited specialized skills of a hunting tribe admit.

In Palestine we have most interesting archaeological evidence of a tribe whose economy is changing from the hunting and food-collecting stage to that of food-production. These folk were still largely hunters, in the Mesolithic tradition, and they had (probably seasonal) camps at the mouths of caves, where they also buried their dead. Their flint blades, knives, and skin-scrapers of the ancient hunting manner were found; and bone spear-tips, barbed points, and gorges for fish-catching. But in addition there were found small flint blades set with gum into grooved shafts of bone, the blades finely notched and set in a line to make a continuous saw-edge, and the bone carved at one end into a convenient handle shaped as an animal's head. These composite tools are in fact sickles, or corn-cutting knives, and the silica in the grass or corn stalks has polished the edges of the flints into a bright lustre from constant use, a feature we know to be distinctive of any flint tools used for straw-cutting. And on the flat rock floor at the cave mouth were

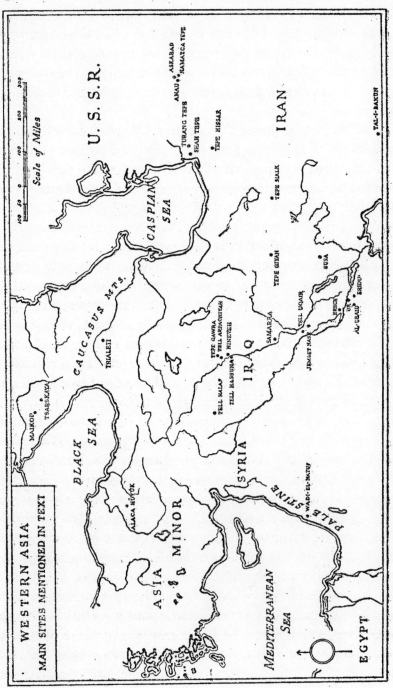

FIG. I

hollows made by pounding out the grain into flour, and other stone mortars were found for the same purpose. Whether these Natufians (named from one of their camp-sites in the Wadi-el-Natuf) grew grain themselves or were reaping wild seed is unknown, but the well-made sickles look as if agriculture was already developed.

These Natufian sites cannot be dated accurately, but all probabilities together imply a date well before 5000 B.C. Our earliest historical dates in Western Asia are round about 3000 B.C., and all we can say of the prehistoric cultures is that they are earlier than this date, and that one thousand years seems the very least space of time into which we can compress the long series of successive prehistoric phases in Mesopotamia or Persia. The relationship of these phases, marked by innovations in pottery styles, tool types, archi-tectural or burial customs, can be established from the strati-fication in the ancient settlement sites, where village after village or town after town was built and rebuilt on the rub-bish of its ruined predecessor, until a mound or 'tell' is formed which may be as much as a hundred feet high. Ex-cavation of such a 'tell' may give a sequence A, B, C, D, E from the first to the last settlement on the site: another mound may begin at D and continue on not only through E but to F, G, and H. And recently it has been found that the 'A' level (i.e. the earliest human occupation recognized) in one area, such as Southern Mesopotamia, may be preceded by earlier occupations, I, II, III, in country to the north that was habitable at a time when Southern Mesopotamia was still under the ancient Persian Gulf. To continue this diagrammatic way of describing stratification, if in phase 'E' we find evidence of an actual concrete date, known from recorded history and represented by an inscription or some object whose style can be fitted into a historical phase, we can at once say that A, B, C, and D phases are earlier than this, and that F, G, and H are later. The more sites on which we find the same relative sequence, the more sure can we be that the scheme is valid for a large area, and not just for a single site or a few close together. (Table I, p. 65).

In Mesopotamia such a sequence has been pretty well established to cover at least five prehistoric periods before the Early Dynastic period, about 2800 B.C., and this can be fairly closely correlated with a similar sequence in Persia and Syria. For the moment it will be instructive to look at the earliest of these farming communities in each area.

Not far from Mosul a site has recently been excavated which has revealed the most ancient agricultural community yet known in Mesopotamia. In the earliest level, on the original ground surface below the mound known as Tell Hassuna, were found what seem to be camping sites of a not wholly settled people, with hearths and indications that any habitations are likely to have been tents. But these people were already mixed farmers, for not only were abundant bones of cattle and sheep found, but stone hoes, still retaining traces of the bitumen that fastened them in their handles, and stone rubbers and pestles and mortars for grinding or pounding corn into flour. The people were using stone tools and making a rough but quite good pottery ornamented with incised lines.

But very soon there was permanent habitation on the top of the old camp-fires, with little houses of rooms set round a courtyard, one clearly recognizable as a kitchen, with its bread oven and storage jars still remaining, another the living-room, another a detached bake-house with two sunk storage bins for grain in the courtyard nearby. More than thirty such grain-storage bins were found in the area excavated, and they recall similar structures, probably of about the same age (or rather later), in Egypt. In this village too were found sickle-flints, like the Natufian ones already mentioned, which had been set in slightly curved wooden hafts. The houses' had been built of the tempered mud which makes such an excellent building material all over the Orient.

In Northern Persia a very similar settlement was found to have existed at the base of the Tepe Sialk mound near Kashan. Here again there were no recognizable traces of permanent dwellings, but layers of charcoal and ash were thought to represent the carbonized wood and branches of rough shelters. The people were still in the Stone Age – a burial was found with a man holding a polished stone axe in his hands – and there were slotted bones for flint blades which may be part of sickles of the Natufian type, as well as stone hoe-blades. Some of the pottery found was painted with black designs, and was hand-made (as was that of Hassuna). Immediately above the layers containing these remains began settlements with mud-built houses, and here too were found the first tiny objects made of copper.

These sites, and that at Mersin in Cilicia (known in less detail) do show in a very interesting manner just that transition from a hunting, semi-nomadic way of life to that of the settled agriculturalist that one might expect, and in Baluchistan a settlement of precisely this type, though not necessarily of such great antiquity, has been found as the lowest occupation in the Rana Ghundai tell in the Zhob Valley. We shall see that in India we have constantly to be on our guard against making comparisons between the local cultures there, and those which seem comparable in Mesopotamia and Persia, and then considering that this implies contemporaneity in the two widely separated areas.

The concept of the 'zoning' of cultures outside the areas of higher and more ancient civilization is one with which European archaeologists are familiar when working in their own continent, but it applies just as much to the countries lying eastwards of the most ancient centres of agriculture (such as the sites described in Mesopotamia and Persia, and others of about the same date in Syria and Asia Minor) as it does to the lands to the west. It seems unlikely, on the whole, that the elaborate techniques of agriculture and, slightly later, of the invention of metallurgy were evolved independently in several areas of the Old World, and in the present state of our archaeological knowledge the origins of these basic contributions to human civilization must be assumed to lie in the area between Asia Minor and Turkestan.

So far as India is concerned, therefore, we must look westwards for the introduction of the arts of agriculture, and it will be seen throughout this book how the Indian material can be properly understood only in terms of its general Western Asiatic setting. And as the relative chronology of the Indian prehistoric cultures is still in a provisional stage, we must continually make reference to the Mesopotamian and to a less extent the Persian sequence, using the generally agreed names of the successive phases to indicate the approximate chronological position in the absence of actual dates. Only in North Baluchistan, where the stratified sequence in the Rana Ghundai tell has been worked out, can we attempt anything of a local Indian time-scale.

But, before turning to the prehistoric and early historic sequence after the time of the first occupations of Hassuna and Sialk, there is an important point to be touched upon. We have said that these earliest agricultural settlements were in a 'stone age', implying by this that the people who lived in these settlements, and tilled the adjacent fields, knew nothing of any metal for making tools or other objects. The sequence Stone, Bronze, and Iron Ages, originally worked out for Northern Europe, is, as it happens, relatively valid in many other regions, especially in so far as the use of chipped or ground stone invariably seems to have come before the use of any metal. But people may move straight out of a 'stone age' into an 'iron age' when this new substance is suddenly introduced to them from outside, or the addition of the knowledge of metal may have no effect on their general economy. The Chenchu tribes of Hyderabad at the present day live a food-gathering, nomadic existence to which iron has contributed nothing but a spike to go on the end of the digging stick with which they dig up the edible roots on which they mainly live.

Nevertheless, in the ancient prehistoric communities of Western Asia we do find that, fairly soon after the agricultural way of life is flourishing, a secondary revolutionary discovery is made – the discovery that certain stones can, under special conditions of firing, be made by heat to turn into a tough substance which can be hammered or cast into any desired form, and take on a keen cutting edge. This recognition of the relationship between copper ore and the metal is one with far-reaching consequences: it is the basis of chemistry and of all metallurgy.

Copper may occur in the form of ores (such as malachite) or it may appear as the native metal on top of the veins or lodes, and by weathering be exposed on the surface. It must soon have been discovered that this native metal could be hammered into shape, and as it is widely distributed in the upland areas of Northern Mesopotamia and Persia, it is not surprising that the earliest copper objects found at, for instance, Sialk, are little pins, awls and bits of wire hammered from the unmelted metal which had been picked up from the surface.

To smelt copper from the ore a relatively low temperature, 700° to 800° C., is needed, in a reducing atmosphere – i.e. one in which access of free air (oxygen) is prevented. Now it has been pointed out that primitive pottery kilns would provide just these conditions, and although simple rough pots can be baked quite satisfactorily in an open fire, as soon as any attempt is made to control the colour of the exterior, and above all to paint it with patterns, a closed kiln is absolutely necessary. The transition from a closed kiln to a smelting furnace involves no great mental labour to conceive and it is not surprising, therefore, that we should find evidence of the earliest copper smelting among the makers of painted pottery in the Ancient Orient.

But there is another process involved if full use is to be made of copper, and that is melting it when in metallic form so that it can be cast. Now this requires a much higher temperature, 1,085° C., and one which could be reached only in a more advanced type of kiln than would produce the heat necessary for smelting from the ore. So for a long time copper must have been worked by hammering and cutting only, whether from the natural metal or from metal smelted from ore, and the further development of furnace types seems to have taken place in Mesopotamia. Certain metallurgists think that smelting may have been invented as a technique only after native copper supplies were worked out, but the evidence for this rather contradictory sequence is not conclusive.

By the time the earliest agricultural communities were being founded in Western India it is unlikely that the lack of copper tools in them means anything more than poverty, and that their 'stone age' was forced on them by sheer lack of purchasing power. At all events it is not long before Indian metallurgy gets under way, using local copper and also tin ores, and in general terms all the prehistoric Indian cultures we shall have to deal with are formally in a Bronze Age.

The classification of the prehistoric cultures of Mesopotamia, with which we must begin, is made by using convenient *type-site* names for the various phases, so that, for instance, Uruk is not only a place (the Biblical Erech and the modern Arab Warka) but it can be used when talking of the 'Uruk Culture' – that is, the various types of architecture, pottery, tools, sculpture, and so on made by a certain group of people at a certain time – and we can also say that another culture is of 'Uruk date': that is, contemporary with

the place the Uruk Culture holds in the whole Mesopotamian sequence. This is a fundamental method of archaeological terminology, and we shall use it similarly in describing the Indian cultures; with it there goes the system of
numbering successive strata in a site or tell of many periods
of occupation. Here the normal and most rational practice
is to reverse the actual sequence of excavation, in which of
course the topmost (and latest) occupation is dug into first,
and number from the earliest settlement to the latest.

This, then, gives a handy method of reference to the sequence, Roman numerals being used after the type-site
name, so that one has Sialk I, Sialk II, and so on as names for
successive occupations. A form of subdivision is necessary
when we find that there are successive levels of rebuilding by
the same group of people on the site, but where there is no
sign that the continuity has been broken, and this can be
done by using IIa, IIb, and so on. A new Roman numeral
should indicate a new group of people living on the site, a
letter after a numeral that there has been no change of population, but that the existing folk have rebuilt their town.
Unfortunately this method of numbering has not been uni-
formly adopted by excavators in the Orient, so that certain
sites are numbered 'backwards' – their latest occupation is I
and their earliest may be XX or so. It is impossible to re-
number these sites without causing untold confusion, so the
reader must be on his guard, and remember for instance
that Giyan V is early but Sialk IV is late in the general
sequence.*

The earliest phase in Mesopotamia we have already described, and it is best known from its type-site as *Hassuna*.

* The following are the main sites numbered 'backwards': in Mesopotamia, Arpachiyah (I–X), Gawra (I–XX, a–f), Uruk (I–XVIII),
Uqair (I–VIII); in Persia, Giyan (I–V). Susa has been reclassified
recently as A–D, but A is the earliest settlement. In India, Mohenjo-
daro and Harappā have extraordinary systems of reference, which are
described in Chapter V.

Although the economic structure of Sialk I in Persia is so similar, distinctions in pottery types, etc., make a complete equation with Hassuna I inadvisable, and the same applies to sites such as Mersin in Asia Minor and Ras Shamra in Syria. But the earliest level at Nineveh (Nineveh I) and perhaps that at Tepe Gawra (Gawra Archaic *f*) seem likely to be more strictly comparable. Of these sites, Sialk I alone has painted pottery, and on this point we must make a necessary digression.

After the very early and primitive 'Stone Age' phases, such as Hassuna I, the most distinctive feature of the prehistoric cultures of Mesopotamia, and even more of Persia, is the frequent and sometimes exclusive occurrence of pottery painted with designs in one or, less frequently, two or more colours. Such painted pottery, with its enormous repertoire of designs and styles, forms the basis of much of our classification of prehistoric Western Asian cultures, and in Baluchistan, where so little scientific excavation has been carried out, comparison of painted pottery styles is the only method of disentangling the various regional groups of people and their trade and movements.

The invention of the technique of pot-painting, with the attendant necessities of more elaborate kilns for baking the vessels, seems to have taken place in the highlands of North Persia, Northern Mesopotamia, or Syria, and we shall see that its appearance in the south of Mesopotamia, when that region became habitable, owing to the shrinking of the Persian Gulf in prehistoric times, is due to immigration from the mountain regions into the plains. Cultures using painted wares have been traced northwards into Turkestan and south-eastwards through Persia into South Baluchistan; Afghanistan is an archaeological blank at present, but in North Baluchistan again the painted pottery reappears. On the basis of a comparative examination of the great mass of material from sites spread over such a wide area, the American archaeologist Donald McCown has been able to show that it falls into two basic groups, distinguished by a predominantly buff or red background to the painted design. These Buff Wares and Red Wares have, on the whole, a contrasted distribution, with the Buff Ware in the south and Red Ware in the north – a distribution which is repeated in Baluchistan, as we shall see.

To return to the Mesopotamian sequence the *Halaf Culture*, known from Syria and from North Mesopotamia, shows already an early use of copper, stone, and mud-brick buildings (including some remarkable structures that may be a form of temple), and a very fine painted pottery which often uses red and black painted designs on a buff base. The origins of this pottery, and probably the culture, may be in Syria or Kurdistan, but there is an allied type of ware, *Samarra Ware*, which is black-on-buff only, and which has strong affinities with certain wares in Persia. At Hassuna, Samarra Ware is stratified below true Halaf pottery, but elsewhere it seems to be in the main contemporary, and the two styles may represent two groups of people, the Halaf folk being indigenous to their northern region (with possible contacts with North Persia), and the Samarra Ware indicating the arrival of allied, but distinct, drafts of population from farther south. The best-known sites are Tell Halaf in Syria (strata below the historic city), Arpachiyah (levels VI to X), and Samarra, where there was a prehistoric cemetery beneath the Abbasid town of the ninth century A.D.

The pottery of the *Al Ubaid Culture* shows clearly that it is derived from the Persian highlands, and its appearance marks the first colonization of the southern parts of Mesopotamia. The stratification of sites in the north shows that its spread to this region followed the Halaf phase, and its establishment in the south is not likely to be much earlier. Settlements and cemeteries are known; there was some use of copper; fields were tilled with stone hoes like those of

Hassuna I; and houses built of stone or mud bricks. Recently too it has been discovered that monumental temples were built by the Al Ubaid folk, the plans of which foreshadow those of later times. At Ur, a 'Flood' occurred during this time, covering the site with a thick layer of river mud, and other important sites are Eridu (Abu Sharain, where the temples were excavated in 1946), Tell Uqair (Area IV), Uruk IX–XVIII, and Tepe Gawra XIII–XIX.

The next phase is one of peculiar interest in the prehistory of Mesopotamia, though we cannot dwell on it here. One of its outstanding characteristics is the sudden change over from painted pottery to wares which are plain, and either red or grey, frequently with a polished surface. This *Uruk Culture* (occupying levels V to X on the type site) clearly marks the appearance of new people with new elements of civilization in the region; engraved cylinder-seals, writing on clay, sculpture in the round and stone-built temples are among the innovations, and these in many ways foreshadow the achievements of the civilization which we can call Sumerian. Settlements of the Uruk Culture appear stratified above those of Al Ubaid, not only on the type site but at Gawra (VIII*b*–XI), Nineveh (IV–III), Uqair (V–VIII), and elsewhere.

What blending of cultural traditions took place between the ancient peoples whose individuality is shown by their painted pottery and the newcomers, whose style of pot-making must indicate a sharply contrasted cultural heritage, we do not know, but from the amalgam painted styles of pottery certainly re-emerged, and in the probably rather short *Jemdet Nasr* period we find a characteristic ware with designs in black and plum red. This phase is recognizable at Ur, at Uruk (II–III), Gawra (VII–VIII), Uqair (II–IV), and other sites, and the Uruk innovations of writing and seal-making were developed. We are now approaching so near to the recorded history and king-lists of Mesopotamia that we can give an approximate date in years for Jemdet Nasr – about 3000 B.C. – for it was followed by the period of the Early Dynasties: the period of the Flood which figures so largely in Sumerian and Hebrew tradition, and the days after the Flood when 'kingship again descended from on, high'. But, before treating the early historical periods of Mesopotamia in more detail, it will be convenient to turn to six main stratified sites in Persia and Turkestan and compare their sequence with that we have already established, from Hassuna to Jemdet Nasr.

Near Kashan, *Tepe Sialk* has already been mentioned for its earliest occupation, Sialk I, which may at least be chronologically, though not culturally, equivalent with Hassuna. Sialk II shows a development from the earliest culture and evidence of trade connexions with the Persian Gulf, and is contemporary with Halaf; and after this the site seems to have been temporarily abandoned, but reoccupied in early Ubaid times into the middle of the Uruk period, with a culture again developed out of the earlier phases seen on the site. But by the latter part of Sialk III a full Copper Age with cast tools is established, the architectural styles suggesting comparison (and perhaps contact) with Uruk and Uqair in the Uruk period. In Sialk IV there is actual Jemdet Nasr pottery (though not the well-known painted ware) and early inscribed tablets.

Tepe Giyan, near Nihavend, begins its occupation in V*a* with painted buff ware which seems to be early Halaf in date, and continues through Ubaid times to mid-Uruk in V*d*, when the site was temporarily abandoned. Giyan V is generally comparable with Sialk III and in its last phase with Hissar I, described below – Giyan IV belongs to Early Dynastic Sumerian times and will be mentioned later.

The site of *Tepe Hissar*, just mentioned, is near Damghan, and Hissar I has black-on-red painted ware with patterns similar to the black-on-buff pottery of Giyan V*d*, and the cast metal tools and other features fit in with Sialk III, so Hissar I cannot be much earlier than late Uruk times. In the next phase, Hissar II, the old painted pottery tradition is interrupted by the appearance of plain, burnished grey or black ware, not like the grey ware of Uruk, but indicating newcomers from outside the painted pottery territory, probably in Jemdet Nasr or even later times. With the Hissar III settlement, when this pottery becomes dominant, we will deal later.

Susa is a famous site excavated many years ago, when its stratigraphy was not properly understood. McCown has shown that the old 'Susa I', which he re-names 'Susa A', is contemporary with Ubaid, Hissar I, Sialk III and Giyan Vc; above this Susa B has actual imported Uruk pottery and so is definitely dated to this phase, Susa C is equated with Jemdet Nasr, and Susa D (which used to be called 'Susa II') can be shown to be contemporary with Early Dynastic Sumer.

In Southern Persia, in the Fars district, two prehistoric sites have been excavated near Persepolis, *Tal-i-Bakun* A and B. The B site proved the earlier, and BI may equate with Hassuna, BII with Halaf, while on the A site AI begins in early Ubaid times and the occupation goes on into Uruk times in A V.

There is one important site which has been excavated in Russian Turkestan, at *Anau* near Askabad. Here the first settlement, Anau Ia, seems to be of Halaf date and has connexions with Sialk II and Giyan Va, and in Ib copper first appears and the painted pottery tradition already present in Ia continues, through Ubaid into Uruk times. As at Hissar, grey wares appear to mark an intrusion of new people into the area at the end of Ib, and the two types continue side by side in Anau II, when other innovations in pottery styles might point to trade or immigration from Baluchistan. By Anau III a culture is established which has many points of similarity to that of Hissar III, and they will be discussed together later on.

It will be seen, therefore, that in Persia and Turkestan there is a series of cultures which show significant relationships between themselves, and which can be equated in date with the Mesopotamian sequence. It has not been possible, however, to group these under inclusive type-site names following the Mesopotamian practice, and we must still refer to them by their site and sequence-number in the stratification. It sounds complicated, but in assessing the position of the prehistoric Indian cultures in the general Western Asiatic picture, we shall have constantly to refer to them in terms of Persia or Mesopotamia. This chapter is an attempt to clarify this background to the Indian material, so that the reader will have some appreciation of what 'trade relations in Early Dynastic times' or 'pottery of Giyan V types' may mean when he encounters these phrases later in the book.

But we must return to the Mesopotamian sequence after Jemdet Nasr times, at which point we enter the realms of recorded history. Lists of kings and of dynasties were beginning to be compiled at least by 2000 B.C., and, though much of the earliest part is fabulous, especially the estimated length of reigns (for example the pre-Flood dynasty of eight kings together reigning for 241,200 years!), nevertheless a fairly coherent chronological skeleton has been pieced together from about 2800 B.C. The *Early Dynastic Period* of the Kingdom of Sumer appears to begin at this date, and on the evidence of archaeology and stratigraphy has been divided into three (E.D.I to E.D.III). These subdivisions need not concern us very much in dealing with the Indian material, and there is no place here to describe in any detail the achievements of Early Dynastic Sumer, with its fully literate urban culture, advanced metallurgy, and monumental buildings and sculpture.

In E.D.I has been found at several sites in the Baghdad

region a type of painted pottery called 'Scarlet Ware', with
some affinities to its predecessor, Jemdet Nasr pottery, but
with a bright scarlet paint instead of the deep plum red used
in the earlier period. This pottery turns up again in Susa D,
and we shall see that very important comparisons can be
made between Scarlet Ware and certain pottery in South
Baluchistan. Another link between Mesopotamia and Baluchistan in Early Dynastic times we shall see to be certain
stone vessels with carved surface ornament which turn up in
E.D.III, once in one of the famous 'Royal Tombs' of Ur,
which must rank as the best known sites of ancient Sumer
and belong to the E.D.III phase.

Ancient Mesopotamia was divided into a kingdom of
Sumer in the south and of Akkad in the north. The next
important point in its early history is the rise of the Kingdom
of Akkad under Sargon, and his conquest of Sumer, thus
forming an Akkadian dominion over all Mesopotamia. This
event probably occurred shortly before 2300 B.C., and the
period of a century or so under Sargon and his successors is
usually known as the Akkadian Period, sometimes as the
Sargonid. And afterwards came break-up and insecurity –
'who was king, who was not king?' asks a contemporary
writer despairingly, as the unified autocratic rule of Sargon
gave way to immediate civil wars and the rise and fall of
city-states. By shortly before 2100 B.C. the so-called Third
Dynasty of Ur was established with wide authority, and
there followed the divided rule of the city-states of Isin and
Larsa. Beyond this date (round about 2000 B.C.) we need not
follow the fortunes of Mesopotamia under the rulers of Babylon and Assyria: we have little concern in India with the
great civilizations before the time of Cyrus, and after the end
of the Sumerian empire we are concerned more with barbarians than with the city-dwellers.

Giyan seems the only site in Persia where a succession can
be traced from cultures which can be equated with the pre-

historic sequence of Mesopotamia to the Early Dynastic
period and beyond. The beginning of Giyan IV seems contemporary with Susa D, and therefore with some phase or
phases of the Early Dynastic period, and it probably ended
in Akkadian or later times. Giyan III contains a cylinder-
seal of a type known in the First Dynasty of Babylon (about
1800–1600 B.C.), and there may be a gap between its end and
the beginning of Giyan II, which seems to go on to 1400.
There may be another gap before Giyan I, which goes on to
the introduction of iron, and includes the grey polished pottery already referred to in connexion with Hissar III and
Anau III. The final occupation of Giyan (or rather its use as
a cemetery) must be about 1300 B.C. or later.

. We are left with a problem which must be touched on
before leaving the Mesopotamian and Persian material and
turning our attention to that from India. In describing the
stratification at Tepe Hissar and at Anau I have mentioned
the intrusion of unpainted grey or black ware which cuts
across and finally supplants the old painted pottery. Now
this is more than a change in fashion among the makers or
purchasers of pottery; such a radically different type of
ware, associated with quite different traditions of kiln building and firing, can only mean the arrival of new people in
North Persia and Turkestan at this time. And this is borne
out by the other finds, which show all the innovations that
might be expected from the arrival of fresh settlers – new
types of copper and bronze tools and weapons and, at Hissar
at least, a considerable access of wealth in the form of gold,
silver and semi-precious stones. These newcomers are, as we
have seen, attested at Hissar, Giyan, and Anau among the
sites whose earlier prehistoric occupations we have studied,
and they are also known to have settled at two other sites not
very far from Hissar, at Shah Tepe, where they replaced
makers of painted wares of the Hissar II type, and at Turang
Tepe nearby, where no earlier occupation is attested. There

is also evidence of makers of the same grey pots from Namaz-ga Tepe and Askabad, both near Anau, and there is a cemetery containing similar ware (Cemetery B) at Sialk, overlying the earlier prehistoric deposits. Finally traces of the same folk have been found in Afghanistan, at Nad-i-Ali.

We shall have to reconsider all these sites again when we come to deal with the events following the break-up of the Harappā Culture in India in Chapter VI, but for the present the problem is – what is the date of such settlements as that of Hissar III? It is clear that a great many of the objects found there have close parallels among Early Dynastic Sumerian metal-work, ornaments and other features, and this has led certain archaeologists to regard the date of Hissar III as approximating to that of Early Dynastic – not much after 2800 B.C., and with Hissar III one must take, for instance, Anau III. But this view seems to me very hard to substantiate, and further difficulties will be seen when we come to deal with the Harappā Culture and the succeeding events in India.

The answer seems to depend largely on two things: the concept of cultures zoned outwards in date from the centres of higher civilization, and the relationship likely to exist between the barbarians of the steppes and the rich townsmen of the fertile river-plains. If we look to the north and west of Sumer in Early Dynastic times and the next eight or nine centuries, we can see that, round the edge of the civilized world, as it then existed, are a number of barbarian tribes in various forms of local 'Bronze Ages'. These stretch from Asia Minor to South Russia and the Caucasus and, as I think, eastwards to the other side of the Caspian. From time to time these people buried their kings or chieftains with enormous pomp and with as much treasure as they could amass. Such tombs have been found, for instance, at Alaca Hüyük in Asia Minor, and at Maikop and Tsarskaya in South Russia; less 'royal' but similar are the graves in

Hissar III, while at Turang Tepe there was found, a century ago, a great hoard of objects (known as the 'Treasure of Asterabad') which were quite likely the furnishings of such another princely tomb as that of Maikop. At Troy, the famous treasures from the second (or third) settlement are quite comparable in general terms. In all these finds were gold and silver vessels and other objects (many showing strong Sumerian affinities), and fine bronze or copper tools and weapons. The evidence, from these burials and treasures of warriors (from which one can exclude, as under dispute, Hissar III and Turang Tepe), is quite reasonably consistent as between about 2300 and 2000 B.C., but not earlier.

But should we not therefore place somewhere within these dates the Hissar III and Anau III settlements and the cemeteries at Shah Tepe, Turang Tepe, and in the Hissar site itself? The grey-ware technique is very ancient in Asia Minor, and with the barbarian inroads into Mesopotamia, known from documentary evidence, actual objects could be looted or craftsmen induced to serve under barbarian potentates in a time of trouble. Apart from the normal course of peace-time trade, the sudden acquisition of wealth in Sumerian styles by the northern nomads may reflect raiding and land-piracy along the caravan routes or even across the frontiers into Mesopotamia at a time when its rich civilization was temporarily weakened by internal disruption. In this context the grey-ware settlements at Hissar and Anau are likely to be Akkadian at the earliest.* As we shall see, there is reason to connect these cultures with the dispersion of Indo-European speaking tribes in the early second millennium B.C. The probable chronological relationships discussed above are summarized in Table I (p. 65).

* Since this was written Schaeffer has discussed the date of Hissar III and assigned it to the period 2300–2100 B.C. – a date with which I agree.

Notes to Chapter III

Professor V. G. Childe's *New Light on the Most Ancient East* (1934), still remains the best general account of the prehistoric Orient, but can now be supplemented by A. L. Perkins, *Comparative Archaeology of Early Mesopotamia* (Oriental Institute of Chicago, 1949), and D. McCown, *The Comparative Stratigraphy of Early Iran (ibid.,* 1942), with a full bibliography of excavations and sites discovered since 1934 except for Tell Hassuna, published by Seton Lloyd and Fuad Safar in *Journ. Near Eastern Studies,* IV (1945) 255. In this connexion the Sialk report is of outstanding importance – R. Ghirshman, *Fouilles de Sialk* (two vols., 1938–1939).

The Natufian Mesolithic Culture is described by Professor D. Garrod in *The Stone Age of Mount Carmel,* Vol. I (1937). For the technology of early copper and bronze working, see papers by H. H. Coghlan in *Man,* 1939, 92; *Antiquaries Journal,* XXII (1942), 22–38; H. Maryon in *Amer. Journ. Arch.* LIII (1949), 93–124. I have discussed some of the problems of the Hissar dating in *Antiquity,* XVII (1943), 169–182; see also T. Burton-Brown, *Studies in Third Millennium History* (1946), Chap. VI, and D. H. Gordon, 'Sialk, Giyan, Hissar and the Indo-Iranian Connection', *Man in India,* XXVII (1947), 196–241. The finds from Namazga Tepe are published in *Eurasia Septentrionalis Antiqua,* v (1930), 9–21, and Nad-i-Ali in *Revue des Arts Asiatiques,* XIII (1939), 10–22.

Since this book was written Dr Claude Schaeffer's monumental work, *Stratigraphie comparée et chronologie de l'Asie occidentale,* has appeared (Oxford, 1948).

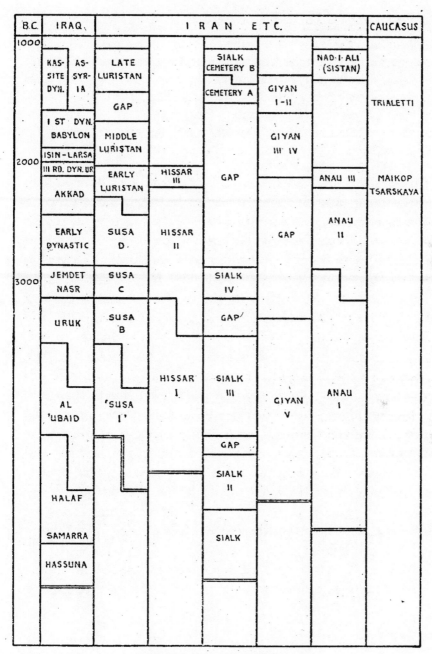

Chronological Table I

CHAPTER IV

Bronze Age Peasant Communities of Western India

> ... through the stones the lizard and the snake
> Rustle their brittle length ...
> Scavenger kites hang waiting for the dead
> Over the old and solitary ram,
> And the mule picks its way up the dried river-bed.
>
> (V. Sackville-West, *The Land*)

THE regions of Western India which comprise Baluchistan, the Makran and Sind are today forbidding, barren mountains, arid desert and sandy waste. But through them, on the eastern boundary of the region, the River Indus, controlled by the Sukkur Barrage and its attendant irrigation canals, brings a strip of rich alluvial lands. The Makran coast stretches eastwards from the Persian border at Gwatar for over three hundred miles of uninviting sandhills and mangrove swamps at the mouths of shallow, turgid streams, while behind the narrow coastal plain the mountains rise stony and bare in fantastic eroded sky-lines like a lunar landscape. Inland, as the massif builds up northwards, it runs in irregular ridges which rise above the 7,000-feet contour: the intervening river valleys, such as those of the Mashkai, the Nal or the Hab Rivers, are isolated one from another, and east-to-west communication must follow the regular routes, which take advantage of the 'laks' or passes across the ranges, or, gaining the valleys of the rivers running eastward into Sind, follow the courses of the Mula or the Gaj obliquely to the plain below.

Around Kalat the mountains narrow to less than a hundred miles from east to west – from the desert of Upper Sind

around Jacobabad to the high plateau above the 3,000-feet
contour stretching from beyond the Pishin Lora River to
Sistan and the Helmund Oasis – and the peaks rise to over
10,000 feet at Koh-i-Maran. The modern Quetta, an
oriental Camberley, sprawls unlovely by the side of the
ancient caravan town at the head of the great Bolan Pass,
linking Kandahar to the Indian Plains; a wide, fertile valley,
between the mountains where in spring the fruit-blossom
rivals in its brightness the snows still lingering on the heights.

Even with its modern irrigation the Sind Desert remains
repellent and inhospitable beyond the limits of the artificial
waterways. The ever-shifting mouths of the Indus lose themselves in a wilderness of lagoons and mangrove-swamps,
while 20 miles inland old shore-lines can be recognized, with
cliffs and promontories looking out over a desert of long-
dried mud. Behind Karachi the foothills of the Kirthar
Range rise stonily from the sand, and hot springs in the little
valleys give rise to unexpected secret oases of lush tropical
vegetation.

Northward, in the dreary country around Larkana, the
soil is so impregnated with salt that, drying in the summer
heat that rises to 120° in the shade, it has a brittle shining
crust that crushes beneath the step like a satanic mockery of
snow. The whole landscape is whitened, and forms a dead
background to the ugly stunted trees and grey-green bushes
that stud the plain.

It is in these mountainous and desert areas that the earliest
agricultural communities yet known in India have been
identified. Human settlement in the region is likely to go
back at least to the beginning of the third millennium B.C.,
and shows from the beginning significant links with the
ancient Bronze Age cultures of the regions farther west. The
abundant evidence of ancient occupation in the Baluchi
hills or the Indus plain implies less exacting climatic conditions in the past than at present, and, though historical

evidence implies that by the time of Alexander conditions in
Baluchistan approximated to those of today, yet we shall see
in the next chapter that there is good evidence for a heavier
rainfall, and extensive forests, in the Indus Valley in ancient
times. The very fact that kiln-burnt bricks were used so
lavishly in the Harappā culture shows that almost unlimited
timber must have been available for fuel in the third millennium B.C. A westward extension of the monsoon rains by
a comparatively small amount could entirely change the
character of this western Indian region.

It is less easy to find evidence of the former climate of
Baluchistan than it is for the Indus Valley. Today the terri-
tories of the Makran, Kharan, and Jhalawan in South Baluchistan, which contain a large number of prehistoric settlements, are very sparsely populated (not more than two persons to the square mile in Kharan), and this population is
partly migratory. The settlements which will form the subject of this chapter are, as will be seen, today represented by
'tells' of accumulated debris which can result only from
settled communities continuously inhabiting one site for
centuries. In the Kolwa region such settlements are particularly numerous, and today this tract is (to quote Stein)
'by far the greatest dry-crop area of Makran, and its export
of barley to other parts in years of good rainfall is considerable. Yet,' he goes on to say, 'how rare such rainfall is, and
how precarious this cultivation in Kolwa, is shown by the
very scanty population of the tract being practically all
nomadic.' This nomadism or seasonal migration is under the
present conditions a marked feature throughout Baluchistan,
and again one cannot do better than to describe it in Stein's
words:

'In consequence of the uncertainties besetting agriculture on all unirrigated land a very considerable portion
of the land-owning or tenant population is accustomed to

move annually for the winter months to the plains of Sind
... in search of employment. They thus avoid also the cutting cold of the winds which sweep down from the higher
valleys at that season. But in the spring when the great
heat of the Indus valley begins to make itself felt, they all
return with their families and with such savings as there
are invested in foodstuffs. But for this seasonal migration
a succession of unfavourable years such as is fairly frequent
would be marked by famine conditions, besides causing
whole areas of cultivation to relapse into the appearance
of a bare clay desert.'

It is clear that such seasonal migration is hardly compatible with the formation of 'tells' which may rise to a hundred
feet and more above the surrounding countryside, in impressive witness of long-enduring continuous settlement. In
the prehistoric past the population must have been enabled,
by successful agriculture, to live in some prosperity in those
same valleys which today support only the most scanty and
nomadic human occupation under wretched conditions.

In his explorations in Baluchistan these problems o.
climate and population were, of course, much before Sir
Aurel Stein's eyes, and he was able to identify a large series
of artificial stone-built dams and terraces, known locally in
Jhalawan as *gabarbands*, clearly designed to aid the irrigation of fields. The date of these is unknown, but, as Stein
remarks, they must reflect not only climatic conditions with
a greater rainfall, but also a large population to provide the
necessary labour for their construction. In the Mashkai
Valley a particularly well-preserved pair of massive, stone-
faced dams were found, 16 yards apart and designed to contain and guide flood-water coming from the hills above; and
these were associated with terraced fields. Near the Lakorian
Pass, farther to the north, a most impressive irrigation work
was found which was in fact a huge barrage, still standing up

to 12 feet high, and having a total length of 348 yards, constructed in such a way as to impound a considerable reser-
voir of water behind it. The dam had a well-built stone
facing containing blocks up to 4 by 3 by 2½ feet in size, and
was backed by an earthen ramp. Even though the age and
culture of these works are still unknown, their presence is
important in indicating greater rainfall in antiquity, and it
is by no means improbable that they do, in fact, date back
to the prehistoric occupation of the Baluchi Hills.

In Sind, even if the rainfall was heavier in prehistoric
times, cultivation must have depended to a large extent on
irrigation works connected with the Indus. At the present
day there is an annual increase in the flow of the river in
spring, owing to the melting of the winter snows in the Himalayas, where the river rises. This would have caused an
annual inundation in primitive conditions, comparable to
but less equable and dependable than that of the Nile and
more comparable with the Tigris–Euphrates floods. And
under these primitive conditions it is important to remember
that there are only two really fixed points in the course of
the river in Sind – at Sukkur and at Kotri, where it cuts
through hard limestone instead of soft soils. Between these
points, where the channel cannot vary its position, the Indus
would, under natural conditions, without man-made em-
bankments, tend to alter its course yearly, after every successive inundation. There is indeed abundant evidence from
the sites of the Harappā Culture that such alteration of
course, with consequent disastrous floods, was not uncommon in ancient times.

Before leaving the geographical background and turning
to an examination of the prehistoric cultures themselves,
attention must be drawn to Lake Manchhar, which lies between the Indus and the foothills of the Kirthar Range of
the Baluchi mountains near Johi. This is normally a lake
about 8 to 10 miles in length, and as much in breadth, but

being connected with the Indus and also receiving drainage from the hills to the west, in the inundation period it becomes enormously swollen, occupying an area of some 200

BRONZE AGE
SETTLEMENT SITES
IN WESTERN INDIA

○ QUETTA WARE ■ ZHOB CULTURES
● AMRI CULTURE ▲ KULLI CULTURE
◉ NAL-NUNDARA ◆ SHAHI-TUMP
　　CULTURE 　　CULTURE

LAND OVER 4000 FEET STIPPLED

0　　50　　100　　150
　　　　　　　　　MILES

FIG. 2

square miles, though nowhere more than 10 feet deep. Majumdar's field-work in Sind revealed a number of prehistoric sites around the edge of Lake Manchhar, some now islanded at 'high-water', though near the edge of the maximum extent of flooding. To the Manchhar region lead two

of the most important routes from Baluchistan in use today –
the more northerly, through the Mula Pass and down the
course of that river, turns south along the edge of the foothills and runs to Johi and the Manchhar region, while the
southern route comes from the Mashkai and Nal valleys over
the Lak Phusi and the Lak Rohel, entering Sind at Pandi
Wahi, near Johi. In addition to these two routes there is
clear evidence of traffic down the valley of the Gaj River to
the same region in prehistoric times.

As we have seen in the preceding chapter, it has been
possible to make a broad classification of the prehistoric cultures in Persia on the grounds of the techniques employed in
pottery-painting – in the south Buff-ware and in the north
Red-ware. In Baluchistan we can observe a similar distinction, with Buff Wares in the south and Red Wares in the
north. In addition, models of human figures in clay, known
from both north and south, differ in character. Within the
Buff-ware province of South Baluchistan and Sind other subdivisions must, I think, be made, and using names taken
from sites where the culture can be well identified, we can
then make a scheme of grouping as follows (Fig. 2) :

A. *Buff-ware Cultures.*
   1. *The Quetta Culture* (from sites in the Bolan Pass).
   2. *The Amri-Nal Culture* (from two sites, the first in Sind,
      the second at the head of the Nal Valley in Baluchi-
      stan).
   3. *The Kulli Culture* (from a site in Kolwa in South Balu-
      chistan).

B. *Red-ware Cultures.*
   4. *The Zhob Cultures* (from sites in the Zhob Valley of
      North Baluchistan).

In addition to these cultures, many probably prehistoric
sites discovered by Stein in Baluchistan and by Majumdar in
Sind produced pottery that cannot, in the present state of

our knowledge, be classified within the foregoing groups. Some of these sites (e.g. the Shahi-tump cemetery in Makran and the culture represented by pottery from Jhukar, Lohumjo-daro, and Chanhu-daro in Sind) are discussed in a later chapter (Chapter VI), where the evidence for their comparatively late date is given.

Our survey of prehistoric Baluchistan can therefore begin with the *Quetta Culture*. So little, however, remains of this most interesting phase that it can hardly be dignified with the name of a 'culture'; we are dependent on a characteristic pottery and a few fragments of alabaster cups, occurring as surface finds on five 'tells' in the immediate neighbourhood of Quetta. The largest of these was about 600 feet in diameter at the base and from 45 to 50 feet high, and could never have been more than a small village. As far as it was possible to determine on this and the other sites, the houses had been made of mud, or mud bricks, which had disintegrated again into homogeneous loamy soil.

The pottery recovered from these sites is, however, of great interest (Fig. 3). It belongs to the Buff-ware group, and is painted in a fine, assured, free style in a purplish-brown ('black') paint. No use is made of a second colour (e.g. red), and we shall see that this is a most unusual feature in Baluchistan, where two-colour schemes in black-and-red are very usual. The shapes of the pots, where these can be recovered, include beakers with a slightly flaring mouth, rather squat biconical or globular bowls, shallow dishes, and at least one fragment of a raised foot-stand perforated with triangular openings. The ware ranges from pinkish-white to greenish (from over-baking), and there are one or two fragments from fine shallow bowls of grey, very hard ware with black painted ornament.

The designs are wholly geometric and representations of animals or plants have not yet been discovered. Chevrons

formed by combining thick and thin bands occur, an overall
pattern made up of diagonally divided squares, pairs of

FIG. 3. Typical Quetta Ware

opposed triangles, and, most distinctive, various stepped
and oval motifs.

Now the outstanding feature of this group of pottery is
that, despite the very large number of sites discovered by

Stein in Baluchistan and by Majumdar in Sind, sites which
yielded an aggregate of many thousands of potsherds, there
is nothing strictly comparable to the Quetta material as a
group. The grey-ware bowls with black painted ornament,
it is true, appear also in certain Zhob Valley sites (e.g. at Sur
Jangal) and in Sistan, but for parallels to the predominant
Buff ware we can only look outside India, to the west. Here
we immediately find precise parallels – in a group of early
pottery from sites in the Fars province of Persia, notably
at Tal-i-Bakun near the site of Persepolis. We shall see, when
dealing with the Shahi-tump cemetery at a later stage, that
certain forms of this pottery had a very long survival in
Southern Persia and Baluchistan, but this derivative ware is
distinctively unlike that from the Quetta sites. Quetta ware
really does seem comparable to that represented by the Tal-
i-Bakun site itself, Susa I, Giyan V, and Sialk III, and may
be equally early in date. This is supported by the evidence
from Anau in Russian Turkestan, where intrusive elements
appearing between Anau I and II include black-on-red
painted ware, buff ware with ornament in red-and-black,
and buff ware with distinctive stepped motifs – an assemblage which seems to point strongly to Baluchistan as its
probable point of origin.

Pending further field-work and excavation, the fuller content of the Quetta Culture, which seems to be the earliest
yet identified in Western India, must remain unknown to us.
When we turn to the next group of cultures within the Buff-
ware class we have relatively abundant information on a
number of sites scattered over a large area, though the evidence is none of it derived from scientific or large-scale excavations.

The composite title adopted, the *Amri-Nal Culture*, indi-
cates the two extremes of variation which can be seen in an
otherwise allied group of pottery types, which can be divided
into three phases. The earliest typologically (though, as will

be seen, not perhaps chronologically in all instances) is
represented at Amri in Sind, where characteristic ware was
first identified by Majumdar, the latest by the cemetery of
Nal in Baluchistan excavated by Hargreaves; and the site of
Nundara, discovered by Stein in South Baluchistan, is a convenient representative of a middle phase. It is clear, however, that these pottery types are really linked, and this, with
other factors (notably the absence of clay figurines of animals or humans in all three phases), seems to justify their
treatment under one inclusive head.

The geographical distribution of the Amri phase is repre-
sented mainly by sites in Sind at the foot of the Kirthar
Range and between the Baran and the Gaj Rivers. In its
later phases its main area of occupation is in South Baluchistan, from the headwaters of the Kech Kaur north-eastwards through Kolwa, up the Mashkai Valley to Nal in
Jhalawan, and with sporadic sites farther north up to the
Bolan Pass at Quetta, and others at the headwaters of the
Kolachi, and down the Kolachi-Gaj valleys into Sind above
Lake Manchhar, along the routes already referred to. It has
also been recently reported from Las Bela State at the southern end of the Baluchi Mountains.

Turning now to the type and range of the settlements, we
find that in practically all instances the sites take the form of
'tells', formed by the debris of accumulated occupations and
ranging from 10 to 40 feet in height. It is difficult to estimate
the relative areas covered by the individual settlements because quite often the characteristic pottery by which the culture is distinguished was picked up only on the surface of the
mound or comes from trial trenches in the uppermost level.
Such an occupied area on top of a tell will of course be far
smaller than the overall dimensions of the mound at its base.
For instance, the Kargushki-damb in Rakshan is a tell some
530 by 360 yards at its base and 40 feet high, but Stein's
trial trenches (which yielded typical Nal sherds associated

with the walls of buildings) were made above the 30-feet contour, where the area available for occupation had diminished to about 200 by 100 yards, and one cannot assume that the preceding 30 feet of unexcavated material was necessarily the product of the same culture.

However, at Nundara itself the settlement producing the pottery of the type designated from this site seems likely to have occupied an area not far removed from the total 220 by 180 yards of the tell, while at Bandhni in Sind the area of Amri occupation may have been as much as 400 by 230 yards. But at the Sind sites of Pandi Wahi and Ghazi Shah, where excavation showed that the Amri ware levels were definitely at the base of the mounds, the areas were about 150 by 115 yards and 170 by 160 yards respectively, and other sites have similar proportions. The average size of the settlements, as far as it has been ascertained at present, seems in fact to have been something under two acres – about the size of the area enclosed by the lowest contours at Tepe Gawra, to instance a well-known prehistoric site in Mesopotamia.

At Kohtras Buthi in Sind there is a small settlement on a hill-spur which has double defensive walls built across the base of the spur to form, in European archaeological terminology, a 'promontory-fort' of the site. This fortification suggests comparison with another Sind site, that on Tharro Hill. Here is an isolated, flat-topped hill, now inland but on what was the prehistoric coast-line, from which it would have projected as a promontory or as an island in tidal marshes. The fortifications, as at Kohtras Buthi, take the form of double walls, curved and of massive construction and 250 feet apart, cutting off the southern headland of the hill in true promontory-fort manner. These walls are now ruined, though a stretch of original face has been exposed at one point on the inner defences, and their nature was unrecognized by Majumdar when he visited and reported on the site. Amri ware occurs on the surface, but there is also evidence of considerable occupation with plain red ware allied to that of Harappā, and it is therefore uncertain to which phase the defences belong, though the Amri period seems the most likely. At Dhillanijo-kot, again in Sind, there are traces of a defensive wall surrounding the Amri settlement, but in general the villages appear to have been undefended by walls or ramparts.

Stone was used for building at least the foundation courses of walls in most of the sites where architectural remains could be identified at all; in some of the Sind sites especially it is probable that the upper parts of the walls were of mud brick or pisée, and that a couple of courses of stones alone formed the foundations. But at Nundara, Kargushki-damb and Rodkan in Baluchistan coursed stone slabs set in mud mortar were used for the walls of houses at least up to window height, and at the latter site large blocks alternated with triple courses of small flat stones to give a decorative effect.

At Nundara some walls of mud bricks were found, as well as the masonry structures, the individual bricks measuring 21 by 10 by 4 inches, while mud bricks of the same dimensions were used to make the rectangular tombs of two infants and an adult in the Nal cemetery. At Nundara, too, the refinement of white plaster over the inner faces of stone and brick walls was observed.

In the Sind sites of Pandi Wahi and Ghazi Shah, where abundant occupational debris was found but no trace of buildings could be identified, it may be assumed that pisée was used exclusively and that it has (as at Quetta) disintegrated in the course of centuries. It is always possible, however, that mud bricks were in fact present, but unrecognized by the excavators.

Owing to the extremely limited excavations which have taken place and the absence of any detailed field surveys of the remains which are briefly recorded as visible on the sur-

face of certain sites, our knowledge of the lay-out of the
settlements is extremely meagre. The published plan of Nundara suggests blocks of buildings comforming to a common
orientation at least in the south-east part of the site, and in
the most interesting hill fortress of Kohtras Buthi, already
mentioned, Majumdar describes the surface indications of
'the outlines of countless rooms, both large and small, grouping themselves into blocks separated from one another by
alleys' inside the cyclopean defensive wall, but apparently
separated from it by an open space. This wall of large,
roughly-coursed blocks has at least four exterior bastions and
the remains of an entrance, while the ruins of a slighter outer
defence wall lie about 100 feet away. The published plan is,
however, very inadequate.

It is possible to say a little more about the plans of individual buildings or groups of rooms. On no site does any building or group of ruins suggest a temple or palace, and the
plans recovered all seem to belong to small private houses.
At Nundara groups of rooms which may constitute associated elements fall into blocks about 40 feet square, within
which there may be eight or ten subdivisions of sizes varying
from large rooms or courtyards 15 by 15 feet or 15 by 10 feet,
to small compartments 8 by 5 feet or less, and in two of the
blocks there seems to be a fairly consistent plan of large
rooms or courtyards, each associated with half a dozen
smaller ones. Rooms of similar proportions also seem characteristic of the Sind sites; at Kohtras Buthi a structure interpreted by Majumdar as a bath occupied the corner of one
room by the entrance, and in the same house the remains of
a stairway, implying access to a flat roof or an upper storey,
were found. Doorways of houses of which only stone foundations remained were rarely possible to identify, as such
foundations would continue to form the door sill; but at
Kargushki-damb a doorway was found still retaining traces
of its wooden lintel, and at Rodkan, in a wall still standing

5 feet high, a window was preserved, 1 foot 4 inches wide, its top formed by overlapping corbelled courses of stone. At Nundara several chambers with walls preserved to a height of at least 10 feet, in one instance, had no openings in the wall and contained a massive square stone-built pillar in the centre. Such chambers can best be explained as cellars, entered by trap-doors from the room above, the central pillar acting as additional support to the floor.

The width of roadways between houses can be measured in a few instances – 6 to 8 feet at Nundara, and narrow alleys 3 feet to 2 feet 6 inches wide at Lohri and Kohtras Buthi.

In addition to this information on the settlement sites, we are fortunate in having knowledge of two cemeteries, one in Baluchistan and one in Sind, both with pottery of the Nal phase, which in fact derives its name from the former site. The Sohr-damb of Nal was excavated on a fairly large scale, but at the Damb Buthi cemetery in Sind little work was done, and it is therefore to Nal that we turn for our fullest information on the burial rites of the culture.

When Hargreaves began his work at Nal the site had already been largely plundered by predatory digging at the beginning of the present century by an English colonel of antiquarian leanings, whose acquisitive enthusiasm for painted pots more than outweighed any vestiges of scientific interest he may have possessed, and to whose discredit the removal and subsequent disappearance of at least 200 vessels from the cemetery must be placed. Hargreaves found that the burials had been made in the deserted ruins of a settlement on the lower slopes of the main tell of the site; this settlement, in which he made several trial cuttings, did not itself yield any artifacts characteristic of the Amri-Nal Culture, and the scanty pottery finds fall in all probability into the Zhob Culture series, under which heading the occupation site is therefore described.

In the cemetery, however (Hargreaves' Sites A and G), between 30 and 40 burial groups were excavated, the greater number associated with characteristic pottery, 270 vessels being recovered. If this proportion of burials to pots is typical, as seems likely, the 300 odd pots found by Colonel Jacobs and other unscientific diggers in the same cemetery must represent another 40–50 burials, so that at least 100 interments must have been made in that area of the cemetery dug into and recorded in some way or other. As we are ignorant alike of the full extent of the burial ground and of finds made but not recorded, the figure is almost certainly an understatement of the total content.

Such a number of burials in one cemetery (and it should be pointed out that some of the Nal burial groups include the skeletal remains of six or seven individuals) implies a settled community of some duration, and the superposition of two layers of burials noted by Hargreaves reinforces this. On the other hand, several of the small communities which the habitation sites described above imply may have used a common cemetery over a proportionately shorter space of time, and there are surface indications of more than one such in the immediate vicinity of the Sohr-damb.

The burial rite was inhumation – at Nal one adult and three infants in the same part of the cemetery were normal burials with complete skeletons (the adult was recorded as on its left side and slightly flexed), but the dominant rite here and at Damb Buthi was that of 'fractional' burial – inhumation of fragments of the skeleton, probably after previous exposure and disintegration. Some of the Nal groups represented several individuals, adults and children together; others comprised merely a few bones from a single skeleton, and at Damb Buthi in one instance at least two adults were represented in a single burial group.

The burials at Nal were normally placed in the earth without any form of protection, but three of the complete inhumations (the adult and two infants already referred to) were enclosed in rectangular mud-brick graves, the individual bricks measuring 21 by 9 by 3½ inches. No trace of covering was detected. At Damb Buthi the fractional burials were contained in contiguous small rectangular stone-built chambers, about 5 by 8 feet, presumably analogous to the brick constructions at Nal, though the possibility of their being really rooms of abandoned dwellings must not be excluded.

Grave-goods with the fractional burials at both sites consisted in the main of pottery vessels, and a flat copper axe accompanied one burial at Nal. Animal bones, mainly sheep or goat, were found in at least six graves at this site, and there were bones of ox at Damb Buthi – no doubt food offerings. At each site there was a burial with red pigment – placed in a pair of mussel shells at Damb Buthi and with a colour-grinder at Nal. A great number of beads were found at Nal in the same areas as, though not directly associated with, the fractional burials; shell and pottery bangles were a distinctive feature in the Sind site.

The complete inhumations at Nal had no pottery associated with them, the only grave-goods being bead necklaces with the two infants, but there was no direct evidence that these burials were not contemporary with the remainder of the cemetery.

In the cemetery area at Nal two hoards of copper implements were found, with no directly associated skeletal remains. These again are presumably contemporary with the burials and pottery, and the axe found with one of the fractional burials is of a type similar to those in the hoards.

As we have already seen, we have to rely mainly on pottery in distinguishing one culture from another (Fig. 4). The two pottery types, Nal ware and Amri ware, seem to me to be parallel, slightly divergent, products of a single culture, the economic and architectural aspects of which (as far as

they can be studied) have just been discussed as the Amri-
Nal Culture. In South Baluchistan sites such as Nundara
yield sherds of vessels which, in forms and more particularly
in ornament, seem to represent an ancestral stock, from

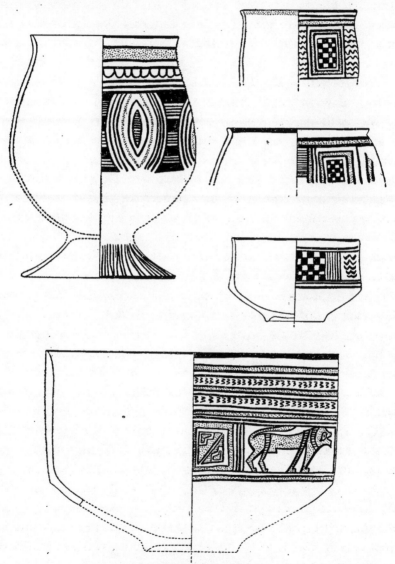

FIG. 4. Amri and Nundara beakers and Nundara bowls
(red paint stippled)

which derived on the one hand the only slightly evolved
Amri ware found across the mountains in Sind, and on the
other the highly developed Nal ware which seems to reach
the height of its specialization at the type-site in Jhalawan,
at the head of the Nal River – the cemetery just
described. But despite the divergences, even in their most
extreme forms the two pottery styles show traces of their
common origin. In the following description of the wares in
greater detail we shall look first of all at the features shared
by the sub-groups and then at the characteristic divergences.

The vast majority of all vessels of Nal and of Amri ware
have a distinctively very fine soft buff or pinkish paste,
which may sometimes approach an off-white and occasionally have a green tinge. On this, a white slip is frequently
applied as a background for painted ornament. At Nal itself, where the larger scale of excavation and the abundance
of intact vessels provided by a cemetery gave a more extended series than is otherwise available, a limited number
of vessels of grey or even dark-brownish colour, sometimes
verging on black, were found, either unornamented or with
motifs in relief or light paint, quite unlike the more abundant vessels of pale paste. The excellence and homogeneity
of the paste in all the vessels are shown by the extremely thin
walls often obtained. The pots are normally wheel-turned.

When we come to examine the forms of the pots divergence is more apparent than in ware, or ornament. The
scanty potsherds permit few complete restorations of the
Amri vessels, but the tall globular beakers from, for instance,
Lohri and Damb Buthi in Sind, taken in conjunction with
numerous rim and shoulder fragments of the same type from
all the Sind sites seem likely to be one characteristic form.
Similar pots are suggested by sherds from Baluchistan, for
instance at Zila and Hor-Kalat, associated with more specifically Nal forms, and, as will be seen, the ornament on these
beakers also presents close parallels to Amri patterns.

' A distinctive type which can be identified on at least two Amri sites (Amri itself and Pandi Wahi) is a shallow pedestal foot, which may belong to vessels of beaker type or, less probably, to bowls not otherwise identified. At Nal a single pedestal-foot has been recorded, though higher and more columnar than those suggested by the Amri sherds, and almost certainly from a bowl or 'offering-stand' type of vessel.

.. In such Baluchistan sites as Nundara, where the pottery is domestic and does not present the high degree of stylization present in the funerary vessels from the Nal cemetery, a straight-sided 'bucket' type occurs together with simple beaker forms, less globular than the norm of Amri ware. Neither of these forms appears in the Nal cemetery, where the bulk of the vessels are variations on bowl types with the diameter greater than the height. Actual bowls range from shallow open forms (also characteristic of a dark ware peeuliar to the site), globular bowls in which the rim incurves so that the shoulder diameter exceeds that of the mouth, small straight-sided cups, and squat shouldered pots rather similar to the bowls. A very remarkable form, found not only at Nal but also at many other sites of the culture in Baluchistan and in Sind, is the straight-sided 'canister' type of vessel, which is the most distinctive of all the Nal pottery types. Most of these types recur at the cemetery of Damb Buthi, mixed with other forms, such as tall beakers, more specifically characteristic of Amri ware. Peculiar to Nal itself are small saucers, pinched in on four sides to form vessels so like the modern Indian *chiragh* that one may assume that they, like their recent analogues, were used as lamps. A couple of double cylindrical pots from Nal may also be noted.

The painted ornament on the two groups of pottery appears at first sight to present a bewildering complexity of motifs, but there are certain main classifications which simplify the issue. Designs representing animal or plant forms are absent on Amri ware, but on the other hand are typical on Nal pots. An Amri sherd with part of the representation of an ox from Tando Rahim Khan, and a possible second example from Chauro serve merely to emphasize the total absence at all other sites except where (as shown below) it is derived from Kulli ware. Again, the material from Nal not only has motifs peculiar to itself, but lacks several patterns which appear farther south at Nundara and other sites and also in Amri ware. The decorative motifs may therefore be divided conveniently into two heads – first, motifs common to Amri and the southern Nal culture sites (such as Nundara), with a small sub-group of motifs peculiar to Amri itself, and, secondly, motifs common to all Nal sites but not present at Amri, and a subdivision of motifs peculiar to the Nal cemetery itself. All motifs are firmly outlined in a black or brownish paint applied with a stiff brush. Red paint is used as a secondary colour in Amri and the Nundara group of sites, and at Nal itself and a few other sites this red paint is augmented by yellow, blue, and green pigments to form an elaborate polychrome style. This use of blue and yellow is very remarkable, as it is almost unknown elsewhere in prehistoric Western Asia.

The ornamental features common to Amri and to such South Baluchistan sites as Nundara, Kargushki-damb, and some others are in the main as follows. First, a panelled arrangement is common, the panels being outlined horizontally and vertically with multiple lines. Then, within the rectangles so formed, a frequent motif is a secondary panel of black-and-white chequers, outlined by concentric rectangles of alternate red and black lines. Finally there is much use of horizontal (less commonly vertical) bands made of such motifs as solid diamonds corner-to-corner, hatched diamonds, small chevrons, loops (sometimes multiple), the 'sigma' ornament, and 'scale' pattern.

In Sind, but apparently not in Baluchistan, there also appear motifs peculiar to the Amri ware of that region, beginning with the use of red paint in a broad horizontal band between black lines at the top (and in one example at least the bottom) of the decorated area of the pot. There are two interesting variations on the chequer motif – a criss-cross of vertical and horizontal lines, arranged in panels, and panels of squares half-filled diagonally. One example at least shows large pointed oval forms outlined by multiple alternating red and black lines. But these divergent types of ornament (except the use of broad red horizontal bands, which is almost constant) are distinctly uncommon, and most pots have ornamental motifs in common with the Nundara style.

When we turn to the decorative motifs distinctive of the Nal style the main feature noticeable is a tendency to use multiple parallel lines to form not only panels but such patterns as diagonal steps or stepped chevrons, equal-armed crosses, diamonds, circles, and numerous variations of over-all curved motifs in multiple wavy patterns. These geometric motifs are most distinctive of the Nal style, combined in the Nundara region with the use of red, and at Nal itself and analogous sites with red, blue, green and yellow paint used in flat blocks of colour, but not in lines (Fig. 5).

In addition, striking representations of animals occur – in Nundara ware there are animals, probably lions, fishes, and birds represented, the bodies often being filled in with red paint. A single representation of an ox occurs (at Hor-Kalat: Fig. 8, bottom centre), and heart-shaped motifs, based on the forms of the leaves of the *pipal* tree, also occur, and may owe their origin, as we shall see, to influence from the Indus Valley. The pipal, or sacred fig, was accounted a holy tree in prehistoric India and still retains its sanctity today. At Rohel-jo-Kund, Pandi Wahi, Kerchat, and other sites in Sind decorative motifs, such as animals or rows of stylized ibex heads, which appear to be derived from the Kulli Culture, appear alongside the normal Nal ornament.

In the mature Nal phase as seen in the cemetery itself the

FIG. 5. Polychrome Nal Ware (red paint stippled, yellow
horizontal and blue vertical shading)

decorative repertoire is at once more limited and more complex. The simple patterns of chequers, diamonds, red-out-
lined panels, and 'sigma' signs seem to have been forgotten,
the multiple-outlined rectilinear and curved figures have
become complicated and dominant, and overall intersecting-

circle ornament is also seen. The animal representations now include new types of birds, ibexes, and scorpions: a curious yoke-shaped symbol, perhaps stylized from the 'sigma', frequently appears. Colours now extend not only to red but to blue, green, and yellow. Though these latter tend to be fugitive and easily rubbed off the surface of the pot, the fact that no trace of colour other than red can be detected on the abundant sherds at Nundara seems to justify the conclusion that a two-colour decoration was all that was in vogue there.

Although we have described as a stylistic sequence the relationship between the Amri, Nundara, and Nal styles of pot painting, it is not possible to say that these stages actually followed one another in time. The decisive evidence, of course, would be that of stratigraphy, but, as we have seen, the lack of good stratigraphical sequences is one of the troubles in Indian prehistory, and we can throw little light on the relationships of the three styles by this means. At the sites in the Nundara region, Amri types appear to be associated superficially with those distinctive of Nundara itself, and in Sind Nal motifs and potsherds do occur in a stratigraphical context, which implies that they are contemporary with at least a late phase of Amri. On the whole, the impression one gains is that while the curious and elaborate Nal style evolved in the mountain fastnesses of Jhalawan, the less distinctive Amri motifs enjoyed a long popularity with little change in Sind, and that the Nundara style may well have continued to exist side by side with both of these.

Turning now to other aspects of the material culture, we have important evidence of metal-working in the Amri-Nal group. In the Nal cemetery two hoards of copper implements were found, the first (in Room A3 of a house of the deserted settlement into which the cemetery was dug) containing five objects, three of which were flat axes, the cutting edges not splayed, and the butts tapering. The other two objects were a very long, parallel-sided chisel with unsplayed edge, and another fragment of a tapering axe or chisel. The other copper hoard, in Room A5, comprised two axes with slightly splayed and curved cutting edges and narrow elongated butts, an axe or chisel with slightly splayed edge and a very elongated bar-shaped butt, a straight-sided saw, part of a tanged knife or spear-head, and another fragment, probably of a knife. No analyses were made of these tools, but a fragment of a similar type of axe found near gave:

Copper	..	..	..	93.05 per cent.
Lead ..	..	..	..	2.14 ,, ,,
Nickel ..	..	..	..	4.80 ,, ,,
Arsenic	..	..	..	trace

A few other fragments of copper implements were found at Nal (and as we have seen, one axe was found with a burial), and a copper bangle at Nundara. At Ghazi Shah in Sind there was a copper bead in the Amri levels.

These copper tools are interesting from several points of view. The composition of the metal, with its surprisingly high proportion of nickel, should prove to be a valuable pointer to the source of the native ore when more is known about the distribution of impurities in native copper deposits of the Orient. We know that certain copper objects from Mesopotamia had a relatively large proportion of nickel in their composition – two Early Dynastic specimens, from Ur and Kish respectively, had as much as 3.34 and 2.20 per cent., though the average is below this – and a possible source for Sumerian copper, the mountains of Oman, yield an ore with a perceptible nickel content. On the other hand, nickel is sometimes present in the copper used at Mohenjo-daro and Harappā, rising to 9.38 per cent. in one object and to 3.34 in another, and its presence is attested in the ores of Rajputana and Afghanistan. There is, therefore, in the present state of our knowledge an unfortunately wide field over which we can look for a probable origin for the Nal copper: it may be a local Baluchi ore, for ancient copper workings are alleged to exist in that area. The comparatively small amount of arsenic suggests a source different perhaps from that which produced the copper of the Harappā Culture.

The types of tools will be commented on at a later stage when we come to discuss the affinities and date of the culture, but for the present it is sufficient to notice the primitive form of flat axe, similar in general terms, though not in detail, to those of equally primitive type from the Harappā Culture. As we shall see, the more sophisticated shaft-hole axe, known in Mesopotamia from Early Dynastic times, is a late-comer to Western India.

In contrast to their abundance throughout most of the ancient Bronze Age cultures of Persia and Mesopotamia, the virtual absence of stamp-seals in Western India is very marked – except, that is, in the Harappā Culture, with its very distinctive series of square seals, so well known: In the Amri-Nal Culture there is only one seal certainly recorded, and that is from the Nal cemetery. Here was found a curious seal of irregular shape engraved with a vulture, outlined and cross-hatched in the technique of the bird drawings on the pottery, with its foot on a snake. The material of the seal is steatite, the surface artificially bleached white in a manner very common in the Harappā Culture. There was also a copper stamp seal found during the Nal excavations, but there is nothing to associate it directly with either the earlier settlement or the later cemetery on the site, though, as we shall see in Chapter VI, it is likely to be relatively late in date.

Beads were found in some abundance in the Nal cemetery, biconical or barrel-shaped and made of agate or carnelian, and an agate bead was found at Ghazi Shah in Sind. Lapis lazuli was also used for beads at Nal, and a bead of this stone

was also found in Sind, at Pandi Wahi. Lapis, as we shall see
in Chapter V, is an exotic substance much valued in the
ancient Orient, and probably obtained mostly from Persia
or Afghanistan. It was used by the Harappā folk, and there
are lapis beads from other sites in Baluchistan. An important
substance used at Nal for making beads, especially tiny
discs, was the artificial paste with glass frit known as faience
– a substance well known in the Harappā Culture but not
elsewhere in prehistoric Western India, and fitting in with
the evidence of the whitened steatite seal. Another point of
contact may be afforded by a perforated stone weight from
Nal and two others from a site probably of the same culture
at Nichara, all of which are very similar in shape to weights
from Mohenjo-daro. As we shall see, the system of weights in
the Harappā Culture is curious and distinctive, but the Nal
weight does not fit into the known series, though the type is
distinctly similar to the Mohenjo-daro specimen.

In the Damb Buthi cemetery were pottery and shell bracelets similar to those of the Harappā Culture, and in at least
seven Amri sites in Sind were found chert blades and cores;
this pre-metallic industry of stone tools has been mentioned
in Chapter II and need not necessarily imply a particularly
great antiquity, for there is a noticeable survival of such
blades in the Harappā Culture itself. Finally it should be
noticed that there was no evidence that any of the clay
figurines of animals found in the Nal excavations were associated with the cemetery, and in view of their total absence
from all other sites of the Amri-Nal Culture, they may safely
be attributed to the previous settlement (of Red-ware folk),
into the ruins of which the cemetery was dug.

We are now in a position to summarize our knowledge of
the Amri-Nal Culture and to review it in its relationship with
other Indian prehistoric cultures and those of the Bronze Age
Orient at large. The small settlements, with houses built of
stone or mud brick, compare, as we shall see, with those of

Kulli or the Zhob Valley people: the lack of burnt bricks suggests that any contact with the Harappā Culture was not of so fundamental a character as to introduce this way of building. Of lay-out and house-plans we know little, and we can only say that here, as with the other Baluchistan cultures, there is a generalized resemblance to the village or small urban communities known throughout the Ancient East in the prehistoric periods, which, even though not contemporary in date with those of India, represent the background from which they emerged.

The burial rites as seen in the cemeteries of Nal and Damb Buthi, with either total or fractional inhumations, do not give us many points of contact elsewhere. Cremation seems the rite in the Zhob Culture, and probably again in Kulli. On Tharro Hill, in Sind, there are burial cairns near the defended settlement presumably covering inhumations, but the associated pots suggest a form of the Harappā Culture rather than relationship with the Amri ware from the site. At Harappā itself the burials in the R 37 Cemetery were extended inhumations, contemporary with the occupation of the city, and in the later H Cemetery at the same site the earliest phase had both normal and fractional inhumations laid in the earth with accompanying pots, the second phase fractional burials in pots. Both phases appeared to be subsequent to the main occupation of the city.* On the whole, then, the rites of the Nal cemetery suggest comparison with the first phase of the H Cemetery at Harappā rather than with other sites, but this can hardly be taken as signifying any close connexion between the two in culture or chronology.

In Sind there is a certain amount of direct stratigraphical evidence for fixing the position of Amri ware at least in relation to the Harappā Culture. At the type-site of Amri itself,

---

* To anticipate a point argued in greater detail later on, I should say that I do not accept the so-called 'post-cremation burials' in the Harappā Culture as being burials at all.

at Ghazi Shah, Lohri and Pandi Wahi, the stratified sequence showed on each site an earlier occupation with Amri ware (and a small proportion of Nal types), later superseded by a Harappā Culture settlement. At Pai-jo-Kotiro in the Gaj Valley, however, the two cultures seem to be mixed, and chronologically indistinguishable. At Ghazi Shah the later occupation is of extreme interest as containing not only Harappā types of black-on-red pottery, but others which show motifs derived from Kulli sources, and on one pot even Nundara (or Nal) patterns painted on in black on a strong red background. This all suggests that there was approximate contemporaneity between at least the later phases of the Amri-Nal Culture and that of Kulli and perhaps with the earlier settlements of the Harappā Culture in Sind; further Kulli influence is perceptible at Rohel-jo-Kund in the Gaj Valley on sherds contemporary with Nundara or Nal styles, and on several other sites in Sind. But in the Nal cemetery, as we have seen, there is clear evidence of contact with the Harappā Culture, and for what it is worth there is a single sherd of Nal ware from the post-Harappā (Jhukar Culture) level at the site of Lohumjo-daro.

The animal ornament at Nundara (and to a less extent at Nal) offers a very interesting point of comparison with the Kulli Culture. On the Nundara pots the animals (mainly lions, but once an ox) are painted with curious horizontally banded stripes down their forequarters and loins, and this same peculiar trick occurs not on the painted pots, but on the painted animal figurines in the Kulli Culture (Fig. 8). The use of broad bands of red paint at the top and bottom of the main ornamental zone of a vessel is again an arrangement common to Amri ware and that of Kulli, and the Nal 'canister' is comparable with the squat bottle form known in Kulli-Mehi sites (Fig. 6). But the use of the *pipal*-leaf motif, and that of intersecting circles, at Nal must again be related to Harappā, and so must the faience beads, the whitened steatite stamp-seal and perhaps the stone weight. The polychrome pottery of Mohenjo-daro and Harappā is vaguely comparable to Nal, but no more; the single sherd from Chanhu-daro, however, with its use of a yellow background, may be rather more to the point.

The Nal copper tools are in part comparable with Harappā types, though the axes are dissimilar in outline. But the spearhead and the saw can be matched in the Harappā series, as can the long bar-chisels, and we shall see in Chapter VI that these tools provide a most important link between Nal and the mysterious copper implements of the Ganges Basin, which seem related to those of Harappā, but perhaps later in date.

When we turn to the prehistoric cultures of Persia or of Mesopotamia for parallels to the Amri-Nal Culture we meet with vague correspondences, but never more. The pottery is clearly a member of the Buff-ware group, but while there is a generalized resemblance in motifs (especially in Amri ware) there is nothing of the precision which exists between Quetta ware and that from Fars. Indeed, the Fars material is akin to Amri only in the broadest terms, and the almost constant use of ancillary red paint in the Indian pottery divides it off completely from the rest of the Persian series; the Jemdet Nasr wares of Mesopotamia provide the only parallel, and those again only in very general terms. The drawing of the animals at Nal and Nundara might be compared with the firm, competent outlines seen on engraved bone and shell plaques in Early Dynastic Sumer, but in no other respects can Sumerian contacts be traced. If, in its early stages, the Amri-Nal Culture has a vaguely Iranian origin, its later developments either took place in isolation or were the result of contact with the Harappā Culture to the east. The firm, assured style of Nal, with its sense of design and spacing, is very remarkable, and unlike most Western Asiatic painted pottery. There is more than a suggestion of familiarity with incrustation and inlay techniques such as those of Early Dynastic Sumer, and the total effect is extremely sophisticated and competent.

The third distinctive culture within the Buff-ware group which can be identified in Western India is that named from a South Baluchistan site in the Kolwa region as the *Kulli Culture*. As before, it is distinguished mainly on the grounds of a very characteristic painted pottery style, and is known from a relatively limited number of sites in South Baluchistan, lying mainly in the Kolwa district (where trial trenches in the type-site of Kulli were made by Stein) and that of Mashkai, with outliers on the Dasht River and at least one sporadic occurrence far away near the headwaters of the Korakan River.

While traces of its influence in pottery styles are perceptible into Eastern Persia, the culture does not appear to have crossed the mountain barrier eastwards into the Indus plain, though the influence of its pot-painting traditions are recognizable on alien wares in the Lake Manchhar region and in the Gaj Valley. Over most of the area of settlement in Baluchistan, Kulli ware is largely coincident with the Nundara and Nal wares of the Amri-Nal Culture, but it does not seem to occur in regions as far north as those inhabited by the makers of Nal ware between the type-site and the Bolan Pass, nor, as has been noted above, do its makers appear to have made the eastward move in Jhalawan which is attested by Nal ware in the Kolachi and Gaj Valleys. In addition to the distinctive character of the pottery forms and ornament, the Kulli Culture is given further definition, and its independent status *vis-à-vis* the Amri-Nal Culture is strengthened by a difference of burial rite and the abundance of clay figurines of women and animals on almost every site of the culture identified.

Notably at the site of Mehi in the Mashkai, two strains can be observed in the culture, one represented by the normal painted wares and the other by plain wares and associated artifacts of types derived from the Harappā Culture of the Indus Valley and the Punjab. Interaction between the two strains is also apparent in a most interesting fashion.

As with the Amri-Nal Culture, the sites characterized by Kulli ware are normally tells, and the same factors already noted as limiting the area of settlements occupying the upper part of such a sub-conical mound apply equally here. At the type-site of Kulli itself the area of visible ruins yielding characteristic finds of the culture, above the 20-feet contour, is about 200 yards square, while at Mehi the excavations, which sounded an occupation layer and a small cemetery (both apparently of the same culture), were all within the 30-feet contour of the great mound; the 25-feet line, within which this phase of settlement might more reasonably be supposed to lie (the 30-feet contour enclosing only a small 'acropolis' rising to 50 feet), encloses an area about 175 by 150 yards. The tell of Shahi-tump, in which excavations were carried to the base and remains of the Kulli Culture found in the lowest levels, was not more than 80-90 yards across. The size of typical settlements, in fact, seems, like those of the Amri-Nal Culture, to have been not greater than about two acres.

At Shahi-tump two building phases, and a possible third, were identified in superimposed deposits, all apparently of the same culture. At two sites probably of the Kulli Culture, Teji and Mazena-damb in South Baluchistan, indications of a probable defensive wall around the settlement were noted by Stein, and similar walls may have existed at the Shahi-damb of Jhau. The normal building material employed was stone, ranging from rough rubble masonry set in mud mortar to the carefully squared shale and sandstone ashlar blocks, arranged in decorative courses and brought from at least

2 miles distant, at the type-site. A somewhat similar use of
stone is seen at Adasta-jamb, which, surface finds suggest, is
of the Kulli Culture. Mud bricks (of unspecified sizes) were
apparently used in addition to stone at Mehi, while a wall of
the latest occupation-level at Shahi-tump had stone foundations and an upper structure of mud bricks each 19 by 10 by
3 inches.

At Kulli, where the most extensive architectural remains
were found, a flagged paving was found at one point, and
there were indications of a wooden flooring over a cellar at
another. Here, too, as at Nundara, stone walls were sometimes faced internally with white plaster. Owing to the
scanty excavations in the sites of the culture little can be said
of the houses. At Kulli rooms ranging from 12 by 8 feet to 8
by 6 feet were found, and the same type of windowless and
doorless cellars as at Nundara occurred. The lower treads of
a stone stairway at Kulli imply access to a flat roof or to an
upper storey.

Information about burial rites is even more scanty. A
flexed inhumation burial was found at Kulli at a depth of 4
feet in the debris of the settlement; there were no grave-
goods and consequently its association with the culture is
unproven. At Mehi, however, Stein cut a trench through a
cremation cemetery, the burials of which had been deposited
in the superficial 6 feet of debris on the western slope of the
tell. Here minor variations of the cremation rite (which
seems to have been performed on the spot) were observed:
in some burials the cremated bones were in pots; in others
deposited directly in the soil; while in one six children's
skulls had been placed over a single cremated adult. Pottery,
clay figurines and copper objects comprised the grave-goods,
but as only ten burials were found in a trench 75 feet long
by 6 feet wide, there does not appear to have been a marked
concentration. The position of the cemetery, on the slope
of the mound and so outside the settlement area, would

allow of its being coeval with the final phase of occupation of the site.

The discussion of the pottery from the Kulli settlements is complicated by the presence of varied traditions which cannot be separated stratigraphically. Majumdar saw the danger of considering the material from Mehi as necessarily of one period, and stylistic considerations suggest that there are two ceramic strains, representing an earlier painted ware local to the region on which impinged a plain ware, manifestly an offshoot of the Harappā Culture. Of these two, the decorated pottery alone should perhaps be credited with the title 'Kulli', and the hybrid types which are formed with this and the Harappā ware, be distinguished as a 'Mehi' phase, from the site where it is best represented. But it is safer to separate out only the unmistakable Harappā ware and to treat the hybrids along with the rest of the painted pottery.

We shall return to the Harappā Culture elements in South Baluchistan when dealing with this culture and its colonies in a later chapter; for the present we may notice that distinctive pottery appears at three sites — at Sutkagen-dor, which appears to be a settlement of the Harappā Culture practically unmixed with any local features, at Mehi, and to a lesser extent Kulli. The pottery is not only mixed with actual Kulli-style painted sherds, but the adaptations of Kulli decorative schemes appear on vessels whose shapes are those of Harappā, notably the 'offering-stands' or footed plates, and there is more than a suspicion of influences from the Indus Valley on the ornamentation of certain sherds. In the discussion of Kulli ware below, Harappā elements in the pottery collected by Stein are referred to only in so far as they combine to form genuine hybrids with the local ware.

The actual paste of the pottery is normally buff or pinkish, the former relatively soft but the latter, especially in those pots showing influence from Harappā ware, usually somewhat harder. There is frequently a pale red or sometimes a whitish slip, on which painted ornament is placed, mainly in black but with an occasional use of red in broad horizontal bands. Apparently under Harappā influence, black-on-red wares appear, the red, however, being paler than the strong red slip characteristic of Harappā or of so much of the Zhob Valley wares. There is a small proportion of hard, fine, pale grey sherds, sometimes with burnished surface and of simple profiles, and grey ware is also used for large storage jars, and in one instance for a vessel with incised ornament copying a stone original.

There is a varied repertoire of forms, the only type certainly due to Harappā influence being dishes-on-stands. Globular beakers, small-based flasks, tall bottle-shaped vases, small flat dishes and straight-sided cups are common, and an individual and distinctive form is a squat straight-sided jar (Fig. 6). Large storage vessels, sometimes painted and sometimes plain, have a globular profile and applied cordons on the shoulders, sometimes with an applied wavy band as well. The tall, cylindrical, perforated vessels, which might be braziers or cheese-presses, are, however, so similar to Harappā types as to be probably intrusive.

The typical painted decoration on Kulli ware consists of zones of non-representational motifs between which, in many instances, runs a frieze of naturalistic representations of animals and plants. This frieze forms the major content of the pot's ornament, and forms a single, continuous band around the pot. Metaphorically it is conceived in the manner of a cylinder-seal rather than the arrangement in Nal ware of animals within close square metopes, which might be compared to the stamp-seal idea. The frieze represents a standard scene, in which two animals, usually humped cattle but sometimes felines, dominate, in grotesquely elongated form, a landscape with formalized trees and sometimes ancillary rows of diminutive, very stylized goats

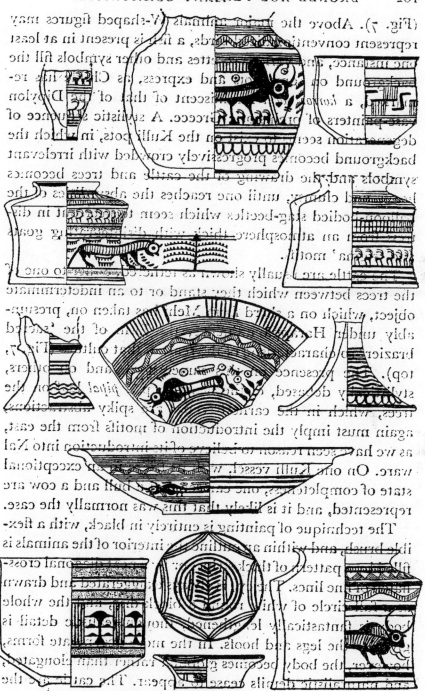

FIG. 6. Typical Kulli Ware (red paint stippled)

(Fig. 7). Above the major animals W-shaped figures may represent conventionalized birds, a fish is present in at least one instance, and various rosettes and other symbols fill the background on some pots and express, as Childe has remarked, a *horror vacui* reminiscent of that of the Dipylon vase-painters of prehistoric Greece. A stylistic sequence of degeneration seems to exist on the Kulli pots, in which the background becomes progressively crowded with irrelevant symbols and the drawing of the cattle and trees becomes heavy and clumsy, until one reaches the absurdities of the balloon-bodied stag-beetles which seem to peer out in distress from an atmosphere thick with disintegrating goats and 'sigma' motifs.

The cattle are usually shown as tethered, either to one of the trees between which they stand or to an indeterminate object, which on a sherd from Mehi has taken on, presumably under Harappā influence, the form of the 'sacred brazier' so characteristic of the seals of that culture (Fig. 7, top). The presence on this same sherd, and on others, stylistically debased, of the heart-shaped *pipal* leaf on the trees, which in the earliest scenes are spiky abstractions, again must imply the introduction of motifs from the east, as we have seen reason to believe of its introduction into Nal ware. On one Kulli vessel, with its frieze in an exceptional state of completeness, one can see that a bull and a cow are represented, and it is likely that this was normally the case.

The technique of painting is entirely in black, with a flexible brush, and within an outline the interior of the animals is filled by a pattern of thick stripes or by a neat diagonal cross-hatch of fine lines. The eye is always exaggerated and drawn as a full circle of white round a black disc, and the whole body is fantastically lengthened, though realistic detail is given to the legs and hoofs. In the more degenerate forms, however, the body becomes globular rather than elongated, and naturalistic details cease to appear. The cattle are the

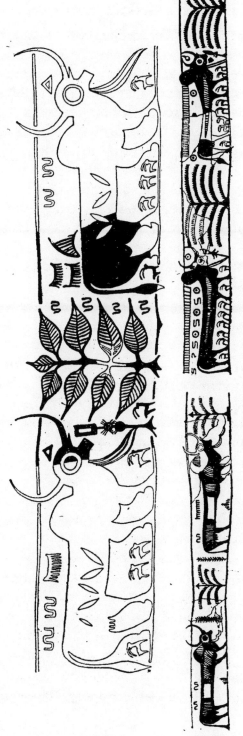

FIG. 7. 'Animals in Landscape' motifs on Kulli ware

typical humped form (*Bos indicus*) which appears everywhere in the Western Indian prehistoric cultures. The goat
figures, which so often accompany the cattle on the vase-
paintings, are more stylized, and may equally well represent black buck or ibexes with curved, swept-back horns.
Fishes are sometimes used to form a continuous band of
design on shallow plates, where they follow one another
head-to-tail in a narrow circular zone. The rather uncommon felines have clawed feet, but other distinctive features
are hard to find. The heads show ears and the large circular
eye in the manner of the cattle. There are various forms of
the tree motif used, some certainly modified by Harappā
contacts, and the birds shown on one fragment of pottery
certainly seem of Harappā derivation.

The geometric ornament, used in conjunction with the
foregoing motifs, or by itself, is varied, very rarely in panels
and normally in zones. A wavy hatched band between horizontal lines is characteristic, and this is sometimes carried
out in relief on raised cordons applied to the body of the pot.
Double triangles, point-to-point, form one of the rare meto-
pic patterns; hatched triangles and diamonds and lines of
solid triangles point-to-base are frequent. A band of pendent
loops is another common pattern, and the 'sigma' and the
'eye' motif of a dot within a circle or oval are also common.
Red paint is sometimes used as a second colour in the form
of broad horizontal bands above and below the main
decorative zone of the vessel.

A single fragment from the occupation layers at Shahi-
tump (of the Kulli Culture and earlier than the cemetery on
the same site) is of hard grey ware with channelled incisions
in straight lines and zig-zags, and belongs to a peculiar class
of pottery imitating stone vessels, which is described later on.
Similar fragments come from other sites in Baluchistan and
the adjacent regions of Persia and Sistan.

Outside the western boundaries of Baluchistan, and so

strictly outside the bounds of this book, which is confined to
prehistoric India, there are at least two sites which must be
mentioned before leaving the discussion of Kulli pottery, as
they show strong signs of contact and fusion between the old
tradition of the painted wares of Fars, and of Persia generally, and that of Kulli ware. In the Bampur region of Persian Makran there are cemeteries and settlement sites, and
settlements occur again in Sistan, which produce vessels
with characteristic raised wavy bands between cordons,
rows of stylized buck or ibexes, tree motifs and an occasional naturalistic large-scale animal, all so reminiscent of
Kulli ware as to suggest interchange of ideas and perhaps of
actual population between the Mashkai–Kolwa region and
that farther to the west. Stone vessels and their pottery imitations already referred to form yet another link between the
two areas, and these are discussed at a later stage. Certain
exceptional vessels with a high shoulder and a plain, bright
red slip from the Khurab cemetery near Bampur again have
exact parallels at Mehi, in the cemetery there, and in both
places may owe their presence to the intrusive Red-ware
traditions of the Harappā people.

A most interesting and attractive feature of the Kulli Culture, and one which marks it off from the other regional
groups we have studied, is the frequent presence of baked
clay figurines of women or of cattle. It must be confessed at
the outset that we have no certain knowledge of the use or
purpose of these little figures, and in some instances at least
they can be regarded only as toys, but the female figurines
at least have some claims to be thought of as deities or household shrines. The use of such clay figures as votive offerings
or as the constituent deities of rural shrines is common in
contemporary popular Hinduism, whose roots strike back
into the prehistoric past; once in the Dekkan I remember
finding remote from any village a shrine consisting of a shelf
of rock on which stood a dozen or fifteen clay figures of

horses and elephants, which constituted the sole visible evidence of sanctity save for the grease of libations over the rock face.

The Kulli figurines are of clay, and the animals are painted, though not the women, and the detailed modelling of the latter is more elaborate than that of the animals. The ware is usually pinkish buff, sometimes almost white.

Cattle figurines were found in very large numbers – 66 were found, for example, in the restricted areas Stein dug into at Kulli, and no less than 85 were found in a restricted area on the lowest occupation-floor at Shahi-tump, which looks more like offerings massed at a shrine than the stock of a toy-shop. The size of the figures is from 3 to 4 inches long, and the characteristic features of the humped cattle are well enough suggested. The eyes are painted in, and additional ornament takes the form of vertical stripes across the body, and a line of short transverse strokes down the shoulders and forelegs (Fig. 8). This decoration, which, as we have seen, recalls the treatment of the animals painted on the Nundara pots, may be purely an adornment of the figurine, or may imply a prehistoric custom of painting the real animal in the manner of the gay ochre spots and stripes that on festivals adorn the grey-white Brahmini bullocks of the present day. From one site (Men-damb) comes a bull figurine with the stumpy stylized legs pierced for wheel-axles and with a hole through the hump for a string to pull it along; clay wheels have also been found on other sites; and in this case we are obviously dealing with a child's toy. This is a convenient place to mention the little modelled representation of a dog on the edge of a pot from Mehi, and there are also certain model birds, often hollow and with a hole at the 'tail' which, if adroitly held to the lips, can be blown into in such a way as to produce a surprisingly loud hooting noise, as I once found to my own astonishment (and even more to that of the attendants) in the Central Asian Museum one day in

1942. But these bird-whistles are more common in the
Harappā Culture, and it is probably there that we should
look for their origin in the Kulli sites.

The female figurines, although less abundant than those of
cattle, are widespread among the sites of the Kulli Culture
and are of very great interest (Fig. 9). They all terminate at
the waist in a slightly splayed, flat-bottomed pedestal, and
the arms are akimbo with the hands on the hips (once only

FIG. 8. Painted bull figurines, Kulli Culture and
animals on Nundara pottery

raised above the breasts). There is no attempt at naturalism
in the face, which is pinched out of the clay into a fantastic
aquiline profile, making an absurd caricature resembling
nothing so much as a scared hen, with the eyes made from
centrally pierced applied pellets and no indication of the
mouth. The breasts are shown on several figurines, but there
is no exaggeration to suggest stress on the maternal aspect,
and indeed in many examples no indications of breasts at all
are given beneath the heavy strings of beads which the

figurines are so often represented as wearing; but one figurine is represented as holding two infants in its arms.

Although the faces of these figures are so sketchily presented, a great deal of care was lavished on the representation of their hairdressing and ornaments, and we can

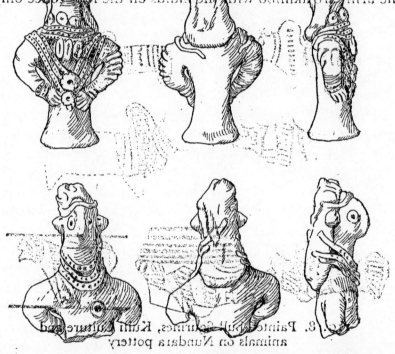

FIG. 9. Clay figurines of women, Kulli Culture

reconstruct with some accuracy from the rather crude clay modelling the appearance of a young woman of Kulli in her finery. Her hair was dressed to a high pile of curls in front, and held back by a fillet above the forehead, and the greater part was looped into a thick, heavy tress which rested on the nape of the neck. This was the standard style, but two figurines show the hair brought down in two long braids or plaits on to the shoulders in front. Over the ears were worn conical ornaments (such ornaments have been found in the Harappā cities), and round the neck a complex arrangement of beads. In the more elaborate, this begins with a 'choker' of large beads beneath the chin, and is followed by three rows of necklets of smaller beads, the lowest having a series of oval pendants hanging from it which seem likely to be cowrie shells. Below these again hang long strings of beads reaching to the waist, each with a central pendant.

And ornament did not stop here, for the bangles or armlets still so beloved of Indian girls are shown on the wrists and arms of these Kulli figures. Several of these bangles are shown at each wrist, but the left arm only has further bangles (above or at) the elbow, which might imply a garment of *sari* type worn in such a manner as to leave this arm bare. Otherwise there is no indirect or direct evidence of clothing to be derived from these figures, but, roughly modelled though they are, they do give us a most entrancing glimpse of the people of prehistoric Baluchistan, who otherwise are such shadowy archaeological abstractions behind the potsherds and ruins from which we reconstruct their story. We seem at least to have come face to face with the women of the Kulli folk when we have studied these little clay figures, and when we are describing the Harappā Culture we shall, I think, recognize a Kulli girl in a foreign city.

Before leaving the clay figurines and toys of the Kulli Culture we must notice one important type of model more likely to be a toy than a votive offering. We saw that a bull on wheels was found at one site – clay wheels for such movable models have been found more than once, and at Mehi and Shahi-tump there have also been found bits of clay models of carts. Now clay carts are very common indeed in the Harappā Culture, and fragments of them turn up on almost every site of the culture, however small, so their presence at Shahi-tump and Mehi may be explained in terms of Harappā imports. The Shahi-tump fragment is, indeed, very much of the Harappā type, and though that from Mehi is of a less common form, there are pretty good parallels for it at Chanhu-daro at least, so that on the whole the carts in the Kulli Culture cannot be claimed as necessarily an integral part of the culture, and are more likely to belong to Harappā trade and traders in the Mashkai and the Makran regions. In the hill country of Baluchistan, carts would be less essential to the farming communities than in the Indus plain.

A very important group of vessels carved out of soft stone comes from Mehi, and, as we shall see, has the most interesting connexions not only with the Harappā Culture to the east but also with Mesopotamia to the west (Fig. 10). There are several types of vessel represented: small cylindrical pots between 2 and 3 inches across and a couple of inches or less deep; a larger one, 4 inches in diameter, divided into four compartments; another, also in four compartments, but square; and some simple cups, one unfinished. The more elaborate pots are decorated with fine engraved patterns of chevrons and hatched triangles, and seem likely to have held cosmetics such as eye-paint or ointment of some kind, like the alabaster box of ointment in the New Testament story. Now pots similar to these from Mehi appear in the sites near Bampur and in Sistan, already mentioned as showing in their pottery types evidence of Kulli contacts, and in both places imitations of the stone in hard grey pottery are also found, recalling the fragment from Shahi-tump. When we come to discuss the connexions of the Kulli Culture with Mesopotamia we shall see how important these stone pots are. A fragment of a circular vessel was found at Mohenjodaro in the earliest settlement reached, and part of a square one in a later occupation level. On the whole, these vessels

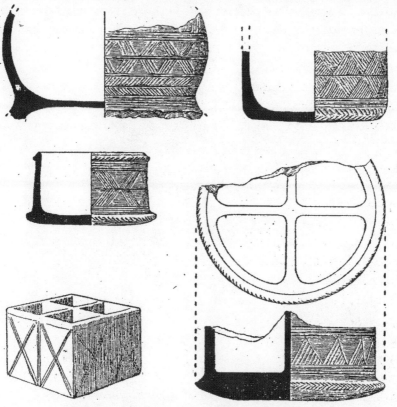

FIG. 10. Incised stone vessels, Kulli Culture

form one of the most interesting links between west and east, from the borders of Syria to the Indus, that we have yet touched upon.

The Mehi cemetery was surprisingly rich in copper and bronze objects among its grave-goods deposited with the cremations, though not themselves burnt, and the most outstanding find is the copper mirror, 5 inches in diameter, with the handle (also of copper) representing a stylized female figure in the manner of the clay figurines, with breasts and conventionalized arms akimbo, but with the head provided only by the reflection of the user of the mirror (Fig. 11). This amusing trick and the sophistication of the metal-work make the Mehi mirror stand out among the toilet accessories of the whole Ancient East – there is nothing like it in the otherwise more advanced Harappā Culture, and the use

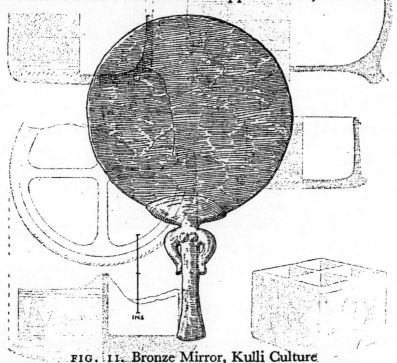

FIG. 11. Bronze Mirror, Kulli Culture

of a human figure as a mirror-handle, though familiar in Egypt in the XVIII Dynasty (from about 1570 B.C.), is unknown in Western Asia. The close resemblance between the Mehi mirror-handle and the clay figurines of women from the same site, and from other sites of the Kulli Culture, increases our confidence in claiming it as a local product, and as a very considerable tribute to the inventive genius of the Baluchistan metal-smiths of the period. There was another mirror from the Mehi cemetery, but this was merely a circular disc 5 inches across and without a handle — a simple mirror form known for instance in the earliest cemetery at Susa in Elam, and also at Mohenjo-daro, where handled types also occur, though without ornament or distinctive shape to the handle.

In the Mehi cemetery were also found two copper pins (one with each mirror), one with a flat, disc-shaped head and the other a head made of a small lapis-lazuli bead. Fragments of simple copper bracelets, and of a small bowl (which on analysis showed traces of nickel), were also found at Mehi, and a pin with roughly bent-over head at Kulli.

Finally, there are a few miscellaneous objects in the Kulli Culture to be mentioned before discussing its place in the Indian and Western Asian setting. Stone saddle-querns and riders from Kulli attest corn-growing; chert blades from Shahi-tump and Mazena-damb are comparable to those in the Amri-Nal Culture and seem to be archaistic survivals. Beads including lapis-lazuli and agate were found at Kulli, and from this site also came an odd 'ritual pillar' of polished purple-red and white variegated stone, 8 inches high and 2 inches in diameter at the base. From Mehi comes a cubical banded grey chert weight, 0·85 inches square and 0·6 inches thick, of exactly the Harappā type, and a clear example of an import which in its very associations suggests traders in Baluchistan. Clay bangles occurred at Mehi and Siah-Damb, and bone fragments came from Kulli. A bone stud with a drilled cruciform design occurred among the grave-goods in the Mehi cemetery, and finally we may note a single fragment of sheet gold from Kulli.

When we come to a comparative assessment of the Kulli Culture, we see, as far as information is available, that the few settlements of which we have knowledge differ in no way from those of the Amri-Nal Culture, nor indeed from the smaller peasant communities of Mesopotamia or Persia. The Harappā element is much more strongly defined in

Kulli than in Amri-Nal, taking the form of actual imports and evidence which implies the presence of Harappā traders in South Baluchistan, but nevertheless there is no trace of the burnt brick architecture which is so characteristic of actual Harappā settlements wherever they occur. As we shall see, at least one Harappā trading-post containing burnt brick buildings is known in the Makran, but at Mehi, apart from modifications of the local pot-painting styles, the connexions with Harappā are no more than could be provided by the visits of caravans and the occasional sojourn of merchants in the town. There is good evidence that trade exchanges did take place, and goods and even people found their way from the Baluchistan hills to the Indus plain.

These Harappā connexions imply, of course, that there was an approximate contemporaneity between the cultures in the two areas, and as far as can be deduced from the Harappā motifs, such as *pipal* leaves, introduced on the native pots, it looks as though this contact took place when the Kulli pot-painting style was well developed and perhaps even past its prime. At Shahi-tump there is stratigraphical evidence of a sort, for the three Kulli building levels (dated as approximately contemporary with Harappā by a bit of a cart-model to which reference has already been made) are themselves earlier than a cemetery that has been dug into the ruins of the last phase settlement. Now the Shahi-tump cemetery is, as we shall see, pretty well dated, and is contemporary with the end of the Harappā Culture in the Indus Valley, so this fits in well with the other evidence for the relative date of the Kulli Culture.

There is further evidence from Sind, which gives the reverse side of the interchange of painted motifs and styles on the pottery. At Rohel-jo-Kund in the Gaj Valley and at Ghazi Shah near Lake Manchhar, animals painted in the Kulli style appear on pots which are not themselves Kulli ware. At the former site they seem to be some form of the

Amri-Nal group, and at Ghazi Shah they are vessels with a background of bright red slip typical of the painted wares of the Harappā Culture. At this site the stratification shows that a settlement with Amri ware was followed by one making or at least using black-on-red painted ware, sometimes with the Kulli type of animals and spiky trees, but also with other motifs characteristic of Mohenjo-daro and Harappā. So by these interesting borrowings between pot-painters we can get a fair idea that Kulli and Harappā were, by and large, flourishing side by side, and we have already seen that the decorated stone pots found in South Baluchistan and associated with the Kulli Culture were also occasionally imported to the Indus Valley.

Nor does that exhaust the Harappā-Kulli connexions. One of the outstanding pieces of Harappā art is a bronze figure of a dancing-girl, described in a later chapter, and it is most interesting to find that her hairdressing is just that seen on the Kulli figurines, with the heavy loop of hair carried over the nape of the neck, and that (again following the Kulli fashion) she wears a couple of bangles at her right wrist, but has her left arm loaded with bracelets from the wrist to above the elbow. The merchants returning from the Baluchi hills may well have brought back with them women as well as merchandise.

When we look beyond India to the ancient civilizations of Western Asia we find clearly defined and most important points of similarity between the Kulli Culture and the lands of Elam and Mesopotamia. The 'landscape with animals' frieze on the Kulli pots finds close stylistic parallels on pots known from Susa and Khuzistan and also from the Diyala region near Baghdad, and named, from their use of a bright red paint in addition to black, 'scarlet ware' (Fig. 12). On these vessels we find large animals standing about in a landscape of spiky trees, and often with the spaces between their legs or over their heads filled in with smaller figures –

usually birds. The animals are not as a rule bulls, but cattle do occur, as well as black buck and goats; in other pots from the Susa region round Musyan, there are long files of goat or ibex figures in the abbreviated 'shorthand' of the Kulli style. Recent finds of 'scarlet ware' at Susa include one pot which shows a war-chariot drawn by an ox depicted

FIG. 12. 'Animals in Landscape' motifs on Early Dynastic Scarlet Ware from Susa and the Diyala region

in a style very close to that of the Kulli pot-painters, with the characteristic exaggerated circular rendering of the eye. There is no doubt of the common feeling in composition and spirit, and to some extent in technique, in the two groups of pottery, which in Mesopotamia is accurately dated to Early Dynastic times (about 2800 B.C.). Nor do the points of contact cease here. In Mesopotamia and just over the Syrian border at Mari some eight or ten stone vessels have been found (again in Early Dynastic contexts), which are of precisely the same type of those from South Baluchistan, and here similarity gives way to identity in certain instances. From Shub-ad's grave at Ur came a small stone cup of this class with elaborate carved ornament probably imitating some kind of woven fabric, and this is exactly matched by a fragment from the Dasht River in the

Makran; other cups carved to imitate basketry occur at Kish in Mesopotamia, at Susa in Elam and at Mohenjo-daro. A common form has carved on the surface the representation of a reed hut with door and windows the lintels of which, made of reed bundles in the original huts, are shown realistically sagging in the carved versions. Now these "house-urns" are common in Sistan and at Khurab in the Persian Makran, and in Early Dynastic Sumer turn up at Mari, Khafajah, Lagash and Adab, and at Susa in Elam — again always in Early Dynastic associations. Here we must be dealing with exports from the Makran to the west, pots presumably originally containing some unguent fragrant with curious spices and rare in the eyes of the Early Dynastic Sumerians, who treasured the little carved vessels, thinking them worthy to be buried with a queen among the great Royal Tombs. What form did this trade take? Did Sumerian ships (perhaps taking advantage of the monsoon winds) put in at the mouth of the Dasht River and barter lapis-lazuli or gold for the fashionable grey-green stone pots with their sweet-smelling contents? Or did there come to the quays of Ur foreign ships of merchants speaking an uncouth tongue and worshipping strange gods? There is some evidence that this did indeed happen, and that Baluchi traders settled in Sumer, a little closed society with its own rights and customs. On a scarlet-ware pot there is a scene of bull-worship, a religious rite not illustrated elsewhere in Sumer; there is a steatite cup from Tell Agrab in the Diyala region carved in the true Sumerian manner, but with a great humped bull who looks uncompromisingly Indian despite the fact that he was carved by a Sumerian artist. Then there is a cylinder-seal from Ur — there could be nothing so distinctively Sumerian as a cylinder-seal — which has on it a bull whose great round eye betrays his kinship with the bulls on Kulli ware and the hand of an Indian gem-cutter. Again, at Susa are clay figurines of humped bulls: the humped bull, *Bos indicus*, so essentially a

symbol of Indian religion then as in contemporary Hindustan; from Susa, too, comes the scarlet-ware pot so similar
in treatment to Kulli ware.

This evidence of Sumerian trade with the Makran and
Baluchistan and the presence of Indian merchants in the
great cities of Elam and Sumer in Early Dynastic times is, of
course, of first-rate importance. That the connexions were
with South Baluchistan and not with the Indus Valley or
the Harappā Culture seems clear enough, and we shall see
that it was not until five hundred years later that the trade
between the Indus and the Twin Rivers was established.
Again, it seems likely that trade was by sea and not overland,
for there is no trace of Kulli contacts landwards farther
west than Bampur, just over the border into Persian Makran,
and the Fars province of Persia, though explored by Stein,
has produced no evidence of Kulli colonization or trade, but
only cultures characterized by a long-persisting painted pottery style, based on that of Tal-i-Bakun, but surviving for
many centuries. An ancient Indian legend which found its
way into the *Jātakas*, or reincarnation stories of Buddha, was
of the merchants who went by sea from India to the land of
Babylon, bringing with them among other rarities a peacock
trained 'to scream at the snapping of the fingers and to
dance at the clapping of the hands', which 'stood in the
forepart of the vessel and, flapping its wings, uttered a sweet
sound and danced'. In such stories may be enshrined the
vague traditions of prehistoric trade, and of the merchants
coming with ivory, apes and peacocks, precious ointments in
strange stone pots, an alien tongue and religious customs,
from the Makran to the wharves of Sumer early in the third
millennium B.C.

We must now turn to North Baluchistan, and particularly
to the valley of the Zhob River, which runs north-eastwards
from the mountains behind Quetta and the Bolan Pass.
Here and in the Pishin-Lora region north-west of the Bolan

Pass are a number of tells which have yielded evidence of
prehistoric occupation. The sites are not as numerous as
those of Sind or South Baluchistan, but they nevertheless
show clear evidence of a group of cultures which, although
allied to those we have been describing in general terms, yet
have distinctive points of difference which justify us in class-
ing them as a separate group, connected with the Red ware
Cultures of Persia rather than the buff wares characteristic
of the South Baluchistan sites. It is very probable that further exploration would enlarge the geographical boundaries
of these *Zhob Cultures*, as we can call them: there is certainly
an extension southwards to the head of the Nal River, well
to the south of the Bolan Pass.

Thanks to work carried out by the late Brigadier Ross at a
site in the Zhob Valley, we have an invaluable stratified
sequence of human occupation in a large tell, that of Rana
Ghundai, which can serve as a framework into which can be
fitted the material known from surface finds elsewhere. We
are therefore in a much better position than in South Baluchistan to form some sort of a chronological scheme for the
various pottery styles, a scheme which may be uncertain in
terms of actual dates in years, but which does give a relative
local sequence.

Ross's work at the Rana Ghundai tell is an excellent
example of what can be done by intelligent observation on
such a site, without excavation in the ordinary sense of the
word – work which might have been carried out on a dozen
Baluchi sites, but has not been attempted so far. The Rana
Ghundai mound is up to 40 feet high and is being actively
dug away by the local villagers, who use the ash-laden soil
from the ancient occupation levels as manure on their fields.
This fate is one common to most tells near modern villages,
and, though naturally it means the destruction of the site, it
nevertheless does provide, in many instances, a complete
cross-section of the mound and its strata. From the exposed

more or less vertical surfaces it is possible to collect potsherds and other material representing human occupation and, by relating these to the levels from which they have been derived, build up a stratified sequence from bottom to top. By patient observation and collection over some years Ross was able to identify five main periods of occupation at Rana Ghundai, with sub-phases or building levels bringing the whole number of strata to nine, and, once this sequence was recognized, it was possible to match surface finds from other tells against this or that period on the key site.

For the convenience of reference in this book I have altered slightly the nomenclature of the Rana Ghundai sequence into a form rather more convenient than that in the original publication of the site, and one which is in accordance with the general practice in describing such ancient stratified sites. Expressed in a table, this will be our key to the interpretation of the Zhob Cultures.

THE RANA GHUNDAI SEQUENCE
(From earliest to latest strata: the letters in brackets are the pottery groups of the original report)

Rana Ghundai I   (bottom of mound on virgin soil)
Rana Ghundai II   (A)

Temporary desertion of site?

Rana Ghundai IIIa   (B)
Rana Ghundai IIIb   (C)
Rana Ghundai IIIc   (D)

Break in pottery continuity

Rana Ghundai IV   (E)

Cessation of painted pottery

Rana Ghundai Va   (F)
Rana Ghundai Vb   (G)
Rana Ghundai Vc   (H)

It will be convenient to refer to the various periods as R.G. I, R.G. II, etc., and, although the sequence at the type-site seems likely to be valid for the whole area of settlement, it must be stressed that, until other sites are explored in the same manner, caution must be used in equating the various settlements.

R.G. I is at present represented only at the type-site, but it may await discovery at the bottoms of yet unexcavated tells. But there were over 14 feet of deposits in R.G. I, consisting of soil in which no structural remains could be traced, though there were frequent layers of ash representing hearths; and the excavator suggested that intermittent but recurrent occupation of the site by semi-nomadic people with imper-manent huts or tents seemed likely. The pottery found was all unpainted (except for a single sherd roughly painted with a lozenge pattern) and had not been turned on the wheel. There were flint blades of the types we have already en-countered in South Baluchistan, but none showed any evi-dence of having been used as sickle-flints, and there were also two bone points and an eyed needle. The animal bones were very interesting, comprising the humped ox (*Bos indi-cus*), domestic sheep (*Ovis vignei*), the ass (*Equus asinus*), and, most surprising and important, four teeth of the domesti-cated horse (*Equus caballus*). Nomadic, horse-riding herds-men using the site as a camping-ground are suggested by the finds in R.G. I; an infant's skeleton was also found buried at this level.

In R.G. II we see newcomers arriving at the site, building houses with boulder footings over the compacted debris of R.G. I, and making a superb painted pottery, turned on the wheel and decorated with fine stylized figures of humped bulls and of black buck, painted with great skill in black paint on a background which varies from pinkish or buff to a dark terra-cotta colour, and without the use of any secon-dary red colour (Fig. 13). A few sherds of the typical 'Bull' pottery of R.G. II have been found elsewhere in the Zhob Valley, notably at Sur Jangal, but the new material from

Rana Ghundai enables us to see that the pots were very fine,
well-made bowls, with either a foot-ring or a pedestal base,
and each with a frieze of stylized bulls or black buck, in
which the vertical elongation of the legs and horns is a contrast to the horizontal elongation of the Kulli animals.
There is a crisper, less naturalistic handling of the RG II
animals than of those in the Kulli Culture, and as we shall
see there are good parallels to the style of bowls and the
treatment of the animals found in Northern Persia.

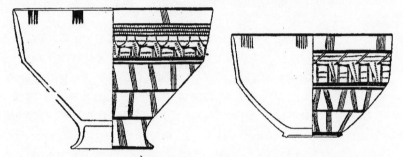

FIG. 13. Bowls painted with cattle and black buck, Rana
Ghundai II phase

The occupation of RG II does not seem to have been of
very long duration, and only one building level can be
traced, followed by sterile material implying temporary
abandonment of the site. RG III, however, is a period of
some length, with three phases of building and a continuous
pottery evolution which in its turn is derived from the wares
of RG II. In RG IIIa the fine brush-work of RG II continues and becomes almost an affectation – one could almost
use the terms applied to a similar stylistic sequence in Danish Neolithic pottery and talk of a 'grand style' followed by a
'pretty style'–and red paint appears, being used as a second
colour, even though the background is itself a red slip, producing a curious 'red-on-red' technique. Among other patterns executed in this two-colour style are multiple-lined
squares in red and black, which recall those of Amri and

which might indicate approximate contemporaneity and interchange of ideas; in Amri ware too there are small pedestal feet with groups of vertical lines just in the manner of RG II and IIIa. The main occupation of the Sur Jangal site seems to be comparable with RG IIIa and with the succeeding IIIb, where tall carafe-like vessels appear, which occur also at Sur Jangal (Fig. 14). In this phase and in the

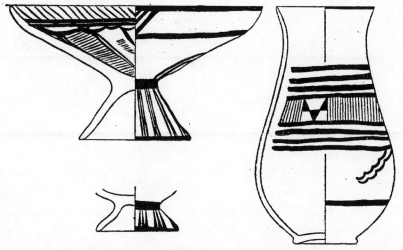

FIG. 14. Bowls and carafe, Rana Ghundai IIIa and IIIb phases

next, RG IIIc, the brush-work on the pottery painting coarsens and the background is almost invariably a deep red; comparable sites of this period are Periano Ghundai and Mogul Ghundai near Fort Sandeman (Fig. 15).

The end of the RG IIIc phase seems to have been violent – as we shall see in Chapter VI, there is evidence of burning, and the site may have been sacked – and at all events in RG IV and V we encounter quite different traditions in pot-making, and the continuous sequence from RG II to IIIc is broken. Before discussing these later phases, however, we can broaden our knowledge of the RG III period as a whole by considering the evidence from those other sites which have yielded pottery referable to one or more of the three sub-phases of RG III, notably Periano Ghundai, which in the main seems to be RG IIIc, and the settlement site at Nal into which the later cemetery was dug, which on the few

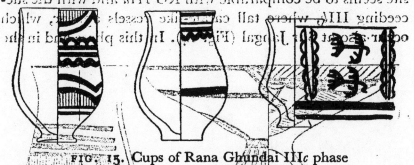

FIG. 15. Cups of Rana Ghundai IIIc phase

available pots seems also to be approximately contemporary with RG IIIc.

The same reservations with regard to estimating the size of the settlements which I have already made for the South Baluchistan sites apply of course equally here, but on the whole the average size of the tells is much the same in both areas. Sur Jangal is very small, only about 40 yards across and 16 feet high, and at the other end of the scale is the enormous mound of Dabar Kot south of Loralai, 500 yards in diameter and 113 feet high. As this latter site has as the final occupation a Harappā settlement or trading-post, its size implies a long series of important prehistoric towns on the spot, all apparently earlier than the middle of the third millennium B.C.

Practically nothing is known of the layout of the settlements of RG III date except at Nal, where houses with rooms or courts varying from 11 by 9 feet to tiny, thick-walled chambers only 5 feet square or less were found; at Moghul Ghundai there were traces of a possible defensive wall to the settlement. Building materials seem to have been of boulder foundations with mud bricks above on all sites where any trace could be seen, and the sizes of bricks range as follows:

12 by 7½ in. (Nal)
9 by 8·9 by 4½ in. (Rana Ghundai)
... by 9 by 4½ in. (Periano Ghundai)
23 by 6 by 3½ in. (Nal)
11 by 9 by 4½ in. (Dabar Kot)

The larger bricks at Nal compare in size with those from Nundara in South Baluchistan. In some rooms at Nal were rough pavings of pebbles or small stones carefully laid on gravel, and at the same site and at Rana Ghundai charred wooden beams were found. The Nal settlement had in fact been burnt down (the red colour of the earth of the tell gives it its modern name of Sohr-damb, the Red Mound); the charred remains of wooden beams and rafters, circular in section, with diameters of 9 and 5½ inches respectively, were found still in position forming two floors, 6 feet 3 inches apart, in one of the small chambers already mentioned.

The pottery of RG III, on which we have already touched, is a consistent development from the Bull wares of RG II. At Sur Jangal we find open bowls on a high pedestal foot painted with grouped vertical strokes; the interior of the bowl is painted with a frieze of humped cattle whose fantastically elongated legs and tails trail down to the centre of the area. This pattern often degenerates until its origin in animal forms becomes only faintly recognizable, and its original significance must have been forgotten by the painters of the more extreme examples of these abstract patterns. The two-colour painting at Sur Jangal is most attractive, with a brighter and more orange tone used than the deep plum-red of South Baluchistan, so that in the red-on-red pots the painted strokes show up lighter against the rich red slip. We have already noted the panels of chequers enclosed by multiple red and black lines, so similar to those of Amri

and Nundara, but on the whole this class of pottery is peeuliar to North Baluchistan. Also from Sur Jangal are one or two
pieces of thin, hard grey-ware bowls with painted ornament
in black, best paralleled in the Quetta sites and in Sistan.

The development of the pottery in RG IIIc is very well
shown at the site of Periano Ghundai. Here the red slip as
a background is constant, and painting on this is in black
alone, while the brush-work has become coarser. A common
shape is the small beaker or bottle with a solid pedestal foot,
and this type serves to link the Nal settlement with this
phase (Fig. 15). There are a couple of sherds from Periano
Ghundai with fairly naturalistic animals painted on them
(probably a deer and a bull), and two more have fishes depicted, but otherwise the decoration is all geometric. Some
fragments with hatched zones suggest comparison with Sistan
sherds, though at these sites the painting is black on buff.

In common with the Kulli Culture of South Baluchistan,
the Zhob Valley sites have produced a number of clay
figurines of cattle and women, and, though the stratified
deposits of Rana Ghundai contained none of these, their
occurrence at Sur Jangal, Periano Ghundai, Moghul Ghundai and Kaudani, as well as at Dabar Kot, suggests that
they should be assigned to the RG III phase. Little need be
said of the few figurines of humped bulls, but one clay figurine (from Periano Ghundai) seems to represent a horse, and
is interesting in connexion with the finds of horses' teeth in
RG I at the type-site.

The female figures are, however, of great interest (Fig.
16). Like those of the Kulli Culture, they end below the
waist in little pedestals, and they are also in several instances
adorned with several necklaces, though these are more
schematically shown than those from the southern region.
But the faces are totally different – hooded with a coif or
shawl, they have high, smooth foreheads above their staring,
circular eye-holes, their owl-beak nose and grim slit mouth.

The result is terrifying, even in a tiny model not more than 2 inches high, and in two from Dabar Kot all pretence is thrown aside and the face is a grinning skull. Whatever may be said of the Kulli figurines, these can hardly be toys, but seem rather to be a grim embodiment of the mother-goddess who is also the guardian of the dead – an underworld deity

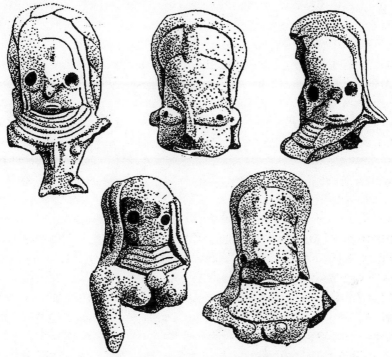

FIG. 16. Clay figurines of women, Zhob Cultures

concerned alike with the corpse and the seed-corn buried beneath the earth.

The fertility aspect so often connected with such underworld gods is indeed represented by other models, for which no parallels can be found in South Baluchistan. From Moghul Ghundai is a phallus carved in stone, and there is another probable example in rough pottery from Periano Ghundai, and from this site too comes a figurine consisting of an enormously exaggerated female vulva and thighs.

Analogous evidence of fertility symbols comes from the Harappā Culture.

Of the other elements of the material culture of the RG III phase we have a little, not very illuminating evidence. The flint blades already found in RG I continue throughout RG II and III on the type-site, and are also found at Sur Jangal and Periano Ghundai. From these sites too come flint points and a good leaf-shaped arrowhead, another of which was found in the nineteenth century by Noetling at Dabar Kot. Small cups of alabaster are attested by fragments from Periano Ghundai, and beads of unspecified stones from Dabar Kot and Moghul Ghundai, and of lapis and (allegedly) jade from Periano Ghundai. Bone beads were found at Dabar Kot, and bangles, needles (recalling the RG I specimen) and small disc-beads of the same substance occurred at Periano Ghundai. Metal is scarce and in no instance certainly dated to RG III, but copper objects (a rod and a ring) come from Periano Ghundai, and fragments of a copper cup from Dabar Kot, the same site producing a gold pin and fragment of sheet metal, which may, however, be better referred to the Harappā occupation on the site.

Probably to Harappā contacts must be attributed two small, square stamp-seals, one of greenish stone and the other of unknown substance and known only from a drawing by Noetling. The former is from Dabar Kot, and has a voided equal-armed cross set between small square panels at the corners, and the latter, probably from Periano Ghundai, seems from the drawing to be very similar. Harappā material is, of course, present at Dabar Kot in the form of a distinctive settlement, but scattered traces of imports from the Indus Valley can also be seen at other sites, such as the etched carnelian beads from Moghul Ghundai and Tor Dherai, and the clay bracelets from Periano Ghundai with a wavy outer edge, paralleled in the Harappā levels at Chan-hu-daro, are presumably likely to be of similar origin.

PLATE I. Harappā 1946: Section through
mud-brick defences of citadel

PLATE 2. Harappā 1946: Section through
defences of citadel (detail)

PLATE 3. Harappā 1946: Corn-pounding platform of brick with traces of central wooden mortar visible in section

PLATE 4. Harappā 1946: Inhumation burials in cemetery R 37

PLATE 5 Harappā 1946: Inhumation burial with remains of reed shroud, cemetery R 37

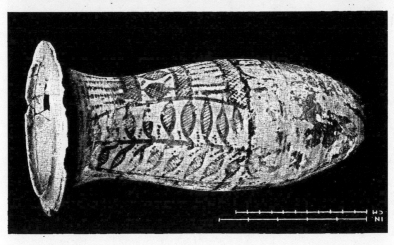

PLATE 6. Harappā 1946: Painted Pots (black on red)

PLATE 7. Harappā 1946: Painted Pots (black on red)

PLATE 8. Harappā 1946: Clay figurines

Burials which can be referred to RG III have been found at Sur Jangal, Periano Ghundai and Moghul Ghundai. At the first site a cemetery of about twenty small cairns was identified 60–70 yards away from the settlement, covering deposits of cremated bones associated with typical RG III potsherds and in one instance a flint blade, lying on the old ground surface. Somewhat similar cairns near Moghul Ghundai may also go back to this period, though the one or two dug into by Stein produced evidence of a late date, contemporary with the 'B' Cemetery at Sialk; but at this site and at Periano Ghundai cremation burials were found in pots, one at least under the floor of a room and another by a wall, accompanied by smaller ancillary vessels. The subsequent occupation-levels on the type site will be discussed in Chapter VI.

When we look to the other prehistoric sites in Western Asia, in Persia and Mesopotamia, we can see that the Rana Ghundai sequence is by no means without parallel. The presumed camping sites in RG I may be compared in type to the first settlement at Tell Hassuna in Mesopotamia, though it must be stressed that the resemblance is no more than one of general similarity, since the Hassuna settlement is immensely older than even the most adventurous chronology could make that of RG I. But, with the newcomers implied by the appearance of the fine painted pottery in RG II, we can make rather more precise comparisons, for the pottery of this phase has very close affinities, in the shape of the vessels and in the style and content of the vase-painting, with that of Hissar I – the first settlement on the Hissar site near Damghan in Northern Persia. Hissar I is a typical site within the Red-ware province, and as we have seen there is a large proportion of black-on-red ware in RG II, and the red background becomes constant in RG III. The animals depicted on the pots in the two regions – North Persia and North Baluchistan – differ, presumably in response to the natural fauna and the differing types of domesticated beast in the two cultures, but apart from this the similarities are so striking that we can claim Hissar I and RG II as parallel developments within the Red-ware area. Whether we can also equate the dates of the two phases is not so certain, but the Baluchistan evidence does show that RG II must have a fair degree of priority over the Harappā Culture, and its date should therefore be well back in the fourth millennium B.C., perhaps contemporary with Jemdet Nasr. RG III would begin in Early Dynastic times and continue to overlap with the Harappā Culture in Akkadian times, or even later.

As we shall see in Chapter VI, there was evidence of violent destruction at the end of the RG III*c* settlement; this and the similar tale told by the burning of the settlement on the Sohr-damb of Nal have some significance when we come to discuss the movements of peoples into India from the west in the second half of the second millennium. The total change in pottery types implies an extinction of the earlier culture at least at Rana Ghundai, and the barbarous quality of the pottery heavily decorated in relief which follows on the painted wares forms a striking contrast to the earlier traditions. It did not mean the end of human settlement in Baluchistan, but it must have meant a considerable reduction in the population, and yet the ancient craft of pot painter never entirely died out. From sites in the Quetta region have come pots painted with designs copied from Sassanian fabrics of the sixth and seventh centuries A.D. brought by traders through the Bolan Pass, and one has only to walk through the bazaars of Quetta or Peshawar to see set out for sale painted pots, gay with their black and red designs that so disconcertingly resemble the ancient patterns, but made the day before yesterday in the local kilns.

Postscript. Since this book was written, **Miss Beatrice de**

Cardi has read a paper to the Society of Antiquaries of London describing her work of reconnaissance in central Baluchistan since the war. She has extended the known distribution of Quetta Ware southwards, and amplified our knowledge of the other cultures considerably, distinguishing also a new pottery type (Togau Ware). Her discoveries on the later prehistoric sites in Baluchistan are referred to in Chapter VI.

Notes to Chapter IV

The basic account of the Baluchistan pottery was that of Professor Childe in *Ancient Egypt*, 1933, summarized in *New Light on the Most Ancient East* (1934), Chap. IX, and based on first-hand study of the material in India as well as the original reports by Sir Aurel Stein (*An Archaeological Tour in Waziristan and North Baluchistan* (1929) and *An Archaeological Tour in Gedrosia* (1931)) and N. C. Majumdar (*Explorations in Sind* (1934)). My own studies in the light of more recent work, and a detailed re-examination of the original material, are summarized in *Ancient India* I (1946), 8–26; *ibid.*, no.4 (1948), 26–40; *Antiquity*, XVII (1943), 169–182, and, in a more popular form, in *Some Ancient Cities of India* (1945), Chap. II.

Sir Aurel Stein's discussion of former climatic conditions in South Baluchistan is contained in his *Gedrosia* volume, 7–13, 24–25, 113–114. The description of the Lake Manchhar region is given by Majumdar, *Explorations in Sind*, Chap. V.

The Quetta pottery is described by me in *Ancient India*, no. 3 (1947), 113–142, and the remainder of the Baluchistan wares in *ibid.*, I (1946), 8–26. I have also utilized unpublished material obtained by Majumdar on his last journey in Sind, by the kindness of Mr Krishna Deva, and the account of Tharro Hill is based on my own field-work there in 1943. The Nal cemetery is described by Hargreaves, *Excavations in Baluchistan 1925* (1929), and that at Bampur (Persian Makran) by Sir Aurel Stein in *Archaeological Reconnaissances in N.W. India and S.E. Iran* (1937), 106–110.

The story of the Indian merchants at Babylon (the *Bāveru-Jātaka*) is from *The Jātaka*, trans. E. B. Cowell, etc., III, 83. The Rana-Ghundai sequence is described in *Journ. Near Eastern Studies*, V (1946), 284–316.

CHAPTER V

Cities and Towns of Sind and the Punjab

Now the land between the Jhelum and the Beas is said to hold
nine nations and five thousand cities, every one of them as
large as Kos; but I think this is exaggerated.

Strabo, *xv, fr. 701.*

FROM the hills to the plains; from a difficult mountainous
country where each secluded valley is cut off from its neigh-
bours to a great region linked from north to south by a river
system forming a natural highway of communication; from
villages, or at the most rustic market-towns, to cities which in
size and organization rank high among the urban achievements of the whole Ancient Orient; this is the transition we
make in turning from Baluchistan, and the prehistoric communities described in the last chapter, to the plains through
which flow the Five Rivers of the Punjab and, to the south,
the Indus. In this great area, where India really begins, eastward of the Baluchi mountain barrier, we encounter another
group of prehistoric settlements which, though they share
with the Baluchistan villages a common agricultural background and certain features of cultural affinity, yet in most
respects present a contrast rather than a similarity

The variety in styles and techniques among the products
of the Baluchistan communities – the strongly individualized
groups of pottery types, for instance – permits us to visualize
the existence of little peasant states, each more or less self-
contained, within a natural area such as the Zhob Valley, or
those of the Kolwa and Maskai. The similarities we can detect between the localized cultures are the outcome of common necessities among farming peoples working a difficult
land; there is no evidence of any uniform arbitrary stan-

dards accepted or imposed throughout the territory. The settlements of the Amri folk in Sind repeat the story of Baluchistan – another localized culture with its own traditions in the household crafts and, one suspects, in other less tangible aspects of its life as well.

But, as we shall see, these very Amri settlements are succeeded by those of folk whose allegiance is not to a petty state, but to an empire. Diversity is replaced by uniformity over an area incomparably vaster than anything we have yet seen in prehistoric India; a complete agreement in details of material culture is found over an area stretching from the Makran coast to Kathiawar, and northwards to the Himalayan foothills: a huge irregular triangle with the sides measuring 950 by 700 by 550 miles. From end to end of this territory, from some forty settlement-sites, come pottery vessels of identical mass-produced types; houses are built of baked bricks of standard dimensions; stamp-seals are used engraved with similar scenes and a uniform script, as yet unread; a standard system of weights is recognizable. While some sites are villages, others are small towns, and 350 miles apart stand two cities, each covering at least a square mile of ground, twin capitals of an empire. To a British archaeologist the inevitable parallel is the Roman Empire supervening upon the prehistoric Iron Age barbarian settlements of his own country. Under the jejune archaeological nomenclature of the 'Harappā Culture' there lies concealed one of the greatest nameless kingdoms of Western Asia.

The natural conditions of the area within the bounds of the Harappā Culture in ancient times are of some interest. Today the Punjab is one of the greatest corn-growing areas of Asia, but Sind is a desert reclaimed only by the elaborate irrigation works which utilize the waters of the Indus. The main weight of settlement, as known by field-work up to the present, seems to have been in Sind, west of the Indus, but there are a dozen sites of settlements, some evidently of quite large towns, along the line of the now-dry Ghaggar River in the desert areas of Bahawalpur State. The northern 'capital', Harappā, is in the Punjab, about 100 miles south-west of Lahore; the southern city, Mohenjo-daro, is on the Indus in Sind, nearly 200 miles north of Karachi. The very existence of these large cities, and of the bigger towns as well, must presuppose a considerable agricultural population producing an adequate surplus beyond its immediate needs for sale to the towns, and the invariable use of burnt clay bricks throughout the Harappā Culture must imply far greater timber resources for firing the kilns than the present vegetation of tamarisk and scrub would afford. Under the present climatic conditions of Sind the Harappā state as we can infer it from the tangible remains could hardly have been achieved. Yet it was brought into being and survived for centuries in this very region, and we can look only to changing natural conditions for an explanation.

Fortunately, we have a rather remarkable amount of evidence for conditions in the third millennium B.C. in this area. The Harappā Culture counted among its achievements representational art which concerned itself largely with animals and natural forms, and these representations of the contemporary wild and domesticated animals are amplified by the actual remains of animal bones recovered from the excavations. From these we see that the climatic conditions were such as to favour a suitable habitat for the rhinoceros and the tiger as well as the water-buffalo and the elephant none of which survives as wild species in the region today (except the tiger, sometimes found in Sind). But on one of the ancient engraved stamp-seals all these animals surround a deity who appears as a lord of beasts with the main species in his domains. Many other representations of these beasts are known from Harappā art, and bones of all except the tiger have in fact been found at either Mohenjo-daro or Harappā.

Among other wild animals known from one or both of
these sources, we may notice the river-crocodile of gharial
type, still an inhabitant of the Indus; some species of bear,
monkey, squirrel, and parrot; the Barasingha deer and the
horns at least of the Kashmir, spotted, Sambhur and hog
deer – but these may have been imported. The jackal and
the wolf were there, not far from the edges of the towns; rats,
mongoose, lizards, and tortoises must have been familiar in
street or courtyard; and fish from the rivers was eaten.
Direct evidence of trees is confined to the lucky survival of a
few charred beams, of which those of deodar must have been
brought down from the hills to the north, though sissoo still
grows in Sind; the cloying sweet smell of its freshly-sawn
wood is an essential part of life in North-Western India
today.

Though none of the evidence is conclusive, yet the inference from the fauna, the wood needed to burn so many
million bricks, and the implication of a flourishing agricultural background, all suggest a climate different from
that of today, when at Mohenjo-daro the range in annual
temperature is between 120° F. in summer to frost in winter,
with a rainfall of less than 6 inches in the year. The very use
of burnt brick as a building material instead of the sun-dried
mud brick common to the Ancient East may imply the
necessity of finding something more durable under conditions of frequent or considerable rainfall, and the elaborate
system of drains in the cities may also be explained in connexion with a greater volume of rain-water.

The record of the chroniclers of Alexander the Great's
campaigns suggests that in the fourth century B.C. Sind (the
region of Mousikanos) was still a fertile tract of country, and
there is even evidence of the persistence of conditions kinder
than now up to the time of the Moghuls. The most reasonable explanation of the climatic deterioration within comparatively recent times is the supposition that the edge of the

south-western monsoon area has shifted eastwards, and that
the Indus was formerly within the area of monsoon rains.
On the whole this explanation seems more likely than the
alternative view that the northern storm-belt was deflected
southwards by conditions in immediately post-glacial times,
and that the effect persisted after the establishment of otherwise normal climatic conditions. Though South Baluchistan
had certainly reached its present conditions of arid climate
by the time of Alexander's retreat, the Indus region may
have preserved its moister climate within the western fringe
of the monsoon until later centuries.

Within the area already described, the uniform products
of the Harappā civilization can be traced with the monotonous regularity of a highly-organized community under
some strong system of centralized government, controlling
production and distribution and no doubt levying a system
of tolls and customs throughout the territory under its rule.
As we shall see, there is no evidence to imply that the cities
of Harappā and Mohenjo-daro were not contemporary: laid
out to a common ground-plan, each with its defenced citadel
towering above the rest of the town, they seem to have been
twin capitals, a northern and a southern, of one united kingdom. One is reminded of historical parallels in North-West
India, when Sakas and Kushanas ruled from Taxila or
Peshawar in the north, and Muttra in the south, over a
single state.

In the region which might reasonably be considered the
Northern Kingdom, fourteen village or small town sites are
known in addition to Harappā, and one suspects that field-
work would produce more in the Punjab, where only two
are now known, the remainder being concentrated east of
the Indus and Sutlej in Bhawalpur State (Fig. 17). In the
Southern Kingdom of Mohenjo-daro there are about seven-
teen such subsidiary settlements, many occupying sites
already lived on by peasants of the Amri and related cultures.

The site at Rangpur in Kathiawar looks like an outlying trading-post, as does that at Dabarkot on the eastern edge

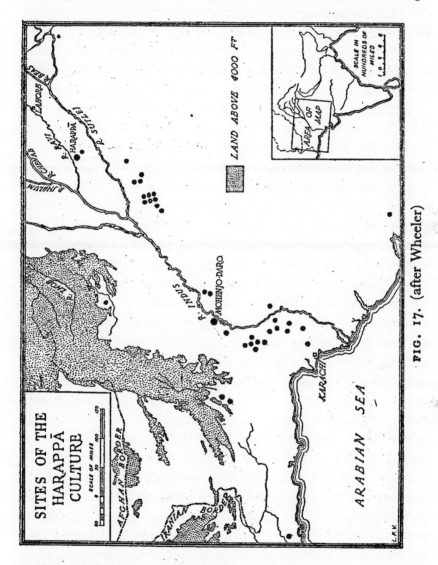

FIG. 17. (after Wheeler)

of the North Baluchistan hills; sites in South Baluchistan, notably Mehi, show clear indications of trading with the Harappā people, and at Sutkagen-dor near the Makran coast is what must be a fortified citadel of Harappā traders, perhaps connected with a port on the shore of the Arabian Sea.

These settlements (such sites as that last mentioned excepted) do not seem to have been laid out for defence, and at the capital cities the defences of the citadels alone have been proved to exist, though town walls are by no means unlikely. Communication by the river would provide a great natural thoroughfare north and south linking the capitals – Harappā on the banks of the Ravi and Mohenjo-daro on the Indus – and pack-trails over the passes into Baluchistan would serve the traders into those parts.

The absolute uniformity in the products of the Harappā Culture cannot wholly be explained by a rigidly enforced set of laws. There must have been a strongly established commercial code and a standardized technique of production which could control the sizes of bricks, the capacity and type of pots (turned out on the wheel in a variety of depressingly utilitarian forms), and the system of weights and measures. At Mohenjo-daro itself the strict observance of street frontages through successive centuries of the town's rebuilding implies heredity of land tenure and trade such as might lie in guilds and a caste system. At Harappā we shall see that the agricultural output was under municipal control, with great granaries strangely foreshadowing those of the Roman Army. In the absence of any effective grinding machinery, flour was produced by organized grain-pounding by coolie labour, which was housed in miserable rows of identically planned two-roomed cottages. There is a terrible efficiency about the Harappā civilization which recalls all the worst of Rome, but with this elaborately contrived system goes an isolation and a stagnation hard to parallel in any known civilization of the Old World, though perhaps not without comparable situations in the New, among the ancient South and Central American civilizations.

The remarkable uniformity of the Harappā Culture is in

fact expressed not only spatially, but also in the dimension of time. At Harappā itself the first town on the site, overlying a peasant settlement related to the North Baluchistan culture area, is already in all its known respects typical of the culture in its full maturity. But here and at Mohenjo-daro, where the greatest depth of accumulated strata has been recorded, there is hereafter no change. In the latter site there were at least nine phases of rebuilding in the city's history, often interrupted by disastrous river floods, but from top to bottom of the accumulated layers of debris no change can be detected in the content of the material culture, and it is reasonable to suppose that the less tangible elements of the people's lives were similarly unmodified. Certainly the script, which should be an index to changing modes of thought, is totally unchanged throughout. As we look today at the unvarying succession of building phases at Mohenjo-daro, towering 30 feet above us as we stand on the lowest street-level, we encounter in monumental form the first instance in the story of India of the innate conservatism of thought that is repeated through the centuries; conservatism that may so easily become stagnation, especially when developed in isolation.*

Although the duration of time implied by this long succession of rebuildings must be at least seven hundred years or more, yet there are no material changes perceptible save in archaeological minutiae. Curiously primitive features, such as the type of flat bronze axe or the spear without midrib, persist unchanged and unimproved. Although there is good evidence of trade between the Harappā kingdom and

---

* As already mentioned on p. 53, the excavation reports on Mohenjo-daro and Harappā use an extraordinary notation in distinguishing the successive phases (true stratigraphy was not recorded). There are three main 'periods,' Early, Intermediate and Late, each divided into three but with the subdivisions numbered in *reverse* order, so that 'Early Period Phase I' is followed by 'Intermediate Period Phase III.' This impossible system is ignored in the following account.

those of Sumer and Akkad, yet the decisive technological advance marked by the making of axes and other tools with sockets for the handle, known in Mesopotamia from the beginning of the third millennium, never reached the metalsmiths of the Indus and the Punjab. Indeed, so far as we can tell, it is likely that the first shaft-hole axe seen at Mohenjodaro was brandished by an invader from the west who took part in the sacking of the city, perhaps about the middle of the second millennium B.C.

This stagnation and uniformity in the Harappā Culture throughout its known duration renders it peculiarly difficult to assess not only the sequence in the larger towns but also their relationship one to another. It is improbable that the nine building phases known at Mohenjo-daro (where virgin soil has not been reached) are all subsequent to the six identified at Harappā, but such a transference of the seat of government to a southern site (or indeed the reverse process, with Mohenjo-daro the earlier site) and a total duration of the two cities between for over a thousand years, is theoretically not impossible. The Harappā Culture is known only in its mature form; it has no known beginnings, no tentative early phases before the outlines are firmly fixed. An origin outside India is inherently improbable, but where and in what form this origin was is quite unknown.

The combination of elaborate social and economic organization over a huge empire with an isolation which rendered many of its technological processes astonishingly primitive makes one think not so much of contemporary Sumer or Egypt, but rather of the Central American pre-Columban civilizations. Here similarly one finds great architectural achievement (far surpassing that of the Harappā civilization indeed); the rigorously authoritarian rule and elaborate religious conceptions that we may be permitted to infer from the Harappā evidence; a primitive hieratic script, and a technological backwardness which in America was so extreme that the use of metals for tools was still unknown. But America in the twelfth century A.D. had more excuse for isolation than Western India in the twentieth century B.C.

In many respects, then, the Harappā civilization is enigmatic to a degree surpassing its contemporaries in Western Asia. In so far as it is an urban and literate culture, using copper and bronze but not iron for tools and weapons, it is comparable with the civilizations known in Egypt, Mesopotamia and Persia in the third millennium B.C. It is indeed unlikely that it springs from any separate ultimate origin – somewhere behind it lie the peasant cultures of the type of Mehi or Rana-Ghundai – and again, in its use of a written script it is likely to be dependent, in the last resort, on the inventions of late fourth-millennium date in Mesopotamia, which seem to have given an impetus to writing not only in Sumer but also in Early Dynastic Egypt. But as soon as it had reached the mature form in which alone we know it, it had become something essentially apart, essentially Indian too. As we examine its various features in detail in the following pages we shall encounter again and again significant parallels with contemporary Hindú Culture, and almost certainly these links were stronger in medieval Indian times.

But before we come to a detailed description of the various features of this extraordinary civilization we may indicate in outline its position in time in relation to the peasant communities of Baluchistan, and of the other cultures of the Ancient Orient in countries lying farther to the west. After a thorough examination of all the evidence this chronological problem is treated in detail at the close of this chapter, but some idea of the general position is necessary to appreciate the setting of the culture as a whole.

In the first place, there is a certain proportion of painted pottery in the Harappā Culture side by side with the mass-produced utilitarian pots of unpainted wares, and these painted wares, with the designs in black on a deep, lustrous red background, suggest that the main relationships should lie with the red-ware group of cultures in North Baluchistan, rather than those using the buff wares of the southern region. But direct connexion is in the present state of our knowledge impossible to prove, though the small amount of material available from the recent (1946) excavations at Harappā shows that the first town on that site overlies a settlement of people using pottery which appears to belong to the North Baluchistan group, in that phase of development seen in the IIIc phase at Rana Ghundai (Fig. 20). The mature Harappā Culture in the Punjab, then, is subsequent to RG IIIc.

Similar evidence is available from sites farther south. One of the Bahawalpur towns of the Harappā Culture overlies a settlement with black-on-buff ware, although this does not seem to be closely allied to any of the Baluchistan wares known to us at present, but at three prehistoric villages in Sind, settlements with pottery of the Amri class have been superseded by those of Harappā folk: this evidence fits in with what we know, or suspect, of the chronological position of Amri in the buff-ware sequence. There is further evidence that Harappā traders, and probably colonists, were in South Baluchistan at the time the Kulli Culture was flourishing there, and the cemetery at Nal seems to be that of people having some contacts with the civilization of the Indus and the Punjab. As this cemetery was dug into the ruins of a settlement of RG IIIc folk, this again fits in well with the evidence of stratigraphy at Harappā itself. It looks as though the urban culture of the plains was approximately contemporary with the hill peasantries making pottery in the style of Kulli, Nal, and Periano Ghundai; only approximately contemporary, as the Kulli style seems to have started before Harappā folk arrived in South Baluchistan, and that of Nal is likely to have gone on rather longer than the period of maximum prosperity of the Harappā kingdom.

At three sites in Sind, on the top of ruined and deserted

Harappā towns or villages, settlements were found which contained evidence of the arrival in the region of new peoples with an alien and more barbaric way of life than that of the complex urban pattern of Harappā. There is a little evidence that similar folk came to Mohenjo-daro in the days of its decline, and at Harappā, as at Chanhu-daro in Sind, there was a final occupation of people building rough huts on top of the ruins of the defences and structures of the citadel, and burying their dead in a cemetery dug into the rubbish-tips of the deserted city. In Baluchistan what seems to be a contemporary cemetery was dug into the ruins of a Kulli settlement containing evidence of Harappā contacts: again the evidence is consistent.

These newcomers, who coincide so suspiciously with the end of the Harappā civilization, came to India from the west. To understand them and to assess the probable date of their arrival we must turn to the countries west of India, with which the Harappā traders had contacts. Here again the detailed evidence will be reviewed at a later stage, when we discuss the relations of the Harappā kingdom with foreign powers, but for the present we may look to Mesopotamia for evidence of connexions between the Indian civilization, prehistoric by reason of its undeciphered script, and those of the Tigris and Euphrates, where some form of written record enables us to regard them as historic from a date not long after 3000 B.C.

As we saw in the previous chapter, there is good evidence for trading contacts between South Baluchistan, and the folk of the Kulli Culture, and Sumer in the Early Dynastic period, about 2800 B.C. That the trade contacts of South Baluchistan were not westwards by sea routes is shown by the abundant evidence at such sites as Mehi of reciprocal mercantile relations eastwards and overland with the Indus Valley and the Harappā Culture. The shifting shoals and the mangrove swamps of the Indus mouths can never have encouraged the establishment of a port there, and the Kulli merchants may have been middle-men in the original trade between Harappā and the west, sailing from harbours on the Makran coast. At all events, there is no absolutely certain evidence that Sumer and the Harappā empire were in touch in Early Dynastic times: clear signs of contact first appear in Akkadian times – that is, about 2300 B.C. In Northern Persia there are certain points of evidence suggesting that some phase of the Harappā civilization was contemporary with the Hissar III period, and at Anau, in Russian Turkestan, Harappā contacts seem perceptible in Anau III – on independent showing contemporary with Hissar III. The dating of these phases is still somewhat controversial, but some time between 2300 and 2000 B.C. seems probable.

The intrusive barbarians responsible for the final occupation of the ruined Harappā sites at Chanhu-daro, Harappā, and elsewhere seem also to have connexions with the Hissar III–Anau III complex of cultures, perhaps indeed representing their final stages, and a migration eastwards from the North Iranian–Turkestan regions. On the whole their arrival in India is not likely to have been until two or three centuries after 2000 – the round figure of 1500 B.C. is conveniently approximate. So the evidence from the west suggests that the mature Harappā civilization – and it must be repeated that this is the only phase of the culture we know at present – flourished within the millennium 2500–1500 B.C. Of its end we are more certain than of its beginning, but we can say that during that millennium there was little appreciable change in the fabric and pattern of this enigmatic civilization. In the following pages, therefore, we are less hampered than we might be by methods of excavation which were stratigraphically uncritical, and we can use the whole body of evidence to build up a picture of the Harappā people and their achievements.

And so, first, the people themselves. For evidence of the physical type and personal appearance of the Harappā folk we can turn to two sources – the actual remains of skeletons and the representations in stone sculpture and bronze-casting found on the excavated sites. About fifty skeletons or fragments of skeletons have been found at Mohenjo-daro, Harappā, and Chanhu-daro, in conditions which vary from ritual deposits to violent massacres in the final stages of the cities' history, and of these a certain number have been reported upon by anthropologists and anatomists. At Harappā the 'R 37' cemetery, belonging to the period of the city's flourishing occupation, has produced about 60 burials, but the anatomical reports on these have not yet appeared. But from the available evidence, mainly from Mohenjo-daro, we can see that more than one ethnic strain was present in the population.

We shall discuss the circumstances in which the Mohenjo-daro people, whose remains were found in houses or in the lanes of the final phase of the city's occupation, met their death, in the next chapter. For the present we are concerned with their appearance in life. Nearly half the skulls which could be classified belonged to a more or less homogeneous group, into which, incidentally, also comes the only well-preserved skull from the Nal cemetery in Baluchistan. This group is that classed as the Mediterranean type, and at the present day includes a large number of groups of peoples stretching from Iberia to India. The characteristic type appears in late Natufian times in Palestine (a Mesolithic phase referred to in Chapter II and perhaps dating back to the ninth or tenth millennium B.C.) and may have been differentiated in the southern steppes of Northern Africa and in Asia, and spread westwards and eastwards. The pre-dynastic Egyptians certainly belonged to this stock, and the purest representatives at the present day are to be found in the Arabian Peninsula. In India it forms today a dominant

element in the population of the north and is widespread
elsewhere among the upper social classes. Such people are
medium to tall in stature, with a complexion ranging from
dark to light olive-brown, a long head and face, and a narrow and relatively pronounced nose; black hair, and eyes
ranging from black to brown and characteristically large
and open. The body is slenderly built.

The archaeological evidence shows that this long-headed
Mediterranean type is everywhere in Western Asia associated with the earliest agricultural settlements: at Sialk or
Al 'Ubaid, Anau or Alishar. The Al 'Ubaid skulls show
singularly close analogies to those from Mohenjo-daro, and
their 'Afghanian' characteristics have been remarked upon.
Just as the evidence from the painted pottery of Baluchistan
and that lying behind the painted wares in the Harappā
Culture points to an eventual homogeneity among these
various simple agricultural economies, so the actual physical
type shows an essential ethnic community over the whole
area, and the appearance of these early 'Mediterranean'
folk in prehistoric India must be related to expansion from
the west.

But there is another and a more primitive element represented in the Mohenjo-daro people. Three skulls belong to
what has been classed as the Proto-Australoid group (the
Veddoid type of some writers), and these have some claim to
represent the aboriginal inhabitants of the country. Here,
analogies lie with the Australian blackfellows and the Ved-
dahs of Ceylon: current opinion tends to the view that Aus-
tralia received her aboriginal population by migration
hrough Ceylon and Melanesia from Southern India, where
the type is well represented today. Of small stature, with a
dark skin-colour approaching black, wavy or curly (but
never frizzy) black hair, long heads, broad flat nose and
fleshy, protruding lips, these people form the main element
in the South and Central Indian aboriginal tribes of the

present day, as well as largely constituting the so-called 'exterior castes' of Hindu society.

The remaining skulls from the Harappā Culture include one (from a burial which may be later than the main occupation of Mohenjo-daro) of a person of typically Mongolian type – by no means surprising, of course: the type has been present in China since Upper Palaeolithic times – and certainly one, perhaps as many as four, which were short-headed and comparable with the so-called Alpine type. This physical type is represented at Sialk as a small proportion of the population during periods II, III, and IV, and its origin has been much discussed; but these round-headed folk may have their origins in an Upper Palaeolithic survival, with reduced head and face size, and parallel to the emergence of the specialized round-headed Mongoloid form. The Sialk evidence suggests that such cranial types may also occur in the Iranian plateau in the third and fourth millenia B.C. The Indian skulls are more likely to be related to a physical type probably indigenous, if rare in Western Asia, than to afford evidence of racial movement from the west towards the valley of the Indus at this time. There is a related short-headed element in the Indian population today, scattered through many regions, and some anthropologists would include in this group the Brahuis of Baluchistan, though others regard them as the result of a mixture between Proto-Australoid and Mediterranean types. In general, however, the Alpine types tend to have a lighter pigmentation than these races, with abundant body hair and a roundish face with strong nose.

The sum of the evidence from the skulls, then, shows that in the Harappā Culture there was, first, the aboriginal Proto-Australoid type, perhaps then, as now, ranking among the 'under-dogs' of the social system; second, the predominant Mediterraneans, presumably the main contributors of the agricultural and urban features of the whole Western

Indian prehistoric world, and with them probably the short-headed Alpine element; thirdly, an occasional 'foreigner' from the north-east – the hill-country of Nepal or Assam, or beyond, possibly from China itself – but he is perhaps present as an invader.

The evidence from sculptured representations must, of course, be handled with some reserve, but it is at least not incompatible with the knowledge gained from the skulls themselves. Four works of art from Mohenjo-daro can really be taken into consideration, and of these the first is the little bronze statuette of a girl, already referred to in Chapter IV as showing close similarities in hair-dressing and adornment to the clay figurines in the Kulli Culture of South Baluchistan. This girl seems certainly of the Proto-Australoid type, with full lips, and if, as seems likely, she is indeed a representation of a Baluchistan type, one may note in passing that the very dark complexion associated with the Proto-Australoid group would be in accord with the name given to Southern Baluchistan in classical times – Gedrosia, the country of the dark folk.

A sculptured limestone head showing a man with a beard and an elaborate coiffure, with a 'bun' at the back, bound round by a fillet, would fit well enough into the Mediterranean facial type, while the treatment of the eyes in another rather similar head might indicate a Mongolian cast of countenance; but this resemblance should not be stressed unduly. But the most important piece of sculpture, that of the well-known bearded man wearing a trefoil-decorated robe, is rather puzzling from an ethnic point of view. It has been suggested that one should see in this sculpture a representation of an Armenoid type with short head – a physical type which appears to be present in Mesopotamia from Early Dynastic times onwards as an ingredient of the population, but which at Sialk is known only from the late Cemetery B, not likely to be earlier than 1000 B.C., and in the main some centuries later. But it is always dangerous to argue from ancient sculpture to ancient skulls, and, as we have seen, there is an earlier short-headed element present at Sialk, and at Mohenjo-daro, in the so-called Alpine types of skull. As many anthropologists regard the Armenoid type as a stable hybrid between the Alpine stock and the Indo-Iranian branch of the Mediterranean race, the early and perhaps sporadic appearance of the type in the third millennium is by no means impossible.

The distribution of Harappā settlements in North-Western India has already been commented on in general terms. Like the contemporary settlements of Sumer and Egypt, the Harappā Culture is essentially linked by great rivers, which have obviously been the decisive geographical factors in its expansion and in the subsequent preservation of its unity over so large an area. The two main cities lie, like the foci of an ellipse, one to the north and the other to the south of the known area of settlement — Mohenjo-daro on the right bank of the Indus in Sind and Harappā on the left bank of the Ravi in the Punjab. Extensive field-work has been carried out in Sind, and we probably have a fairly complete idea of the distribution of settlements there, except those later covered by medieval and modern towns or villages. It seems probable that intensive field-work in the Punjab would bring to light a great many more sites there; at present there is one village known not far from Harappā itself, and another in the Himalayan foothills at Rupar on the Sutlej River. But east of the Indus in Bahawalpur State and along the course of the now dry Ghaggar River, the Sarasvati of early Indian literature, are a dozen sites of villages or towns which, by their position, would seem politically to come within the ambit of the ruler of Harappā, and which might be taken as evidence of a northerly kingdom, to be amplified no doubt by further undiscovered sites in the Punjab (Fig. 17).

Between the most southerly site in Bahawalpur and the nearest site farther south, in Khairpur State, is an interval of 150 miles – but this lacuna may be due to incomplete field-work over the intervening area, and settlement may be virtually continuous. However, from this point southwards and south-westwards nearly to Karachi are clustered settlements of which the chief is the city of Mohenjo-daro, near the northern limit of the area of concentration, suggesting a population owing allegiance to the ruling powers in that city.

It is, I think, improbable that further field-work will bring to light more cities of the first rank, such as the two already known – improbable, though of course not impossible. On the evidence as it stands at present, we are entitled to regard the Harappā kingdom as governed from two capital cities 350 miles apart, but linked by a continuous river thoroughfare. That the Northern and Southern kingdoms, if we like to separate them in this manner, were in fact only subdivisions of a unit is shown by the complete uniformity in material culture from the most northerly to the most southerly site, ignoring any imaginary boundary we may draw between Bahawalpur and Khairpur, for instance. Whatever the system of rule and however enforced, it can hardly be that of two competing city-states, but must represent a common authority having a dual seat of government.

The archaeological evidence of continuous occupation of the city-sites over centuries, with at Mohenjo-daro at least the preservation of the initial street-plan from first to last, with practically no encroachment on the building-lines of houses where they faced upon main streets or subsidiary lanes, shows that continuity of government was somehow assured throughout this long time, and that whatever the changes of dynasty or of individuals in power, the tradition was transmitted unimpaired and of constant validity. While it is dangerous to make deductions from the evidence with any confidence, one can nevertheless suggest that such a

continuity over generations is likely to have been enforced
by religious sanctions, and that, in its remarkable conser-.
vatism and scrupulous preservation of even the details of
everyday life intact for centuries, the texture of the Harappā
civilization has a strongly theocratic tinge, and surely implies
a social system wherein the unchanging traditions of the
temple were of more account than the ambitions of an individual ruler or the secular instability of the court, and in
which the form of land tenure was dictated by the priestly
hierarchy.

In the two cities the impression of centralized power,
already implicit in the distribution and character of the
settlements as a whole, is immediately and overwhelmingly
apparent. The two sites are laid out to a common ground-
plan, in which, on the western edge of the city, rose an impressive citadel, an approximate rectangle or parallelogram
with its long axis north and south, and measuring about 400
by 200 yards (Fig. 18). This was formed of an artificial platform over 30 feet high, of mud brick faced with burnt brick
revetments and strong defensive walls, carrying on its fortified summit a group of buildings which, as we shall see later,
are not private houses, but houses with a ceremonial or
public character. To this high defended citadel belonged
processional terraces and monumental gateways; below it
lay the streets and houses of the town, and the industrial
quarters of a semi-servile labouring class (Fig. 19).

Here, to quote Wheeler, whose work at Harappā has so
forcibly demonstrated the essential character of the cities
and their rulers,

'whatever the source of their authority – and a dominant religious element may fairly be assumed – the lords
of Harappā administered their city in a fashion not remote from that of the priest-kings or governors of Sumer
and Akkad ... In Sumer, the wealth and discipline of the

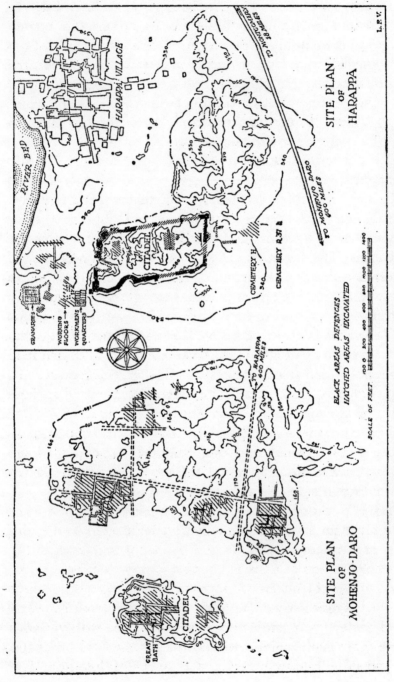

FIG. 18. Site plans of Mohenjo-daro and Harappā (after Wheeler)

city-state were vested in the chief deity, i.e. in the priest-hood or a priest-king. The civic focus was the exalted temple, centre of an elaborate and carefully ordered secu-lar administration under divine sanction ... In essence, the picture is one of a rigid and highly evolved bureaucratic machine, capable of organizing and distributing surplus wealth and defending it, but little conducive to the poli-tical liberty of the individual.'

A state ruled over by priest-kings, wielding autocratic and absolute power from two main seats of government, and with the main artery of communication between the capital cities provided by a great navigable river, seems, then, to be the reasonable deduction from the archaeological evidence of the civilization of Harappā. To maintain the populations of such cities, and of the smaller towns to a large extent as well, an agrarian system sufficiently well organized to produce the necessary surplus must have existed, but there is no direct evidence of its nature, or of the systems of artificial irrigation which might well be expected to accompany it. We know that bread wheat (*Triticum compactum* and *sphaero-coccum*) and barley (*Hordeum vulgare* and the *hexastichum* vari-ety) were grown, as well as sesamum and field peas (*Pisum arvensis*), and a species of *Brassica* (perhaps *B. juncea*, the modern Indian *rai*). The cereal crops are of sufficient interest to merit further discussion.

Barley is a grain which has been cultivated from very early times in Western Asia; it is attested to in Tell Halaf times at Arpachiyah in Northern Mesopotamia, and in the Egyptian Fayum at a time probably contemporary with the Uruk phase of ancient Mesopotamia. The Egyptian finds include, significantly enough, the *hexastichum* (six-row) vari-ety of barley, as in prehistoric India, and the wild varieties of the grass from which the cultivated grain was produced still grow in Turkestan, Persia, and North Afghanistan. The wild ancestors of what is known as bread wheat (with 21 chromosomes as against.14 and 7 in the other two main wheat groups) are unknown, but it is interesting to note that the most primitive forms of the cultivated varieties are grown today in Persia, Afghanistan, the region around Bokhara, Kashmir, and Western India, and there is some reason to think that the *sphaerococcum* and *compactum* forms may be the earliest forms of bread wheat, arising out of hybridization of the other wheats with kindred grasses. On botanical grounds such workers as Vavilov have suggested that bread wheat originated on the Himalayan edge of Afghanistan; others have looked to the region between the Zagros Mountains and the Caspian. The archaeological evidence is slight, but impressions of bread wheat grains of the *Triticum vulgare* group were found in potsherds from Anau I in Turkestan, and point to the early emergence of the type in regions not too remote from Western India, where the Harappā Culture evidence shows that bread wheats were being grown in the third millennium B.C.

We shall see that the storage of grain was, at Harappā at least, and by inference at Mohenjo-daro as well, carried out as part of a government agricultural policy, and that, adjacent to the municipal granaries, the preparation of flour – the equivalent of corn-milling – was also part of a controlled economy using organized labour. It is to be presumed that other state-controlled industries would be brick-manufacture, and that the supply of wood fuel for this and for pottery-baking, both in terms of mass-production, would involve some sort of forestry force. No brick kilns have so far been discovered; as these are likely to have been large, they would certainly have been set outside the main occupied area of the city, where the smoke would not offend the inhabitants. Pottery-kilns are known only in the latest phase of the city at Mohenjo-daro, and bespeak decadence: even quite small pottery-kilns are today set outside the town walls in India – partly to avoid the smoke and partly to obviate the risk of fire to adjacent premises. But in the degenerate days at Mohenjo-daro they were built in the town – even in the street.

One of the most interesting crops grown by the people of the Harappā civilization was cotton, of which a fortunate single find at Mohenjo-daro has given conclusive evidence. Fragments of a true cotton textile, dyed red with madder, were found sticking to the side of a silver vase, and it is clear that the plant which produced the fibre is of the *Gossypium arboreum* type – that grown today as a cultivated form, and. not one of the wild cottons. Cotton cloth is likely to have been an important article of commerce for the Harappā civilization, and it is probable that some at least of the trade with Mesopotamia was in cotton goods. By later historic times in that country Indian cotton was known under the name of *sindhu*, and this in the form *sindon* passed into Greek.

In addition to vegetable crops, the farming economy which lay behind the Harappā kingdom's prosperity naturally included various domestic animals. We are fortunate in having an admirable series of zoological reports on the animal bones from Harappā to form the basis of a detailed survey. The Indian humped bull, or zebu (*Bos indicus*), was domesticated as in Baluchistan; so too was a smaller, short-horned, humpless species. The origin of the humped bull is obscure: wild species are not known, and one can regard it only as a domesticated variety which ultimately goes back to the common stock represented by the Pleistocene *Bos namadicus*. It is a breed specifically Indian in ancient times, the characteristic hump differentiating it from contemporary domesticated breeds elsewhere in Western Asia; and, as we have seen, it certainly goes back to the Rana Ghundai II phase of North Baluchistan, perhaps contemporary with Hissar I and Jemdet Nasr at least.

Other domestic animals in the Harappā Culture include

the Indian domestic buffalo (*Bos bubalis*), goat (*Capra aega-grus*, r. *indicus*), sheep (*Ovis vignei*, r. *domesticus*), and pig (*Sus cristatus* var. *domesticus*). The goats appear to belong to the same group as those of Kashmir which produce the superb wool from which the famous Kashmir shawls are made, and so the possibility of goat wool being used in the Harappā Culture must be borne in mind. The sheep, probably forms domesticated from the wild Urial stock and similar to sheep from Sialk I and Anau, seem likely to belong to a long-legged, long-tailed race which includes various wool-producing forms, and the pigs belong to the lean, brisk, bristly species known in India today.

There is evidence of the domestication of the dog from the earliest days of the Harappā Culture. This animal had in fact been the earliest in Europe to be domesticated, having been tamed for hunting in post-glacial mesolithic times, by 8000 B.C. or so. The evidence of bones and representations from Harappā sites show at least two types of dog, one akin to the modern pariah and the other a mastiff type. The former (*Canis tenggeranus*, r. *harappensis*) comes near the original ancestral type of dog, derived from some form of medium-sized wolf, probably from Eastern Europe or Western Asia. There is very interesting evidence of domesticated cats as well – bones from Harappā, and from Chanhu-daro a brick over which, when soft and unbaked, a dog had chased a cat, both leaving their characteristic foot-prints – 'the deep impress of the pads and their spread indicate the speed of both animals ... the dog's imprint slightly overlapping the cat's shows that he came second'. The cat from Harappā (*Felis ocreata*, r. *domestica*) seems to have closely resembled the ordinary European domestic cat in appearance.

The camel is an animal whose early history as a domesti-cated beast is curiously obscure, though it was extensively used by the Assyrians from the ninth century B.C. onwards. Today no wild camels exist, both species, one-humped and two-humped, being domesticated, and there is a remarkable lack of early representations of the animal in the Ancient East. However, a few camel bones of the Indian one-humped race (*Camelus dromedarius*) were found at Mohenjo-daro and at Harappā, and they have also been found at Anau in Turkestan and in the neolithic Tripolye Culture of South Russia, where they are likely to be approximately contemporary with the Harappā civilization. One of the rare representations of a camel in prehistoric Western Asia comes from a site probably of the second millennium B.C. just over the border of Baluchistan in Persian Makran, at Khurab, where it is modelled in relief on a bronze object.

The domestic ass (*Equus asinus*) and the horse (*Equus caballus*) are both represented, and we have seen that the latter animal was already known to the first inhabitants of the Rana Ghundai site in North Baluchistan; it was also known from Anau and from the second phase of Sialk. The remains suggest comparison with the modern Indian 'country-bred' animal.

Finally, the elephant should be included among those animals almost certainly domesticated by the Harappā people, and it is possible that the representations on the seals show the two breeds recognized today in India, the Komooria Dhundia with its flat back, square head, and stout legs, and the inferior Meergha, less heavily built and with a sloping back.

Apart from specifically Indian animals, such as elephants and water-buffaloes, the most interesting feature which differentiates the Harappā assemblage of domesticated beasts from those of other Western Asiatic prehistoric sites is the presence there of the horse and the camel. Ox, goat, sheep, pig, and dog are the familiar domesticated animals of the Old World wherever the adoption of agricultural economies takes over from the hunting stage of human culture — the dog indeed, as we have seen, was domesticated even earlier. But the origin of the camel is an enigma among the beasts of burden and of transport in the Ancient Orient, and the horse is at least not an original inhabitant of Mesopotamia, but is given the significant Sumerian name of the 'ass of the mountains' when it first appears, probably in Jemdet Nasr times. It was presumably imported from 'the mountains' of Highland Persia or Turkestan, which with Baluchistan formed a common geographical province within which the earliest evidence of horse-taming comes.

Turning now to a description of the actual cities and towns of the Harappā people, we must obviously first consider the two capitals, at Harappā and Mohenjo-daro. Both sites have certain striking features in common, visible even on the surface before excavation, and these similarities have been confirmed by the work of archaeologists during the past twenty years. The situation of the two sites is essentially similar, each by the side of a river. Harappā lies beside an old confluence of two branches of the River Ravi, a tributary of the Indus, and although at the present time the main river-channel is 6 miles away, in the circumstances of heavier rainfall, which we have seen are likely to have existed in the third millennium B.C., the city must have stood on ground liable to be flooded, and it seems probable that the great rampart or 'bund' of mud and mud-brick which forms the earliest phase of the citadel defences on the site was designed primarily as an embankment to keep out flood-water.

Mohenjo-daro stands on what is significantly known in the locality as 'The Island' – a narrow strip of land between the main bed of the Indus and the Western Nara loop – and was subject to flooding until very recent times, when the building of a long embankment prevented a recurrence of floods. There are remains of a prehistoric embankment between the city and the nearest part of the river, running for at least a mile, and the excavations produced clear evidence of several successive floods in the history of the site, with the

consequent deposition of layers of silt. Indeed, so great has
the volume of silt brought down by the Indus been that today the surface of the plain is some 30 feet higher than the
lowest foundations reached. There is some evidence of an
ancient branch of the river washing the edge of the city on
the west in prehistoric times. At Harappā evidence for periodic floods is not as clear as at Mohenjo-daro, but there seem
to have been traces of a protective embankment on the west
of the city here also.

In the matter of actual plan and lay-out the two cities are
strikingly similar, and Wheeler's recent work at Harappā
has thrown much light on the significance of this uniform
planning. In both sites the extant remains consist of an irregular series of mounds towards the east and a recognizably
higher and more compact mound placed more or less centrally and on the edge of the site to the west. In both cities
this mound is roughly a parallelogram in plan, measuring
about 400 yards north–south and 200 yards east–west : at
Harappā it rises up to 50 feet above the level of the surrounding plain, at Mohenjo-daro to 35 or 40 feet at least.
At the latter site enough has been recovered of the original
street plan to show that this high mound to the west stands
centrally between the two main east–west streets and, as we
shall see, it may have formed one of a series of major building
blocks in a symmetrical lay-out (Fig. 18).

We now know that these mounds are the ruined remnants
of impressive fortified citadels, in which, on an artificial
platform of mud brick 30 feet or more high, stood certain
buildings of peculiar plan, defended by a battered wall of
baked brick facing the mud-brick core, with rectangular
towers and great gateways (Figs. 19 and 20, Pls. 1 and 2).
The Harappā evidence is full, and is derived from the first
excavation to be conducted on the Indian prehistoric sites
which follows modern archaeological technique, but here
the buildings on the top are so ruined as to render their plan

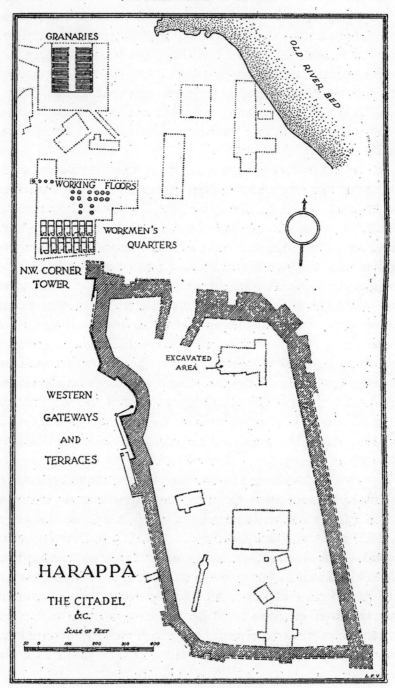

FIG. 19. (after Wheeler)

incoherent. But we can turn to Mohenjo-daro for these details on that site, and interpret the unexcavated remains of the defences there from the discoveries at Harappā.

The sequence at Harappā was found to be as follows (Fig. 20). The first settlement on the site was a village of folk using pottery of North Baluchistan black-on-red type, probably the RG III*c* phase, and there are considerable traces of de-vastating floods. The arrival of folk of the Harappā civiliza-tion is marked by the building of a great defensive wall, overlying but integral with an embankment, of mud and debris with a mud-brick core, evidently made to raise the foundations of the defences above flood-level. The main de-fensive wall was of mud brick, battered internally and exter-nally and faced with a revetment of burnt brick on the outside, the whole structure being 40 feet wide at the base and rising to a height of some 35 feet (Pls. 1 and 2). It retained the great mud and mud-brick platform which carried the main buildings of the citadel, and in plan was a parallelogram 1200 by 600 feet, with a complex western gateway associated with ceremonial terraces and another re-entrant gate on the north – perhaps the main entrance. This defensive wall was reinforced by rectangular salients, some of which were carried higher than the main wall as towers.

The defences showed two phases of reconstruction. After the original work had weathered and suffered some damage, the burnt-brick revetment was rebuilt in first-class fashion (better than the original work) and thickened in some places – work evidently carried out at the height of the Ha-rappā civilization. But in the second phase of rebuilding the north-west corner was reinforced by an additional salient and the two entrances of the western gate system were wholly or partially blocked. 'In this late phase of the city,' Wheeler remarks significantly, 'the Harappans were on the defensive'.

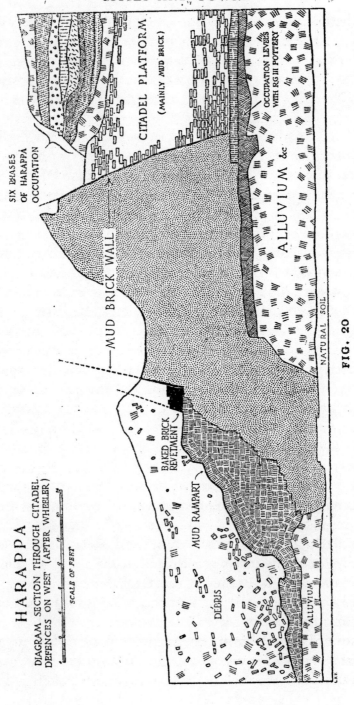

HARAPPA

DIAGRAM SECTION THROUGH CITADEL DEFENCES ON WEST (AFTER WHEELER)

SCALE OF FEET

SIX PHASES OF HARAPPĀ OCCUPATION

CITADEL PLATFORM (MAINLY MUD BRICK)

MUD BRICK WALL

OCCUPATION LEVELS WITH R.G.II POTTERY

ALLUVIUM &c

NATURAL SOIL

BAKED BRICK REVETMENT

MUD RAMPART

DÉBRIS

ALLUVIUM

FIG. 20

At Mohenjo-daro Wheeler was able to show, by a little
field-work rather than by actual excavation, that similar
defences must have surrounded the westernmost mound on
that site, now crowned by a Buddhist stupa of the third or
fourth century A.D. Marshall and Mackay in the earlier excavations had shown that the stupa mound had contained a
great rectangular platform of mud brick, at least 20 feet high,
and built immediately after the earliest building phase
recognized on the site (where virgin soil was not reached
owing to the water-table). On this platform had been some
building now covered by the stupa and its court, which the
excavators unfortunately did not remove: it is a third-rate
architectural monument and it is to be hoped that the site
will be dealt with satisfactorily in the future. But adjacent
to it was a remarkable complex of buildings, described by
Marshall as 'a vast hydropathic establishment'. Memories
of Matlock or Baden-Baden, however, are hardly applicable
to the actual structures on the Mohenjo-daro citadel, though
the central feature is certainly a great bath, or 'tank' in
modern Indian nomenclature, nearly 40 by 24 feet and built
of very fine brickwork. It is 8 feet deep, and steps, originally
with wooden treads on the brickwork, lead down into each
end; the whole walling is backed with bitumen to make it
water-tight, and there is provision for draining the bath
when needed. Around it was a cloister and on three sides a
series of small rooms, like changing-rooms, in one of which
was a well.

In addition to this bath-building, there was another large
building some 230 by 78 feet, planned as a single architectural unit with a cloistered court reminiscent of that surrounding the Great Bath, and containing an arrangement
of rooms that suggested to its excavator that it might be a
communal establishment or 'college' of some sort: its plan
is certainly unlike any of the normal house-plans known
from the rest of the town. To the south of these buildings was

another structure of equally curious plan, much altered and rebuilt but apparently originally a nearly square hall about 80 feet each way, with its roof supported on twenty rectangular pillars of brickwork.

In addition to these exceptional buildings, the citadel area at Mohenjo-daro also contained what appear from their plans to be houses similar to those in the remaining areas of the city. But the general character of the citadel architecture is obviously dominated by the presence of the Great Bath, the Collegiate Building, the Pillared Hall, and, one suspects, by whatever structure lies beneath the stupa. The implication is, in Wheeler's words, that we have here 'a centre of religious or administrative life on a significant scale'. The Great Bath takes its place well in a sacred site when one considers the 'tank' ancillary to every Hindu temple of the middle ages, and, while the actual temple cannot yet be identified, continuity of religious tradition on the stupa site would be by no means unlikely.

At Harappā it was found that the Western Gateway had, like the rest of the Citadel, been terribly robbed and wrecked by the brick-robbers, but enough remained for patient excavation to disentangle the remains of ceremonial terraces and a processional way leading up from a ramp or flight of steps to the actual gateways, the terraces being provided with guard-rooms at the outer angles (Fig. 19). These were all situated in a curious curved re-entrant of the defensive wall, 'not explained by the normal needs of defence. ... We are driven back upon the conclusion that the plan was designed to conform with the needs of some sort of ceremony – religious or secular or both – in which the terrace or terraces played a dominant role, and to which processional access was required ... A variety of processional ceremonies to which the scheme could be adapted suggests itself, but choice is unprofitable until we have more knowledge of Harappan religion and administration.'

Below the citadel in each city lay the remainder of the streets, shops, and dwelling-houses of the main population. Erosion has played havoc with the outer edges of the mounds that now mark these buildings, and traces of city walls, other than those of the citadels themselves, have not so far been identified with confidence, though at Mohenjo-daro part of a wall, with a flight of steps probably going down to the river outside, has been found and claimed as a possible town wall. At this site too the better-preserved buildings, hardly touched by brick-robbing, have enabled a considerable amount of the street-plan and the plans of individual houses to be recovered (Fig. 21).

The mounds which represent the city of Mohenjo-daro today cover a square mile, and surface indications of some of the main streets can be traced and have been confirmed by excavation, which has also revealed the details of the smaller streets and lanes in some areas. Combining these pieces of evidence, the published plan suggests that the basic lay-out was that of a gridiron of main streets running north–south and east–west, dividing the area into blocks of roughly equal size and approximately rectangular, 800 feet east-to-west and 1200 feet north-to-south. The existence of six and probably seven of these blocks has been proved by excavation, as have two main streets at right angles (East Street and First Street), and part of a third to the east of and parallel with First Street. The denudation of the edges of the mounds already mentioned renders the perimeter of the city uncertain in outline and exact position, but if the lay-out indicated by the central street-plan was continued symmetrically, we would have a square city a mile across comprising twelve major building blocks in three rows of four, east to west. The central western block, on this reconstructed lay-out, would be the Citadel, occupying a position commensurate with the distinction implied by its function. The main streets, unpaved, seem to have been up to 30 feet wide, and

within the main blocks was an irregular network of small
roads, lanes, and alleys roughly following the general lines
of the lay-out and dividing the blocks into individual houses.
At Harappā it was impossible to determine any details of

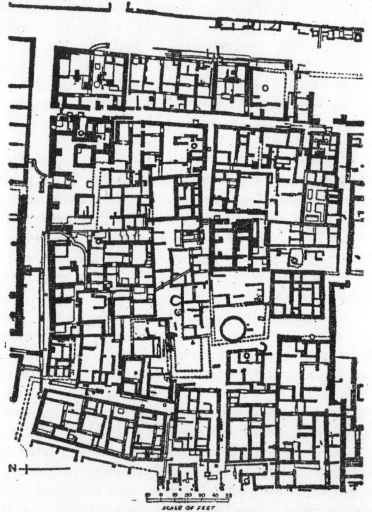

SCALE OF FEET

FIG. 21. Lay-out of city block, Mohenjo-daro (after Mackay)

the general lay-out, and almost none of individual houses.

It has already been pointed out that a series of constructional phases can be distinguished at Harappā and at

Mohenjo-daro, but until the final and decadent phases of
the sites' occupations the original plans of buildings were,
at least in the latter city, strictly followed, and consequently
the street lay-out preserved throughout, although internal
alteration and subdivision were often made to houses. The
stratification is discussed in detail later in this chapter, and
here it is sufficient to note that the material culture is so uniform that for our immediate purpose the entire accumula-
tions of occupational and constructional debris on the two
sites may be considered as a single entity, and architectural
features described in terms applicable to the whole.

While the buildings at Mohenjo-daro which can reasonably be considered as houses or shops, or which combined
both functions, showed variations in size which no doubt
corresponded to the respective status and wealth of their
occupants, their general plan was much the same. Building
in the better-class houses was invariably carried out in well-
fired bricks, normally 11 by 5·5 by 2·5 inches, though there
are variants, and walls were always built solid, not with a
faced rubble core. There seems to have been wide use of mud-
plastering inside the houses, and probably normally outside as well, though one or two instances of more or less decorative bricklaying rather suggest that these particular walls
were left unplastered. The usual method of laying was the
'English bond' of alternate courses of headers and stretchers.

Following normal oriental customs, the outside walls of
houses fronting the streets were as featureless as possible and
broken only by doorways. These had an average width of
about 3 feet 4 inches, and normally had flat timber lintels,
though some were corbelled. Practically no trace of windows was found, even in well-preserved walls, and they
were probably very high in the room and small, with
gratings of which some fragments in stone survived. Marshall commented on the forbidding blank walls of brick
which front one today in the excavated streets of Mohenjo-

daro, and aptly compared the site to the ruins of a Lancashire industrial quarter – even with plaster and colour the smaller lanes and alleyways must have been strange and secret places to walk in.

The normal plan of well-to-do houses seems to have been based on a courtyard, to which access was gained by a door which normally led not from the main street but from a side alley; there is often provision for a watchman immediately inside the entrance. Round the courtyard or on two or three sides only are grouped rooms of varying sizes, including bathrooms with very well-made brick floors and elaborate drains running out to the street, though privies are practically unknown. Rubbish-shoots occur, however, running out through the wall into a brick-built rectangular bin outside, presumably cleared by order of the municipal authorities, who must similarly have been responsible for the elaborate drainage system which ran under the streets and into which house drains communicated. The main drains could be cleared by lifting large, specially made brick 'manhole-covers', and the whole conception shows a remarkable concern for sanitation and health without parallel in the Orient in the prehistoric past or at the present day. Soak-pits took the eventual sewage.

Fireplaces were practically non-existent, and such artificial heating as was needed was presumably obtained from charcoal braziers. Stairways, implying upper storeys or at least flat roofs, were common, and in some instances beam-holes for definite upper floors were found. Charred pine rafters were found at Harappā, and sissoo is also attested from Mohenjo-daro, where putlog-holes for squared beams up to 14 feet in span were found. Wood was also used for door-lintels, and, as we have seen, for the treads of the steps into the Great Bath. Wooden pillars may have been used, though rarely; a few possible limestone capitals and bases have been found. The flat roofs of houses were covered with

bamboo and rush matting coated with mud and earth to
form a solid waterproof layer.

In general the planning of the city at Mohénjo-daro shows
little variation in the type of house, but in one area there is a
very interesting range of what can only be called workmen's
quarters, identically planned and apparently with a special
well by way of a water-supply. This group of cottages lies in
the north-west corner of the HR area of the excavations, and
consists of sixteen identically planned structures, each 20 by
12 feet internally and divided into two rooms, one twice
the size of the other. These are arranged in two parallel
rows, with a narrow lane on one side and a street on the
other, and have thin walls suggesting that they were single-
storey. The whole lay-out is so strongly suggestive of contemporary coolie-lines that one feels that this is a likely explanation, and this view receives confirmation from the
more explicit Harappā evidence.

Here, below the Citadel on the north, was undoubtedly
the workmen's quarter of the city – perhaps one of several.
A double row of cottages arranged much as at Mohenjo-
daro was found, each identically planned on much the same
principle of two main rooms, one larger than the other, but
the individual houses were twice the size of those at Mohenjo-daro. Fourteen such houses were found, and the existence
of many more can be inferred (Fig. 19).

The whole area in which these coolie-lines stood is, in
Wheeler's words, 'marshalled like a military cantonment
and bespeaks authority'. In the areas excavated beyond the
workmen's quarters were orderly rows of circular working
floors carefully built of baked brick, about 10 feet in diameter and originally containing at the centre a massive
wooden mortar sunk in the ground, in which grain could be
pounded to flour with long heavy pestles in the manner still
employed in Bengal and Kashmir. The worn bricks near the
centres of these primitive corn-milling devices showed where

the bare-footed slaves had stood as they pounded the grain, and remains of wheat, barley and chaff were in fact found in some of the central hollows (Pl. 3). Behind these again was a great granary standing on a brick-built podium 150 feet wide and probably at least 200 feet long, with buttressed walls and divided by a central aisle, on each side of which were ranged the individual storage blocks raised on brick substructures above the damp ground, and each measuring 50 by 20 feet. Again, not far from the granary and working-platforms were metal-workers' furnaces, which once more emphasize the semi-industrialized nature of this quarter of Harappā.

It is inevitable that one should mention slave-labour when describing this piece of planned economy: the standardized little houses in dreary rows, the great State Granary, the municipal flour-mills. Probably the nearest parallel to the coolie-lines is the Workmen's Village at Tell-el-Amarna, with its similar blocks of identically planned cottages, but the Harappā lay-out must antedate the Egyptian by at least a millennium. The concentration of various trades and industries into specific quarters or streets is, of course, common in oriental towns up to the present day, as it was in medieval Europe; and there was considerable centralized control of trade and industry in ancient Sumer. But this relegation of a particular group of occupations to a restricted area of the city, with the provision of a housing scheme evidently drawn out in the city architect's office, represents something more consciously organized. To the Harappā civilization we must presumably attribute the first really organized industry in Western Asia, as distinct from that of a craftsmen's guild.

The water-supply of the two cities was obtained from excellently constructed wells with brick lining, and as successive rings of brickwork had to be added as the ground level within the town rose from long occupation and flood-silts, these wells now stand up in the excavated sites like grotesque factory chimneys. Some wells seem to have provided a private supply to individual houses, but others almost certainly were for public use, serving the purpose of the water-stall or *piau* of modern India. Round such well-heads have been found innumerable fragments of mass-produced little clay cups, suggesting that, as in contemporary Hinduism, there was a ritual taboo on drinking twice from the same cup, and that each cup was thrown away or smashed after it had been used.

The elaborate system of drains and the almost ubiquitous bathrooms have already been mentioned. The bath would be taken, as in modern India, by pouring water over the body from a large jar, in the small bath-room with its well-paved brick floor and its outlet drain in one corner. Some of the floors still show the polish of bare feet upon them, probably aided by the oil used to prevent the skin from drying in a hot climate.

Apart from the two cities, the Harappā civilization is represented by a large number of small towns and villages of varying size and status, and at least two fortified sites. There is considerable variation in the size of these settlements, ranging from such sites as Chanhu-daro, whose extant remains cover an area 1000 by 700 feet, to hamlets like Amilano, a bare 300 by 200 feet. It is impossible to estimate precisely the area of the Harappā occupation at Dabar Kot, which, as far as it is known, occupies only the upper part of the great 100-foot-high tell. This tell has a diameter of 1200 feet at the base, but it may have covered an area some 450 feet across, and similarly at Sandhanawalla on the Ghaggar River the Harappā occupation was contained within the top 9 feet only of a 28-foot-high mound measuring 750 by 500 feet at the base.

In the smaller sites the use of burnt brick is not so ubiquitous as in the cities; a circumstance not altogether surprising when the demands on fuel and labour implied by such building material are considered. But it is interesting to note that baked bricks of the standard Harappā proportions occur as far afield as Rupar on the Upper Sutlej, Derawar in Bikaner, and Rangpur in Kathiawar, as well as at Chanhu-daro and in sites in the Larkana neighbourhood. At Dabar Kot burnt bricks were found, but measuring 24 by 16 by 4 inches and 21 by 16 by 3 inches: these are outside the range of variations recorded in the Harappā bricks, but on the same site were also mud-bricks 21 by 10 by 3 inches, which offer a better comparison and are themselves paralleled in size and material on sites of both the Kulli and the Amri-Nal Cultures. At Sutkagen-dor burnt brick structures were recorded in the nineteenth century by Mockler, and some bricks found by Stein not *in situ* measured 16 by 6 by 2½ inches, again not within the known Harappā range.

Several sites in Southern Sind had stone foundations on which walls of mud brick or of terre pisée presumably stood, to judge by the absence of stone debris on the sites and the continuation of the stone footings unbroken by doorways (e.g. at Amilano, where the footings are clear). Mud-brick walls appear to have existed at Sandhanawallah, while at Sutkagen-dor the outer walls of houses were masonry for at least 5 feet, and the inner partition walls had a 3-foot-high masonry foundation supporting mud bricks. At this site, too, the use of wooden pillars was deduced from the stone bases found in position by Stein.

Of the smaller unfortified sites of the Harappā Culture, Chanhu-daro has been excavated to the greatest extent and shows a general resemblance, on a smaller scale, to the cities, with the notable exception that the five successive rebuilding phases within the Harappā Culture occupation of the site are separated by layers of flood-borne debris, and that rebuilding did not follow the plan of the preceding settlement. Drains, wells, and house-plans conform to those of the cities. Of the other sites little detail has been recorded:

a characteristic brick drain and well were found at Dabar Kot, but elsewhere little save incomplete plans of houses has been found in the trial trenches dug. At Amilano stone foundations are visible over much of the site and show that the whole lay-out was more or less homogeneous and oriented roughly on the cardinal points. The very small size of this settlement suggests that it might have been a posting-house or serai on a route leading towards the coast, following indeed the line taken today by the track from Hyderabad to Karachi, which runs past the site.

There are a couple of fortified sites known. Ali Murad in Sind is surrounded by a stone wall 3 to 5 feet thick, which encloses an irregularly rectangular area, within which were houses and at least one well – such slight village fortification must have been the normal provision for safety from robbers and cattle-raiders. At Sutkagen-dor in the Makran, however, there was a more massive fortification, and a rectangular area 125 by 170 yards was enclosed by a stone wall, built of roughly-squared stone blocks in courses, 30 feet wide at the foot and with a vertical inner face, and the outer face battered at an angle of 40 degrees. Stein considered its probable original height to have been from 20 to 25 feet, and the whole site is clearly a very strongly defended citadel. There were traces of an entrance only 8 feet wide, with probable flanking towers or guard-houses, in the south-west corner, and there had been buildings both inside and outside this gateway.

The fortified site of Tharro in Sind has already been mentioned on p. 77, and the defences attributed in all probability to the Amri Culture, which is represented on the site. But the possibility of their being a product of the Harappā civilization must be borne in mind, for among the pottery from the site there is a great deal of rather soft, coarse red ware with characteristic Harappā 'offering-stands' among the forms represented. Furthermore, Majumdar found pictographs approximating to the Harappā script carved on the living rock at more than one point on the hill, and there are burial cairns apparently of some form of the Harappā Culture close by.

The interpretation of these provincial sites does not present any difficulties – they represent the more or less peasant and agricultural background which the existence of the cities presupposes. Some of them must have been chiefly trading-posts – Sutkagen-dor seems a clear case in point, and probably Dabar-Kot as well, and the former may have had an added importance as providing contact with the sea-going trade of the Persian Gulf and the Arabian Sea.

Some indication of what this trade did in fact involve can be gained from the detailed examination and analysis of the various stones and metals used in the Harappā civilization for decorative or utilitarian purposes. From the west bitumen, alabaster, and probably steatite seem likely to have been obtained from Baluchistan; and farther afield Afghanistan may have been a source for silver, though Persia is perhaps a more likely region. From Persia, too, gold may have been obtained, and more certainly silver, lead, and tin. Two semi-precious stones, turquoise and lapis-lazuli, are certainly of Persian or Afghan origin, the latter most probably from Badakshan, famous for its precious stones throughout the centuries, so that the poet Mir, writing in Delhi in the fifteenth century, could naturally say of the features of his beloved:

> Of the beauty of your eyes I shall
> tell the gazelles of Hindustan;
> Of the tincture of your lips I shall
> tell the rubies of Badakshan.

The conspicuous deposits of haematite, the red iron oxide, in the islands of the Persian Gulf and near Hormuz, exploited in ancient times by Sumer, also seem likely to have provided this red colouring matter for India.

Southwards, the Kathiawar region, in which there is, significantly enough, at least one Harappā settlement, would have provided the *chank* shells used for inlay and other decorative purposes, agates, carnelians, onyx and chalcedony for beads, and probably rock crystal as well. The fish of the *Arius* species, today dried and salted in large quantities on the Western Indian coast, and known from the remains of its bones to have been eaten at Mohenjo-daro, may also have come from this region, or that of Karachi.

East of the Indus, Rajputana is most likely to have provided the copper and probably the lead (from Ajmer) used by the Harappā metal-smiths, and from this region, too, steatite, slate, jasper, bloodstone, green chalcedony, and other stones for beads would have come. The Dekkan is likely to have provided amethysts, and a rare stone, amazonite, must have come from the Nilgiri Hills or, less probably, from Kashmir. Kashmir and the Himalayan forests would have provided deodar wood, probably floated down the rivers, as well as the substance *silajit*, used in folk-medicine, and the horns of deer, also believed to have medicinal properties. And perhaps from beyond the mountains, in the Pamirs, East Turkestan, or even Tibet or Burma, came jadeite.

All this trade, quite apart from that within the boundaries of the Harappā kingdom itself, must have involved a considerable merchant class, with the attendant organization of caravans along recognized trade-routes and not improbably the provision of halting-places or caravanserais in the remoter districts: I have suggested that such small sites as Amilano in Sind might represent such serais. In the transport of goods, one would expect camels to take a conspicuous place, though pack-horses may well have been used, especially in the mountainous regions, and what looks like a little clay model of a pack-saddle has been found at Jhukar in Sind, probably of the Harappā period. But many animals can be used for transport in the mountains, as anyone will realize who has seen the flocks of long-haired goats coming over the passes to India from Ladakh, each with a little pack of rock-salt slung across its back.

For slower and heavier transport, the ox-cart was extensively used in the Harappā Culture. Models of carts in clay are among the commonest antiquities on the prehistoric sites of the Punjab and Sind, and the type represented is exactly that which today creaks and groans with its ungreased, nearly solid wheels in the villages round Mohenjo-daro, and in fact carries your luggage from Dokri railway station to the site when you visit it. The type, we now know, is unchanged even in its wheel-base, for the recent Harappā excavations have revealed cart-ruts belonging to an early phase of the city's occupation having a width of some 3 feet 6 inches, which is that of the modern carts in Sind. Such things have a long survival-value – the standard gauge of modern English carts was already fixed by the third century B.C. in these islands.

While river traffic must have been considerable, there is no direct evidence of the use of boats, and only two representations exist. One is a rough drawing scratched on a sherd of pottery, but one can recognize the high prow and stern, a mast and furled sail, and a steersman with a long steering-oar. The other is a more carefully executed engraving on a seal, and shows clearly a vessel with very high prow and stern, and apparently made of reeds, the lashings of which are distinctly seen. Amidships is a square cabin (or shrine), perhaps made also of reeds, or as a tent. A steersman is very sketchily drawn in, seated on a raised platform in the bows. Vessels of similar type, as far as can be judged from representations, were characteristic of prehistoric Mesopotamia.

Though not strictly concerned with trade and the transport of merchandise, this is a convenient place to draw attention to another type of vehicle in the Harappā Culture, known from a charming little bronze model from Harappā itself, and from another almost exactly similar from Chanhu-daro – a striking example of the uniformity of the culture in two places 400 miles apart. These models represent a little covered trap, very similar to the *ekka* of modern India, with a roof and curtains of fabric set up on four poles above the cart-frame: in the Harappā model a driver is seated in front, well forward between the shafts, with one hand on his knee and the other raised to hold the reins, and both models have lost the draught animal. But from Mohenjo-daro come two bronze oxen which evidently came from precisely such models, and provide the evidence missing at Chanhu-daro and Harappā; in both the cart and the oxen, bearings for the wheels are provided by loops of metal below the object, and there seems no doubt that they belong to models of almost identical type.

To the foreign trade and the relations between the Harappā civilization and other powers we shall return later in this chapter. It must always be remembered that archaeology may give us a misleading impression of trade relationships, since its evidence is confined almost entirely to nonperishable materials. How much cotton was exported from prehistoric India is unknown, and, while it is probable that colonies of Indian merchants were settled in Sumerian towns, there is strangely little evidence of what was brought back to India. In the absence of a written record that can be understood we can hardly hope to know whether spices and pepper, for instance, were already in the third millennium a staple of trade with the West, or whether incense was such a marketable commodity then as in later times. Slave-traffic, too, is an archaeological imponderable to a very large extent, except where skull types may give an ambiguous clue. But the bronze of the Dancing-Girl from Mohenjo-daro, so closely representing the type of hairdressing and adornment of the Kulli Culture of South Baluchistan, does at least .

suggest that the merchants returning along the southerly caravan routes may have brought with them girls whose exotic dancing and unsophisticated charms might be thought to tickle the fancy of the tired business men of Harappā or Mohenjo-daro.

From merchants and trade to writing and arithmetic is a reasonable enough transition: Speiser has put the whole relationship into a delightfully cynical phrase – 'writing was not a deliberate invention, but the incidental by-product of a strong sense of private property'. It is not surprising, then, that the bulk of the inscriptions in the Harappā civilization that have survived are cut on stamp-seals, engraved with figures of animals or less often of gods and humans, and evidently used as a means of identifying the property of individuals (Fig. 22). Apart from the seal inscriptions, there are infrequent short stamped signs on pots or inscriptions scratched on after firing. A group of inscribed objects which stand alone are small copper tablets with inscriptions and outline engravings of animals.

Leaving for the time being the type and significance of the seals themselves, we may note a few definite facts about the Harappā script. Once again it is necessary to say that it has not been read or transliterated; the language it represents is quite unknown; the script has no direct affinities with any other known ancient script in Western Asia (or indeed elsewhere). These facts have not, however, deterred the irresponsible theorist, and the Harappā inscriptions have been 'read' with a bland assurance and a complete lack of any authority by more than one person, and given more than one interpretation. One can only say that, apart from attempts to connect it with the nineteenth-century 'script' of the natives of Easter Island in the Pacific, the Harappā script has perhaps suffered less from lunatics than the Minoan. But perhaps it is only the shortness of the available Harappā inscriptions that has deprived us of such entertaining fantasies as the transliteration of the Phaistos Disc into Basque hexameters.

The Harappā script seems to have employed a total of about 400 characters, but, excluding variants, they can probably be brought down to not more than 250 different symbols. This in itself shows that we are encountering the script at a late stage of its development, for if we turn to Mesopotamia for analogies we find that the Early Dynastic Sumerian script employs about 900 characters and the number in the Uruk period syllabaries is believed to be something like 2,000. There is a tendency to reduce the number of characters as language and writing develop, and this evidence of maturity in the Harappā script is in precise accordance with the other evidence, so often stressed in this book, that we know the culture only in its later phases. And one of the most striking proofs of the essential stagnation of the Harappā civilization is the fact that there is no development at all in the script throughout the whole history of the long occupation of the great cities.

The script is essentially pictographic, even though we cannot recognize many of the objects represented. It is stiff and precise, and is exactly comparable in its formality to the hieroglyphic script of Egypt; no equivalent to the more cursive developments such as appeared in the hieratic and demotic hands of Egypt, or in the cuneiform scripts of Mesopotamia, has been recognized in prehistoric India. While this may be thought to be due partly to the absence of any documents of a more or less temporary nature, such as would be written in Egypt on papyrus or in Sumer on clay tablets, yet even in such things as rough inscriptions scratched on pots the signs are still the formal designs known from the carefully cut seal inscriptions.

No inscription of more than twenty or so symbols is known, but it can be deduced that the language was read from right to left, though when a second line of inscription .

is present the *boustrophedon* practice, as known in early Greek, of reading the lines alternately from right to left and from left to right, seems to have been followed. Certain signs can be identified as normally coming either at the end or at the beginning of inscriptions, and others may represent numerals; there may have been some system of accents or diacriticals used. The signs are of course not alphabetic, and by analogy they could represent either syllables, ideograms, or determinatives to indicate the class of thing to which the word belongs.

One might reasonably suppose that the inscriptions on the seals represent personal names and perhaps titles, and there is no evidence to suggest a direct connexion between the device engraved on the seal and the legend, though on the little copper tablets there does appear, as a general rule, to be concordance between the animal represented and the group of signs accompanying it. There are no monumental or public inscriptions known in the Harappā civilization, no hint of anything which could be regarded as a business document, a private letter, an historical record or a literary composition. When bilingual inscriptions are found, and the script is eventually read by their means, it is unlikely that we shall learn much about the life and thought of the people: certainly there will be no new literature revealed.

As it stands, the Harappā script is unique, intrusive and without descendants. Its relationship to the ancient scripts of Mesopotamia is likely to be analogous to the Egyptian system of writing, itself wholly different from anything known in Sumer, but perhaps inspired by it, as far as the idea of representing a spoken language by a fixed set of symbols goes. The apparent priority of Mesopotamia in the invention of writing implies that India, like Egypt, derived the basic idea of a written script from that source, but, as in Egypt, the script early took on a characteristically local form. The type of language likely to have been spoken within the

Harappā kingdom is as uncertain as the details of the script, except that we can fairly definitely rule out any of the Indo-European languages. The persistence of a Dravidian type of language 'islanded' in Baluchistan among the Brahuis has given rise to the supposition that the Harappā language also belonged to this group, but the Munda group now largely spoken by Proto-Australoids in India is another claimant. The fact that Dravidian can, like Sumerian, be described as an agglutinative language has been brought forward in support of the claim for this language-group, but all discussion must remain academic until the inscriptions are deciphered.

A very large number of weights all belonging to a uniform system have been found in the two capital cities of the Harappā civilization, as well as at Chanhu-daro and other smaller sites in Sind, at Mehi in South Baluchistan, and probably (from Mockler's description) at Sutkagen-dor in the Makran. Normally these weights are very carefully cut cubes of banded grey chert, graded extremely accurately in a curious system independent of any other known in the ancient world, and one which seems to have been far more scrupulously observed than was the ordinary practice elsewhere. The weights have been found to run in a ratio of 1, 2, 8/3, 4, 8, 16, 32, 64, 160, 200, 320, 640, and can be recognized as a system in which the unit was ratio 16, equivalent to 13·64 grammes, binary in the lower weights and decimal in the higher, with fractional weights in thirds. This use of the multiple 16 is interesting and curious, and the number had a traditional importance in early Indian numerology, surviving indeed in the modern coinage of 16 annas to 1 rupee!

The smaller weights were certainly used by jewellers and bead-makers, and many were in fact found in a bead-workers' shop at Chanhu-daro. It has been suggested that as they are never marked with any sign to represent the weight, they may have been used among a merchant population largely ignorant of the art of writing or written arithmetic, but this seems a little unlikely. The way in which this weight system was preserved or enforced throughout the whole area of Harappā settlement and from beginning to end of the known duration of the culture is remarkable.

Fragmentary evidence of equally exact systems of measurement has been recovered. From Mohenjo-daro came a broken scale engraved on shell, of which nine accurately divided intervals remained, indicating a decimal scale of 1·32 inches probably rising to a 'foot' of 13·2 inches; and at Harappā a bronze rod was found marked off in units of 0·3676 inch, which can be related to a scale based on a 'cubit' of 20·62 inches, a unit frequently used in the ancient world. The inferences from these two scales were tested at Harappā and Mohenjo-daro by a check series of over 150 measurements of architectural details, with the result that the concurrent use of two units of measurement, a 'cubit' of between 20·3 and 20·8 inches, and a 'foot' of between 13·0 and 13·2 inches, was proved. Measurements resolved themselves into simple multiples of one or other of these standard units – for instance the Great Bath at Mohenjo-daro is 36 by 21 units of a foot of 13·1 inches, and the circular working-platforms for flour-pounding in the Workmen's Quarter at Harappā had a diameter of 10 feet of 13·2 inches.

The late Sir Flinders Petrie, one of the few persons to have studied ancient metrology on a wide basis, pointed out that the 13·2 inch foot was very widespread in Western Asia and in prehistoric and Roman Europe, surviving indeed as the builder's foot used in English medieval buildings. The 'Royal Cubit' of 20·62 inches is equally widespread, and subdivides into palms and digits, the Harappā measure having on it divisions of one half-digit, correct to within 0·3 per cent. Behind these accurately constructed scales, and of course behind the whole lay-out of the Harappā street systems and house-plans, must lie a sound knowledge of practical geometry and land surveying.

The engraved seals already referred to in connexion with the inscriptions cut upon them have, however, other claims to our attention (Fig. 22). The scenes depicted upon them usually consist of representations of animals shown in profile, and frequently carved with a brilliant sureness of touch:

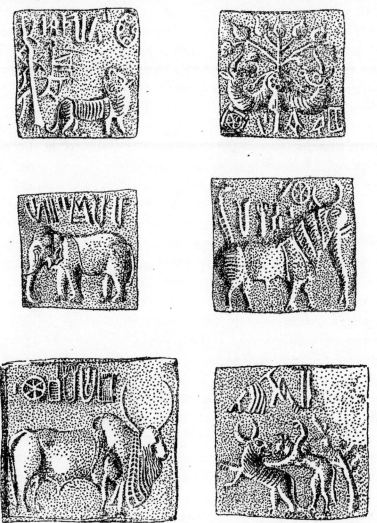

FIG. 22. Impressions from inscribed stamp-seals, Mohenjo-daro

some animals are mythical inventions, such as chimeras and unicorns, but others, notably the magnificent series of humped and dewlapped bulls, monumental for all their miniature size, are of beasts immediately recognizable as likely to be familiar, wild or tame, to the Harappā artists. Some seals show mythological scenes which give us hints as to the possible strains in Harappā religious thought, and these will be commented on later when dealing with the problems of Harappā religion. There is a class of so-called small seals from Harappā which seem to be among the very few objects from any of the sites which show significant stratification, for they are confined to the lower levels.

But the essential feature of the seals is that they belong to the class known as stamp-seals. Such seals were pressed directly on to the soft material used for sealing, in the normal manner of a modern seal or a signet-ring; further than that, the Harappā seals are usually square. Now the seal as a method of marking property is of great antiquity and its use is very widespread in the Ancient East, but one peculiar development, the cylinder-seal which is rolled on to the sealing to produce a continuous band of pattern or an oblong scene, is entirely a Sumerian invention, and its appearance in any ancient culture in prehistoric Western Asia can be attributed fairly confidently to Sumerian influence – as for instance the rare cylinder seals in prehistoric Egypt. The fact that cylinder seals are as rare in the Harappā civilization as they are in Egypt stresses the independence of the Indian culture of any but the most indirect and slight Sumerian influence, and the use of stamp-seals certainly cannot be attributed to that source.

The stamp-seal is known, in one form or another, as early as Halaf times in Syria (with decorative patterns, not naturalistic designs) and similar 'button-seals' appear in the Tal-i-Bakun A phase in Southern Persia, with clay sealings showing that they were indeed used for this purpose, and again in Sialk III, Giyan V, and Hissar I in the north. All these seals are normally decorated with geometric designs, but at Giyan there is a roughly engraved figure of a scorpion. The fact that the Harappā Culture is characterized by stamp-seals should indicate that its eventual antecedents are likely to be found in Persia. But it is curious that stamp-seals are unknown in any of the Baluchistan cultures, the couple from North Baluchistan, already mentioned in Chapter IV, being of Harappā type and probably imported from the plains. While we shall see that there are certain points in common between Harappā painted pottery and that of North Baluchistan, this discrepancy in respect of seals is very interesting, and seems to place a barrier in the way of any more or less direct derivation of the Harappā civilization from any of the known peasant cultures of Baluchistan. The individual technique of the Harappā seals, which were subjected to heat after carving so that the steatite of which they were made acquired a lustrous white surface, can be recognized on the seal from Nal, although there the technique of engraving is not that of the Harappā artist, but that shown in the local pot designs.

In addition to the glyptic art of the seals, the Harappā sites have produced some remarkable pieces of sculpture in the round. The unexpected naturalism of some of these has caused doubts to be thrown on their authenticity as third-millennium work. The red sandstone torso of a man from Harappā is perhaps the best-known piece, and its mature rendering of the human form, no less than the subtle but perceptible stylistic affinities it has to Indian sculpture of later date, has more than once caused its extreme antiquity to be questioned; the treatment of the heavy lines of the abdomen, for instance, is astonishingly similar to some work of Kushan date.

A second sculpture (in grey limestone) from the same city must also be taken into consideration: it is a dancing figure

in which the head has been affixed separately with metal
pegs, the arms and legs are also designed to be in more than
one piece similarly held together, and the nipples are inlaid
in some sort of plaster. The sandstone torso too has had inlaid nipples originally, as well as discs on the shoulders and a
separate attached head. The technique of the sculpture dif-
fers in the two figures, the dancing figure showing facets and
striations absent in the evenly rounded contours of the torso:
it seems unlikely that they are by the same hand.

Archaeologically the circumstances of finding are not
wholly satisfactory, as the stratigraphical record does not
furnish us with precise evidence. But we may turn for comparative evidence to other sites. Mohenjo-daro has produced
several pieces of stone sculpture in convincing archaeological
contexts, and of these the bearded man wearing an embroidered garment is justly famous. Here is an art tradition
more hieratic, more formal than the naturalism of the Harappā torso, but we may note again the use of inlay and
metal – the trefoils on the robe and the disc on the bared
right arm; probably the eyes and perhaps the ears may also
have held inlays, while the sockets for a metal (probably
gold) collar can be seen at the base of the hair on each side
behind the ears. And in at least one other minor piece of
sculpture in steatite from the same site, a charming little
bull, sockets for metal ears, horns and eyes are again provided.

Now this adornment of sculpture with inlay and metal-
work is a frequent fashion in prehistoric Western Asia, but
one not characteristic of early historic Indian sculpture. One
is therefore inclined to accept the two Harappā sculptures
as authentic expressions of prehistoric Indian art in the third
millennium B.C. There is, however, additional evidence to
support this view. From Mohenjo-daro also comes the ex-
quisite little bronze figure of a Dancing-Girl, more than
once referred to already, with a sensitive modelling of the

body and limbs closely akin to the feeling of the Harappā
sculptures. This bronze was found in an unexceptionable
archaeological context, and we have seen that it represents,
in all details of hairdressing and adornment, a sophisticated
version of the female type known in the rough, schematized
pottery figurines in the Kulli Culture, and is likely to represent trade between Mohenjo-daro and South Baluchistan.
The sum of evidence, therefore, suggests that naturalistic
human sculpture which even foreshadows later Indian artistic modes was produced in the Harappā civilization, and
was already essentially Indian.

One thing which needs to be stressed in connexion with
the sculptural art of the Harappā civilization is the complete
lack of any monumental or public compositions – a situation
comparable with the absence of public inscriptions. If the
sculptures, or any of them, represent deities, then they can
have graced only private shrines; if individuals, they can
have played no part in any state ritual. And in the whole
field of Harappā art this privacy, almost secrecy, obtains,
and one has an uncomfortable impression of cities of for-
biddingly blank walls behind which wealth is hoarded and
jealously guarded.

The sculptures give us a little information about the clothing and hairdressing of the people – the short beards worn
by the men, the hair bound back by a fillet with its two ends
hanging down behind, the embroidered robe worn so as to
leave the right shoulder bare. The abundant clay figurines
of women, some probably toys, others godlings in household
shrines, show, as do the comparable figures from Baluchistan, details of elaborate head-dresses and an abundance of
necklets and ornaments, and such rich ornaments as we can
deduce from the figures are in fact known from many finds
in the Harappā sites.

Scattered beads and fragments of jewellery are frequent
finds, but there are several exceptional discoveries that have

preserved intact entire parures, collars, girdles, and necklaces. One such find is almost certainly the result of a very
successful burglary carried out in the third millennium B.C.
For in a hole dug down 7 or 8 feet beneath one of the cottages
in the coolie-lines at Harappā was found a great mass of
jewellery of gold and semi-precious stones – there were
nearly five hundred pieces of gold, ranging from armlets to
beads, and many complete necklaces made up of multiple
strings of beads and metal. The situation of the find makes it
very unlikely that it was acquired by legal means, and it
looks as if a patrician lady's jewel-chest was rifled; or perhaps this was the stock-in-trade of a jeweller (who must have
been the Cartier of Harappā!) carried off by a burglar who
hid the swag but failed to recover it.

Four hoards of similar jewellery from Mohenjo-daro seem,
however, to have a different history, for they are all significantly from the latest occupation of the city, and probably
belong to a time when it was already beginning to go down-
hill. We shall see in the next chapter that there is evidence
that the end of the Harappā civilization was brought about,
or at least precipitated, by barbarian inroads from the west,
and the Mohenjo-daro hoards, some of them packed in silver
jars and wrapped in cloth, are eloquent testimony to
troubled times. They may have been hidden hastily by their
original owners for safety during a raid, or they may represent loot gathered together by the raiders and left behind in
a temporary retreat, but whatever their history they certainly tell of insecurity and the collapse of the old traditions
of the Harappā kingdom.

The actual jewellery worn includes gold plaques with
ornamental white paste inlay, plain gold armlets and globular beads, gold conical ornaments which we know, from the
evidence of the Kulli figurines, were worn over the ears by
women, and a great variety of necklaces or girdles, often
made of multiple strings of beads separated by 'spacers'

which kept the rows parallel. The individual beads were
made with very great skill, and a great favourite was the
very long tubular bead of carnelian; other materials used
include jadeite, perhaps brought from North Burma or
Tibet. Lapis-lazuli was very sparingly used, in contrast to
its frequent use in Sumer, but a curious technique of 'etch-
ing' a white pattern on red carnelian was sometimes employed, and, as we shall see, this type of patterned carnelian
bead is known in Mesopotamia and Persia in the third
and second millennia B.C₂ and has an interesting bearing
on the trade relations and the date of the Harappā civilization.

At Chanhu-daro a bead-maker's shop was excavated, and
the technique of making the long carnelian or agate beads
could be recovered. The rough stone was first split and sawn
into a bar, about 3 inches in length and square in section: a
copper saw using an abrasive such as emery or powdered
quartz was probably used. This bar was then carefully flaked
to a rough cylinder and then ground and polished, and at
the same time the central longitudinal perforation was
bored, by means of tiny stone drills. These were rods about
1½ inches long and 0·12 inch in diameter, with a cup-
shaped hollow at one end to hold the abrasive powder with
which the actual boring was performed – an experiment
showed that it took 20 minutes to drill to a depth of 1 milli-
metre by this means, using emery as an abrasive, and this
would mean that it would take about 24 hours to drill a
3-inch bead! Even allowing for greater adroitness in the
practised craftsman and the probable use of a wooden bow-
drill into which the stone points were fitted, the making of
these beads must have been a slow process, but in the im-
memorial stagnation of the Harappā civilization this would
have counted for little.

In addition to the beads there were ear-rings and probably nose-studs, as in modern Hindustan. Simple copper

mirrors with a handle were used for the toilet; kohl or some
similar cosmetic seems to have been used, and applied with
special little rods; while razors were certainly used for
shaving.

There are some agreeable toys, usually made out of baked
clay, though here it is not always possible to make a sharp
distinction between children's toys and figurines which might
adorn a household shrine (Pl. 8). But cattle with movable
heads that waggle with a string, and monkeys that slide
down a rope and, owing to the deliberately bent perforation,
can be stopped at will by tightening the string, are clearly
for fun and not for worship, and the same may be said of
many of the toy carts. The model cart made of clay was a
favourite toy in early historic India, and indeed *The Little
Clay Cart* is the title of one of the best-known plays of ancient
India, written somewhere before the eighth century A.D.;
the plot turns on the hiding of jewels in a small boy's toy
cart. Then there are pottery whistles made in the shape of a
hen or other bird, which can be made to give a surprisingly
loud coo-ing noise when blown in the right way.

A couple of bricks have been found roughly scored with
lines marking out a game: one contains part of the whole
pattern which might either have been similar to a known
Sumerian games-board or another type from Egypt. The
other brick has a row of depressions into which pebbles or
something similar, such as beans, could be flicked, in the
manner of the games of certain African tribes. Both bricks
probably came from pavements, and contrive to give a convincing picture of household servants playing, and probably
gambling, in a shaded corner of the courtyard. Dice were
certainly used, and must mean games of chance: the arrangement of the 'spots' was not the same as that usual today,
when any two opposite sides add up to seven, but 1 is opposite 2, 3 opposite 4, and 5 opposite 6. Incidentally, a similarly marked piece has been found as far away as Tepe

Gawra in the north of Iraq, with other evidence of Indian contacts. This use of dice is interesting in view of the great popularity of gambling on some game of chance among the Aryans, whose arrival in India, as we shall see, marks the end of the Harappā civilization.

Turning now from the minor arts and crafts to more basic manufactures, we must consider first the pottery. The reader has no doubt felt a certain relief in the escape from the minutiae of pottery styles and ornament that had to occupy so much of Chapter IV, but we cannot altogether leave out of account the pottery of the Harappā civilization, even if it does not have the overwhelmingly important place in the culture that it has in the less fully explored communities of Baluchistan, where so much depends on local ceramic variants in detecting cultural differences.

Potters' kilns are known from the latest phase of Mohenjo-daro, when the slackening of municipal authority in the days of the city's decline permitted their erection within the residential areas. They are circular, with a stoke-hole and furnace beneath a perforated floor originally covered by a domed roof, and represent a rather more evolved type than that found in Sialk III; they are also comparable with those from Susa and Mesopotamian sites of Early Dynastic date. Six were found in a restricted area at Mohenjo-daro and clearly represent a potters' quarter.

The Harappā pottery is for the most part plain, mass-produced wares for purely utilitarian purposes, peculiar in its types to the Harappā kingdom itself, and without recognizable antecedents or analogues outside. Among the types represented, however, one is particularly noteworthy, which consists of a platter on a raised foot, usually referred to as an 'offering-stand'. The appearance of sherds of this type of vessel on a site marks the presence of the Harappā civilization as surely as 'Samian' pottery betokens Roman occupation in Europe. These offering-stands derive from the pedestalled bowls known, for instance, in the Zhob Valley in the Rana Ghundai II phase: this type is not, however, represented among the Buff-ware group of Baluchistan except for possible examples in the Amri phase.

The decorated pottery of the Harappā Culture (Pls. 6 and 7) gives one an immediate clue to its likely origins, for it is a black-on-red ware, the designs being painted on a deep red, lustrous slip. This strongly suggests that its connexions lie with the North Baluchistan wares, such as those of the Rana Ghundai III phase at Periano Ghundai and other sites. But already the Harappā styles have taken on a characteristically individual form which do not in themselves seem to owe much to North Baluchistan styles of pot painting; on the other hand they have certain quite strong similarities with the Kulli style of the south.

Two groups of patterns are of common occurrence: the geometric or abstract forms include the distinctive intersecting circle motif repeated as an overall pattern, and a smaller but significant group employs naturalistic motifs of plant and animal designs. It is difficult to make comparative comment on the first group of patterns, except to note that a certain kidney-shaped motif is common to Harappā shell inlays and gold jewellery as well as to pot ornament, and that the intersecting circle pattern is found on a vessel from the Nal cemetery, though there painted on to a buff background. The naturalistic designs are interesting. They are usually painted in a sprawling, slapdash technique which covers all the available area of the vessel in an irregular mass of foliage and tendrils, among which birds (sometimes peacocks) and less frequently animals take their place. It is an untidy, luxuriant style, and has nothing of the formalism and sense of precise patterning found in so much of the Baluchistan pottery; one almost feels that the hard, arid hill-country produced a taut, muscular style of painting, but that down in the humid plains a lush jungle style grew up.

The treatment of the bodies of the animals and birds is best compared to those of the Kulli style, with thick outlines inside which a cross-hatching or series of parallel strokes fills up the space. There is a tendency to horizontal elongation, more appropriate to Kulli than to the northern region, where vertical distortion can be traced so clearly through the RG II and III sequence; and some of the pots have scenes which really do recall Kulli very remarkably. There is, for instance, a pot with buff slip and from a very late context at Mohenjo-daro which has an elongated deer or goat with cross-hatched body standing in a landscape filled with dot-and-circle and cross-hatched blobs, with a secondary animal (probably a jackal) and a spiky-branched tree. Although the style is not pure Kulli, it looks like an import from that region late in the city's history. But at Chanhu-daro representations of the ibex and antelope occur on pottery of normal painted Harappā type from the main period of occupation of the site, and similar scenes appear at Harappā itself.

But the most remarkable painted sherds from Harappā show scenes with human figures (Fig. 23). One shows a

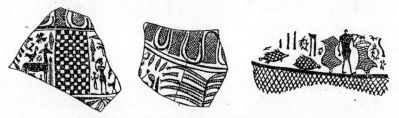

FIG. 23. Sherds showing humans and animals, Harappā

fisherman carrying two nets suspended from a pole across his shoulders, with a fish and what is probably a turtle near his feet, which rest on a cross-hatched band, presumably the river by which he is walking. Fragments of another pot, from a late phase of the site's history, show that it originally had an ambitious series of panels round its circumference, in which

P.I.—8

naturalistic scenes alternated with metopes of chequer-work. The surviving scenes show, first of all the boughs of a tree with a bird seated on one of them, by which is a doe suckling her kid, with two birds, a fish and a star in the upper part of the panel; and secondly a man with one hand raised and the other touching his head, and a child with upraised arms, with two fishes and a cock in the field. Fragments of two other panels show a tree, the head and arm of a man, and perhaps a hooded cobra on one, and on the other a large branching tree.

It is as difficult to pin down the sources of these various motifs as it is to produce a pedigree for any other feature of the Harappā civilization. I have suggested Kulli as a likely source, at least in part, and one may note that large buff-ware pots in which chequer-work panels alternate with branching trees and ibex-figures occur in the Khurab cemetery in Persian Makran: this pottery will be discussed in the next chapter, and may be approximately contemporary with the later phases of the Harappā Culture – i.e. about 2000 B.C. or a bit later.

One other type of painted pottery in the Harappā Culture should be mentioned, that in which the design is painted in several colours. Such polychrome ware is very rare in the Ancient Orient, although painting in two colours, usually black and red, is not unusual and crops up in various cultures at various times – Tell Halaf, Jemdet Nasr, the Zhob Valley or Amri, for instance. But true polychromy, such as we find on the sherds from Harappā and Mohenjo-daro which are painted in red and green on a buff slip, or that from Chanhu-daro which appears to show a naturalistic scene of birds and animals in black, white, and red on a yellow ground, is very exceptional. Nevertheless, as we have seen in the last chapter, polychrome ware employing a very full range of colours, including red, blue, green, and yellow, is characteristic of the Nal Culture of Baluchistan, and it seems difficult to dissociate this from the few examples in the Harappā sites. The Chanhu-daro sherd at least, with its use of yellow colouring, strongly suggests some sort of connexions with the Nal series of painted pots.

An artificial substance manufactured and used in the Harappā civilization, and of some importance, is faience. This is essentially a composition of some base, mixed with a powdered glaze, which is then fired to form a vitreous substance with a glazed surface which can be coloured in manufacture by the addition of various mineral substances to the composition. The process of manufacture is complex, intimately associated with the use of frits and glazes, though not necessarily with the manufacture of glass itself. Such an elaborate technique is not likely to have been invented independently in several areas of Western Asia in prehistoric times. It is nevertheless known at least as early as Jemdet Nasr times in Mesopotamia and Syria, when faience beads are already common, and about the same time it appears in Egypt, while at Susa in Elam it actually appears to have been known to the people of the first phase of occupation and burial on the site. This Susa I phase should in general terms be contemporary with the later part of the Al 'Ubaid and the first half of the Uruk periods in Mesopotamia, so the presence of faience there seems to mark its earliest appearance in Western Asia. But it does not appear in the Baluchistan cultures, except at Nal, where a few beads are an obvious Harappā import; and elsewhere in the regions immediately to the west of India its appearance is sporadic and late – as for instance the solitary bead from Anau III and another from Shah Tepe. The use of faience by the people of the Harappā civilization, then, seems likely to be derived from Mesopotamia or perhaps Elam at some still unidentified stage of the culture's earlier evolution, for it is frequent at all levels in the excavated sites, from the beginning to the end of their occupation, where it was much more extensively employed than, for instance, in Early Dynastic Sumer.

The metal industry of Harappā has many curious and interesting features. Like all the early urban civilizations of Western Asia, that of Harappā was formally a 'Bronze Age' in that copper and bronze were the only metals used for making tools and weapons. In Chapter III we saw how the use of copper seems to have been discovered among the makers of painted pottery in the Persian highlands or some adjacent region, first by using natural pieces of raw metal and hammering them into shape, and later by smelting it from the ore and melting it so that it could be cast. Analysis of the metal from which Harappā tools were made shows certain significant impurities accidentally included which give an indication of the possible sources of the natural ores from which it was obtained, for there is no reason to think that smelting was not known to the Harappā folk from the earliest phase at which we know the culture. In the Harappā copper there is normally a little nickel (usually below 0·5 per cent. and seldom above 1·0 per cent.), but the proportion of arsenic is higher and is sometimes excessive. Now this presence of arsenic shows that it is unlikely that the Harappā people were obtaining their copper from the same sources as the Sumerians, who were working ores with a slight nickel content, but with no significant arsenic, and which may have been obtained in Oman on the south-west side of the Persian Gulf. The Harappā copper most likely came from Indian ores in the Rajputana district, though Persian sources are not absolutely ruled out.

The Harappā metal-smiths were manufacturing objects in copper, either crude or refined; in bronze (copper with approximately 10 per cent of tin deliberately or accidentally added); and in a copper-arsenic alloy, almost certainly accidental but one which gave an added hardness to the metal. Actual representative analyses are as follows:

		Copper	*Bronze*	*Copper-Arsenic*
Copper	..	96·7	85·37	94·76
Tin	.. ..	0	11·09	0·09
Antimony	..	0·88	trace	0
Arsenic	..	0·15	0·07	4·42
Iron	.. ..	0·03	0·18	0·15
Nickel ..	..	1·27	0·16	0·14
Lead ..	..	0·02	trace	0·26
Sulphur	..	0·98	0·11	0

The question of the early use of bronze is interesting. In many instances it seems likely that the introduction of the tin alloy was accidental and that it was used only so long as the rather rare metal could be obtained easily to add to the copper; often the two ores are found together and thus an accidental bronze could easily be produced. In Sumer the first bronze appears in Early Dynastic III times in the Royal Tombs of Ur; its occurrence in Giyan IV*b* may be rather earlier, and contemporary with Jemdet Nasr. At Sialk copper is used throughout the earlier prehistoric periods as it was in the first phases at Anau, but in Anau III a copper-arsenic like the Indian is known. At Hissar, copper was known from Hissar I onwards, and although objects from Hissar III have traces of tin (and one contained nearly 3 per cent) true bronze was not in use on the site.

The techniques employed in Harappā metallurgy included casting and forging – the former process, of course, is dependent on melting the metal before it is poured into a mould. But casting was never developed in prehistoric India to the pitch it was in early Sumer, and this simpler technique resulted in the preservation of certain very primitive forms of tool which soon became demoded in other areas of Western Asia. Copper is a difficult metal to cast in a closed mould, owing to the bubbles of free oxygen which tend to make the casting spongy, but the addition of a very small percentage of tin (under 1 per cent.) or of arsenic acts as a de-oxidizing agent. This permits good castings to be made even by the complicated *cire perdue* method, in which a model is made in wax, coated in clay, and then heated until the wax is melted and absorbed in the baked mould; the molten metal can then be poured in to take the exact shape of the original wax model. Such figures as the Dancing-Girl from Mohenjo-daro must have been cast by this process, with subsequent work in chasing and finishing the surface; and the little model canopied carts were also presumably made in this manner. But the curious fact is that closed-mould casting, either by *cire perdue* or by less ambitious processes involving moulds in more than one piece, was never used in the Harappā civilization to produce tools which gripped their hafts by means of a socket, although this technique was discovered in Sumer in very early times and from this centre its adoption was rapid in most regions round about.

The axes produced by the Harappā metal-smiths in particular are of the simplest flat type which appears in the very earliest stages of the manufacture of metal tools in many parts of the Old World, and can indeed be cast from an open mould of the most primitive type (Fig. 24). Flat axes of precisely the Harappā forms appear in Sialk III, Hissar I*c*, Giyan V*c*, and Susa I – a period approximately contemporary with late Al 'Ubaid – early Uruk in Mesopotamia; they may be dated to the fourth if not the fifth millennium B.C. But rough shaft-hole adzes in copper or bronze were already being made in Sialk III and Susa I, side by side with the more primitive flat type, and in the Al 'Ubaid culture itself and in that of Jemdet Nasr there are models in pottery that appear to represent advanced types of metal shaft-hole axes. It is true that at Mohenjo-daro a similar clay model was found at a low level, which again seems to represent a form of shaft-hole axe, but the absence of the type among the abundant metal-work means that it was never adopted for practical use. In Sumer, however, the

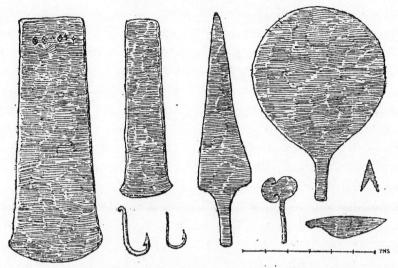

FIG. 24. Copper and bronze tools, Harappā Culture

shaft-hole axe and the application of this principle of hafting to other tools and weapons were universal by Early Dynastic times.

It appears, therefore, that the Harappā civilization was based on some culture which had inherited the early Iranian tradition of the primitive flat copper or bronze axe, and that evolution of the form was arrested partly by the inherent conservatism of the Indian culture and partly by the lack of effective contact with Mesopotamia or immediately adjacent Elam, where the shaft-hole type appears to have had the longest life in Western Asia. Something similar can indeed be observed at Hissar in North Persia, where shaft-hole types first appear in Hissar III together with a large body of material indicating strong influence from Sumer, probably not earlier than Akkadian times (about 2300 B.C.). And, as we shall see in the next chapter, the appearance of these weapons in Hissar III is to be related to the same movements of people that brought the first shaft-hole tools to India.

Within the limitations of conservatism, limitations that

seem almost self-imposed, the Harappā metal-smiths produced a mass of competent workmanship in chisels, knives,
razors, spears (though without the strengthening mid-rib so
soon developed in more progressive centres of metal-working), fish-hooks and the flat axes already mentioned (Fig.
24). At Chanhu-daro especially these axes tend to take on an
elongated form narrower than the archaic Iranian forms,
and they are comparable with the long chisels from the Nal
cemetery and other tools from North India discussed in the
next chapter. There was also a wide range of bronze and less
frequently silver bowls, cups, vases, and other vessels, none
of which, however, shows any subtlety of form, and these
compare all too well in their uninspired mediocrity with the
pottery of the culture.

The general impression we obtain from the Harappā arts
and crafts is indeed one of competent dullness. As I wrote in
another context, the Harappā sites and objects

'imply all too effectively the elaborate organization of an
urban mercantile class whose products lack not only the
barbaric spontaneity of the older and more primitive cultures, but even the cheery *nouveau riche* vulgarity of Early
Dynastic Sumer ... and display instead a dead level of
bourgeois mediocrity in almost every branch of the visual
arts and crafts.'

The dead hand of conservatism in design, rather than in
technique, lies heavy on all the Harappā products. Complex
technical processes were known, well understood, and ad-
mirably organized for production, but the output suffered
from standardization and an almost puritanical utilitarian-
ism. Working within such narrow limits of traditional forms,
fossilized over the centuries into a rigid, inescapable mental
prison, the artist or craftsman could have found little outlet
save in developing technical virtuosity. The pattern of Harappā civilization seems to have precluded great monuments

such as temples, palaces, or tombs, wherein an outburst of
artistic achievement could redound to the glory of the gods
or the pride of a splendid spendthrift monarch. The secrecy
of those blank brick walls, the unadorned architecture of
even the citadel buildings, the monotonous regularity of the
streets, the stifling weight of dead tradition all combine to
make the Harappā civilization one of the least attractive
phases of ancient Oriental history. One can grudgingly ad-
mire the outcome of its ruthless authoritarian regime rather
as one admires the civil engineering of the Roman army in
the Provinces, but with as little real enthusiasm. I can only
say that there is something in the Harappā civilization that
I find repellent.

There remains another aspect of the Harappā Culture to
be discussed before we conclude our survey. It is clear that
the potent forces behind the organization of the Harappā
kingdom cannot have been wholly secular, and there is, as
we have already seen, more than a hint that the priesthood
of some religion played a very important part in the regula-
tion of Harappā economy from within the walls of the citadels of the two capital cities. Such rule by priests, or priest-
kings, would be wholly in accordance with what we know of
other ancient civilizations in Western Asia, where the written record has provided us with an insight beyond the limits
of archaeology, and it is unlikely that the Harappā civilization, individual though it was, differed radically in this
respect from its sister kingdoms.

To the nature of the religion administered by such a
priesthood some of the Harappā relics give us clues. The
numerous clay figurines of women suggest that, as in Baluchistan, there was some form of worship of a Mother-Goddess in which these figures played their part in household
shrines, and there is a sealing which bears a representation
of a female from whose womb a plant issues, and suggests the
idea of an earth-goddess concerned with vegetation. Such

goddesses are common in the Hinduism of the countryside today – the *gramadevatas* of many a rustic shrine; the priests, significantly enough, are not the Brahmins, whose authority dates back to the Aryan invasion of the middle of the first millennium B.C., but outcastes who still know the ways of the gods before the gods.

And this is not the only link with contemporary Hinduism. There is more than one representation on seals from Mohenjo-daro and Harappā of a male god, horned and three-faced, sitting in the position of a *yogi*, his legs bent double, heel-to-heel, and surrounded on one seal by four beasts, the elephant, the tiger, the rhinoceros and the buffalo, with a couple of deer by the throne at his feet. There can be little doubt that we have here the prototype of the great god Shiva as Lord of the Beasts and Prince of Yogis; he may have been conceived as four-faced, and with his four animals looks to the four quarters of the earth. This would indeed recall the symbolical elephant, lion, horse, and bull on the Mauryan column of the third century B.C. at Sarnath. The deer by the god's throne make another significant link with later religion, and with Sarnath for, similarly placed, they are the inevitable accompaniment of Buddha in representations of the Deer Park Sermon.

There is also evidence of some form of phallic worship, with representations of the male and female generative organs; of tree-worship in which a deity is shown in the branches of the sacred fig-tree or *pipal*, still regarded as a holy tree. In ancient times *pipal* leaves provided the motifs for many pottery-painters in the Harappā Culture and others under its influence, such as Kúlli and Nal. The seal representations again show what must be sacred animals – such as the humped bull, whose privileged position today, as he noses his way unmolested through the bazaars, helping himself to whatever takes his holy fancy, must date back to the third millennium B.C. on the banks of the Indus and the

Ravi. Other cult-animals on the seals stand in front of curious 'mangers' or 'sacred braziers' somehow connected with
their worship.

The one or two seals on which a hero is shown defeating
tigers or other beasts (Fig. 22, bottom right) suggest comparison with the Sumerian hero who battles with lions,
Enkidu or Gilgamesh, and here perhaps there may be
evidence of a faint strain of common tradition or even
of Sumerian influence in religious matters during the
time of the flourishing of the Harappā Culture. But, on all
other counts, the religion as implied from the archaeological
remains is significantly distinct from any others known in
Western Asia, and is essentially Indian from the start. The
absence of any building that can be interpreted convincingly
as a temple may be due to the chances that such a structure
may still be concealed beneath the stupa at Mohenjo-daro
and that another has been bodily removed by the brick-
robbers at Harappā; but it is nevertheless curious that no
such building has been traced in these or any other site. We
know that the formal plan of the Sumerian temple was
already fixed in Al 'Ubaid times, and similarly in such a
conservative civilization as that of Harappā one would expect a rigid and recognizable formula of temple-building from
the earliest days. One would expect also to find minor shrines
of recognizable plan outside the citadel areas. The absence of
any such buildings does imply that household shrines were of
more importance than centralized worship in specific temples.

The links between the Harappā religion and contemporary
Hinduism are of course of immense interest, providing as
they do some explanation of those many features that cannot
be derived from the Aryan traditions brought into India
after, or concurrently with, the fall of the Harappā civilization. The old faiths die hard: it is even possible that early
historic Hindu society owed more to Harappā than it did to
the Sanskrit-speaking invaders.

Until recently little was known of the burials of the Harappā people. It is normal in the ancient oriental cities to
find, even in the heart of the occupied areas, burials made
among or under the houses and contemporary with the living
inhabitants, but despite the claims of Marshall and those
who followed him I do not feel that any true burials contemporary with the Harappā civilization were found within
the city precincts on either of the two main sites. It is again
an instance of the Indian individualism, and perhaps another example of strict urban byè-laws. At Mohenjo-daro a
series of skeletons were found, of assorted ages, sexes and
anthropological types, individually or in groups of up to
fourteen persons, and in all instances the bodies lay in
disorder and other circumstances suggested a violent or accidental death, and in no sense a deliberate burial deposit.
At Harappā a curious, tightly-packed mass of human skulls
and a few other bones, representing over twenty people,
was found on the outskirts of the city: the deposit is unex-
plained, but is hardly a normal burial. Fragmentary bones
from another site in this city were claimed as a 'fractional'
burial, but may be modern; and a definite fractional burial
at Mohenjo-daro was associated with a pottery vessel of a
type now known to belong to a phase following the Harappā
civilization. The groups of broken pots cited by Marshall as
allied to fractional burial groups seem to have no claim to
any funerary significance whatever.

There remain the so-called 'post-cremation urns' at
Mohenjo-daro and Harappā, containing a miscellaneous
assortment of sherds, artifacts, ornaments and animal, but
never human, bones. These urns, which were found beneath
streets and houses, were regarded by the excavators as the
burial deposits of bodies completely cremated, and (invoking
modern Hindu practices) were supposed to have been
thrown into a river or otherwise disposed of. With Wheeler,
I cannot regard these as having anything to do with human

burial: I am inclined to think that sometimes at least they may have served some drainage or soak-pit function, which would account for the miscellaneous debris drifting into them. The row of such pots immediately behind (and presumably beneath the eaves or gutter) of the range of buildings immediately within the citadel defences at Harappā on its southern edge certainly suggests such a use.

But in 1937 a cemetery of the Harappā people was found at the type-site south of the citadel and outside the built-up area of the city, not far from the previously discovered 'Cemetery H' of later date than the Harappā Culture and described in the following chapter. The new cemetery, R 37, was further investigated by Dr Wheeler in 1946. It was then established that it was contemporary with the main period of occupation of the city and that it was earlier than the earliest phase of Cemetery H. Fifty-seven graves were excavated in 1937 and in 1946, and a full report is awaited, though the 1946 material (ten graves) is already published (Pl. 4).

Evidence of the continuous use of the cemetery over a fair period of time was afforded by eighteen instances of later graves which had cut into earlier burials, and eight instances of still later graves which had cut these, but the culture represented by the grave-goods is homogeneous throughout. The burials were extended, with the head usually to the north, and a large grave was made to accommodate quantities of pottery vessels, up to a maximum of forty and usually from fifteen to twenty.

Personal ornaments and toilet objects were also occasionally buried with the dead – a copper ring on the third finger of a right hand; necklaces and anklets, bangles or strings of beads, a rod for applying eye-paint. Twelve graves contained handled copper mirrors, and in one was a small lamp and the bones of a fowl at the feet of the dead.

One extremely interesting burial was found in 1946, in

which the body, probably that of a girl, had been buried in a
wooden coffin and wrapped in a shroud of reeds, of which
traces still remained (Pl. 5). Such reed-shrouds or coffins are
a fairly obvious form of protection for the corpse, and are
known in Sumer in Early Dynastic and Akkadian times (that
is, between about 2800 and 2000 B.C., and so contemporary
with Harappā) and the use of such a mode of burial in the
R 37 cemetery has been considered by Dr Wheeler to imply
a link between the two civilizations.

Farther afield, other cemeteries or groups of burials wholly
or partially of the Harappā Culture have been identified,
notably at Derawar on the Ghaggar River in Bahawalpur
State. Here was a cemetery at least 200 yards square which
yielded in trial digging by Stein fractional burials (i.e. skeletons which had been removed from some other place before
the final burial, and so in disorder or incomplete). In the
R 37 cemetery there were groups of Harappā pots, sometimes as many as twenty-one in a single grave. At Derawar
the cemetery, as at Harappā, lies outside the adjacent
mounds, which, up to 40 feet high, represent the ruins of the
settlement. At Sutkagen-dor in the Makran three large pots,
containing cremated human bones and small vessels, a shell
bangle and an ornamented disc, were found buried upright
in the debris of the fort wall on the outside: evidently they
were deposited late in the site's history at a time when the
wall was becoming ruinous. They seem likely to belong to
the Harappā Culture in view of the sherd of a typical 'offering-stand' in one burial.

Outside the defensive walls of the settlement on Tharro
Hill in Sind Majumdar excavated some remarkable stone-
built chambers in small oval cairns, which, although they
contained no trace of a skeleton, seem explicable only as
graves originally containing inhumation burials now rotted
away. The chambers were built of dry walling and were
rectangular, averaging about 10 by 3 feet and with walls

standing up to 2 feet from the floor. They were enclosed in cairns about 12 by 20 feet overall, and contained pottery which included 'offering-stands' not unlike the Harappā type, of plain red ware.

The cemetery of Mehi has been described above in Chapter IV: the scanty material and imperfect record make it difficult to assess the Harappā element there, but certain plain red-ware pots, including vessels shaped like a flower-pot and a shallow footed cup, may have Harappā affinities, and the same should apply to the very similar vessels in the Khurab cemetery over the border in Persian Makran. The rite was cremation at Mehi and probably fractional burial at Khurab.

Apart from the probably Sumerian usages in the R 37 cemetery it is difficult to cite any significant parallels for these various burials – the Baluchistan cemetery of Nal already described has points of similarity to R 37 in the numerous vessels buried with the dead, and in R 37 there was at least one brick-edged grave comparable with those at Nal. But the large groups of pots are a common feature in the prehistoric and historic graves of Western Asia: we shall find them recurring for instance in the Shahi-tump cemetery, later than the Harappā period, in the Makran, and again in the Cemetery H at Harappā itself, similarly of late date.

We are now in a position to consider a final aspect of the Harappā civilization – its relations with foreign powers and, in consequence, its date and position vis-à-vis the contemporary civilizations of Western Asia. We have already seen, in Chapter IV, that there was contact established between the merchants of the Kulli Culture in South Baluchistan and those of Early Dynastic Sumer, probably soon after 2800 B.C., but it is difficult to be sure that connexions between Harappā and Sumer were really established as early as this. At Mohenjo-daro there was found, in a very early

level, a fragment of a carved steatite vessel of a type identical
with those known from South Baluchistan and in Sumer in
Early Dynastic times, and this might be used as evidence for
equating this phase of the city with Early Dynastic Sumer.
But, as we have seen, contacts between the Harappā Culture and that of Kulli (which seems to have originated this
type of steatite vessel) were continuous throughout the life
of the two great cities, and I have pointed out that there is
actual evidence of particularly strong Kulli contact in the
last phase of their history. Together with the pottery on
which I based this suggestion, there were also found at
Mohenjo-daro fragments of two steatite boxes (or vessels)
from the latest levels; we must assume that the type had a
long life in South Baluchistan, and cannot use the presence
of fragments of these stone vessels in the sites of the Harappā
Culture as dating material.

In Sumer there is no absolutely clear evidence of Harappā
contact until Akkadian times – that is, from 2300 to 2000
B.C. or a little later. In deposits of this period, however, a
number of typical Harappā engraved seals have been found,
and one sealing which shows on its back the imprint of
coarse cloth. The seals (and other pieces of evidence, such as
pieces of typical Harappā inlay-work, a die with the peculiar Harappā system of 'spots', and a scratched representation of a humped bull) suggest Harappā merchants established in Sumerian cities and engaged in a trade which may
well have included cotton goods. How long this trade relationship continued is a little uncertain, but it seems likely
to have ceased soon after 2000 B.C.

Unfortunately evidence of the complementary aspect of
this trade, Sumerian goods in the Indus Valley or the Punjab, is scanty. There are three cylinder-seals from Mohenjo-
daro – a purely Sumerian type, here probably made by a
Harappā lapidary for clients who seem to have acquired
outlandish tastes in such matters: can they have been re-

tired cotton-merchants home from Sumer? There is a little bronze toilet-set which could be called Sumerian; there may be the reed shroud in the R 37 cemetery – really there is very little else that can definitely be attributed to Sumerian contacts. Whatever the nature of the Harappā–Sumer trade agreement, the Sumerian contribution must have consisted largely of invisible exports! The etched carnelian beads to which reference has already been made may be imports from Sumer to India, although the fact that they were apparently manufactured at Chanhu-daro, and that their curious technique of manufacture survives in Sind to the present day, rather suggests that they were an Indian invention of the third millennium B.C. Nevertheless, they appear in greater numbers in Sumer, from Early Dynastic to Akkadian times, and a little beyond, than in Harappā sites, and they occur as far afield as Ras Shamra in Syria and Trialeti in the Caucasus in a probably third-millennium grave. As there is a possibility, however, that the technique was re-discovered independently in later times, they could represent a Sumerian import to India.

It is possible to detect Harappā contact, however, with civilizations other than that of Sumer, and similarly there are imports to India which are non-Sumerian. In the Hissar III Culture of Northern Persia, which probably dates from Akkadian times in the main, there are several objects which seem to show Harappā connexions, and the same applies to Anau III – both sites, for instance, have Harappā metal types, and at Anau is a clay cart-model comparable with some from Chanhu-daro. The odd faience bead from this site too and a segmented bead from Shah-tepe might come from Harappā as well as from Sumer, and the etched carnelian beads at Hissar III and Shah Tepe could again be Indian rather than Sumerian in origin, though the evidence is not conclusive. Stone has recently published the results of spectrographic analysis which show identity of composition between an unstratified faience bead from Harappā and another from Crete of *c.* 1600 B.C., and this point is commented on in Chapter VI below.

From Harappā, Mohenjo-daro and Chanhu-daro come bronze pins or rods ornamented in a distinctive manner either with spiral tops or with representations of animals. These seem to belong to a great province of barbarian metal-work which stretched from the Caucasus to Turkestan, around the northern fringes of the kingdoms of Sumer and Akkad, with its main phase of productivity round about 2000 B.C. or rather later, and the occurrence of these pins at various levels in the Indian sites implies that odd imports from the barbarous regions of Western Asia occasionally reached the otherwise almost closed kingdom of Harappā.

To sum up, then, the Harappā civilization, while largely self-sufficient and essentially Indian in its origins, and in the whole fabric and texture of its peculiar constitution, nevertheless did have certain intermittent outside contacts. The trade with Sumer seems almost certainly to have been initiated by the South Baluchistan merchants of the Kulli Culture in Early Dynastic times, and it is not straining the evidence to attribute to these men also the establishment of 'factories' in the Sumerian cities where colonies of Indian merchants lived and worshipped in their traditional way. The Harappā traders acquired a business which was already flourishing by about 2300 B.C., and they again must have had their resident representatives in Ur and Lagash and other centres of trade, using the characteristic seals on merchandise and documents. In connexion with this trade, surely sea-borne up the Persian Gulf, the fortified station at Sutkagen-dor must have played a part, at the convergence of the routes inland from the little harbours between Gwatar Bay and Gwadar – perhaps other ports existed at the mouths of the Indus.

Overland there was occasional coming and going – the

departure of an adventurous caravan to Turkestan, to bring
back lapis and turquoise, a foreign pin as a curiosity, and
tales of unrest and trouble around the far Caspian shores.
What was brought back from Sumer in the ships whose
anchors 'were at Tygris and Euphrates weighed' we may
never know from archaeology alone. Perhaps inscriptions in
one or other land will some day tell us: Indian cotton certainly seems an inevitable export for which some adequate
return must have been made.

While the antecedents of the Harappā civilization still
elude us, we can only say that in its mature form it is not
likely to be earlier than about 2500 B.C., and that the only
reasonably close point of contact with the West, where written records are available, is between the years 2300 and
2000 B.C. It is not improbable that trade relations with
Sumer ceased soon after this time, when the struggles between Hammurabi and Elam may have closed the frontiers
for a time. And just as Sumer was suffering from the inroads
of the barbarians from the hills, so too, in the archaeological
record of the Harappā cities and towns and in the villages of
Baluchistan, we find evidence that kingship and the established order of things come to an end and the barbarians
appear at a date rather later than that of the less successful
attacks on the Mesopotamian kingdoms. Her position farther to the east saved India for a time, and the unchanging
civilization of the Indus and Punjab was left for a century
or two to revolve slowly round the fixed points of authority
in the sacred citadels, as it had done for so long. But the end
was delayed, not averted. In the next chapter we shall see
what archaeology tells us of the end of the Harappā civilization and the coming of the barbarians.

Notes to Chapter V

The basic evidence for the Harappā civilization is contained in
the excavation reports — J. Marshall (and others), *Mohenjo-daro and*

the Indus Culture (1931); E. Mackay, *Further Excavations at Mohenjo-daro* (1938); N. C. Majumdar, *Explorations in Sind* (1934)· (for smaller sites); M. S. Vats, *Excavations at Harappā* (1940); R. E. M. Wheeler, 'Harappā 1946: the Defences and Cemetery R 37', in *Ancient India,* no. 3 (1947), 58–130; E. Mackay, *Chanhu-daro Excavations* (1943); summaries in E. Mackay, *The Indus Civilization* (1935), V. G. Childe, *New Light on the Most Ancient East* (1934), Chap. VIII; S. Piggott, *Some Ancient Cities of India* (1945), Chap. II.

Reports on the skulls with comments on the physical types represented are in the various excavation reports; see also H. F. Friederichs and H. W. Muller in *Anthropos,* XXVIII (1933), 383–406; B. S. Guha, *Racial Elements in the Population* (Oxford Pamphlets on Indian Affairs, 1944); H. V. Vallois, 'Les Ossements Humains de Sialk', in *Fouilles de Sialk,* Vol. II, 113–192. For the Mediterranean type of skull, see C. S. Coon, *The Races of Europe* (1939), especially 146–152, 400–509.

The grain remains have been reported on in the works cited above, and in their wider setting discussed by H. Peake in *Man,* 1939, 36 and 53. The animals from Harappā have been described in a special monograph, D. Prashad, *Animal Remains from Harappā* (1936), and in the individual reports.

For the planning of Mohenjo-daro and Harappā and the significance of the citadels, see R. E. M. Wheeler in *Ancient India,* no. 3 (1947), 58–64, 74–77; for the grain-pounding platforms, *ibid.,* 78. The smaller sites of the Harappā culture are described by Majumdar, *Explorations in Sind* (1934) and by Stein, *An Archaeological Tour in Gedrosia,* 60–71 (Sutkagen-dor); *An Archaeological Tour in Waziristan and North Baluchistan,* 55–64 (Dabar Kot). I am indebted to Mr Krishna Deva for unpublished information on the Ghaggar River sites, briefly described by Stein in *Geog. Journ.,* XCIX (1942), 173–182, and my account of Amilano embodies the result of fieldwork there in 1942.

The quotation from the poet Mir is from a translation by Professor Ahmed Ali, and that by Professor Speiser is from *The Beginnings of Civilization in Mesopotamia,* Supplement to *Journ. Amer. Orient. Soc.,* 1939. The substance of my comments on the Harappā sculpture is taken from my article in *The Burlington Magazine,* CX (1948), 33–37, by permission of the publishers, and the quotation on the character of Harappā art is from my *Some Ancient Cities of India* (1945), 16.

My views on the 'post-cremation' pots are supported by R. E. M. Wheeler (*loc. cit. supra*), and the account of the R 37 cemetery will be found in this same excavation report. The description of the burial cairns at Tharro Hill is based on personal observation in 1943, supplementing Majumdar's comments.

The contacts with Sumer are summarized in my paper in *Antiquity*, xvii, 169–182, and by R. E. M. Wheeler in *Ancient India*, no. 3, 78–80. For etched carnelian beads, see H. Beck in *Antiq. Journ.*, xiii (1933), 384–398; for pins and rods of Western derivation on Harappā sites, my paper in *Ancient India*, no. 4 (1948), 26–40, and for the analysis of the faience beads, J. F. S. Stone in *Antiquity* xxiii (1949), 201–205.

CHAPTER VI

The Time of Troubles and the End of the Cities

A host whose onslaught was like a hurricane, a people who
had never known a city.

(Third Dynasty Year-date at Ur)

THE dual pattern of prehistoric Western India at the beginning of the second millennium B.C., with the great urban
civilization of Harappā in the plains and the simpler peasant
communities in the Baluchistan hills, had endured almost
unaltered for seven or eight hundred years at least; the
Baluchi settlements themselves are likely to have been established as early as 3000 B.C., and some of them perhaps earlier. There is no evidence of violent change in the archaeological record of this time; villages are deserted, towns
rebuilt after a flood, or new settlements are made, but the
small, self-sufficient societies in the remote valleys of the
hills or the vast organization of the Harappā empire in the
plains continue their way of life unaffected by the outside
world.

But an intimation of what occurred to break this long
seclusion of peaceful, if stagnant, communities is to be found
in the stratification of the Rana Ghundai mound. Here there
had been continuous occupation of the site accompanied by
an evolving pottery style from a time likely to be late in the
fourth millennium up to one more or less contemporary
with some part of the Harappā civilization, the RG IIIc
phase, perhaps about 2000 B.C. At this point there is evidence that the settlement was sacked and burnt – 'everywhere overlying the foundation level ... [of the RG IIIc
phase] there are pockets of ashes, as though some great

conflagration had taken place', wrote Brigadier Ross in his
description of the stratification of the site. Above this burnt
layer, in the RG IV phase, the pottery types show a complete break from those below – coarse bowls appear with
painted ornament, 'bold and not altogether unpleasing in a
somewhat tawdry style'. And this settlement was once more
destroyed by fire, and again in RG V a change in pottery
shows new folk settling on the ancient, flame-scorched Rana
Ghundai tell; the pottery is now unpainted, with relief
patterns encrusted on to its surface.

This evidence of violence and of rapidly-changing populations can mean only that the RG IV and RG V phases represent a time of troubles, of insecurity and raiding, arson and
pillaging in North Baluchistan. To the Rana Ghundai evidence can be added that of Nal, where the last phase of the
Zhob-ware settlement on the site was also burnt down, to
such a degree that the tell is still called Sohr Damb, the Red
Mound, from its fire-reddened soil. At Dabar Kot the upper
6 feet of the tell, exposed in section, showed no less than four
thick ash layers, implying repeated destructive conflagra-
tions of the later settlements, and here there occurred abundant fragments of the encrusted ware of the RG V type on
the surface. At this site too one of the later settlements was
that of the Harappā folk, so the sacking of the settlement is
approximately dated.

In South Baluchistan there seems no recorded evidence of
similar burning in the later settlements, but it must be remembered that here little excavation has been done. At one
site, however, a small tell at Shahi-tump, near Turbat, a
cemetery had been made in the ruins of an abandoned
village of the Kulli Culture, which can also be equated with
the presence of Harappā folk in the region by means of a
fragment of a clay toy cart of characteristic type. So the
Shahi-tump cemetery is later than the Kulli Culture and
some phase of Harappā. In the area excavated by Stein

twelve inhumation burials were found, and an additional
seven groups of grave-goods with no recognizable human
remains.

The inhumations where identified all appeared to be of
complete bodies lying on their backs or sides with the legs
flexed. Grave-goods in most instances consisted of groups of
pots, but copper or bronze tools and ornaments, stone beads
and alabaster cups also occurred. Two burials, Stein's A
and B, had richer grave-goods than the others. The skeleton
discovered in burial A seems to have been that of a man
buried crouched on his right side; in the grave there were
more than fifty pottery bowls, cups and beakers, a copper
stamp-seal, a stone pestle, a bead of ruby-like stone, a stone
blade and a group of twelve marine shells (*Natica asellus*)
against the skull. Burial B (certainly male) had again a
wealth of pottery vessels stacked in 'nests' of up to five bowls,
a necklace of lapis, agate and onyx beads, a copper spear-
head and a heavy, shaft-hole copper axe. The presence of
animal bones, some charred, in certain of the vessels accompanying these and other burials suggests that funeral bake-
meats had been deposited with the corpse.

The pottery from all the burials is consistent and characteristic (Fig. 25). The ware is very good, hard and thin,
varying from grey to pinkish and sometimes having a clear,
yellowish-buff colour. The commonest form is a shallow
bowl, usually with a rather sophisticated foot-ring, and
allied forms are deeper bowls which may attain a consider-
ble size, or be represented by small cups of similar profile.
There are two types of beakers, globular or conical, and
characteristic 'squat pots' which merge into small bottles
with small necks and feet and a bulbous body. Exceptional
forms are footed bowls and a bowl on four legs, and a couple
of triple vessels each of three conjoined units.

The painted ornament is executed with a soft brush and
in paint which varies from black through warm sepia to a

reddish-brown, and a very characteristic feature is the soft blurred edge of the painted line, where the thin paint has 'run' into the porous background. The technique is slack,

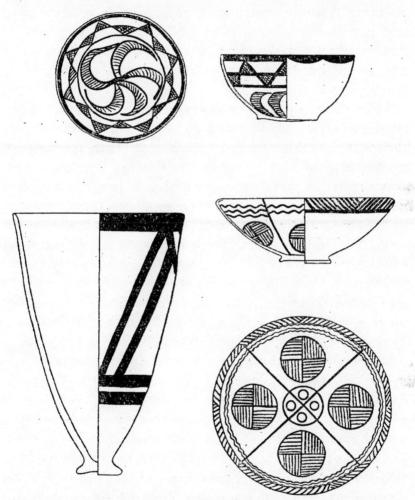

FIG. 25. Painted bowls and goblet (twice scale of bowls), Shahi-tump Cemetery

often sloppy, and we look in vain for the crisp vigour of the Iranian wares which, as we shall see, are its nearest relatives. The ornament on the outside of the vessels is normally in zones, but sometimes in panels, and in the bowls the centre is either occupied by a swastika or allied motif, above which zonal patterns run, or the whole interior is divided into quarters within which circular elements are placed, or the so-called 'Maltese square' is employed. In the exterior zonal and panelled ornament swastikas and angular spirals are used in addition to the more frequent chevrons, lozenges and triangles. One vessel has two-colour chevrons in red and black.

The nearest parallels to this pottery come from the cemetery of Khurab near Bampur, 150 miles to the west over the Persian frontier, the date of which appears to approximate to that of Kulli and Harappā. At Khurab the vessels were very similar to pots from the Mehi cemetery (belonging to the latest phase on that site, even possibly dating from after its abandonment). As a whole, the Khurab and other cemeteries near Bampur are likely to belong to the centuries around, or probably just after, 2000 B.C. But ultimately, the Shahi-tump and similar wares are descended from the pottery of the Buff-ware group best represented in Susa I and other sites in Fars, and, at greater remove, from that of Samarra. The shape of the vessels, the arrangement of the patterns, and much of the actual decorative repertoire remains relatively unaltered, but the degenerate patterns, the flaccid brush-work and the thin paint betray the fact that Shahi-tump ware is archaistic, not archaic, and enable us to accept with confidence the late date implied by its associated finds. It represents in fact the final expression of a tradition persisting in Southern Persia from perhaps the fifth millennium B.C. until the beginning of the second; to this tradition also belong the little conical alabaster vessels from the cemetery, unchanged in form and substance from their earlier representatives.

Of the other objects from the cemetery, the copper spear and shaft-hole battle-axe from burial B indicate that this is the grave of a warrior (Fig. 26). The spear-head, 9 inches

long, has no mid-rib and recalls Harappā types, but the
stoutly-made axe, with a shaft-hole 1·2 inches in diameter,
seems to derive from Sumerian and Akkadian prototypes,
while its nearest parallels, significantly enough, come from
the graves of chieftains of barbarian tribes beyond the fringe
of the oriental urban civilizations at Maikop and Tsarskaya
in South Russia. In the loosely-knit structure of semi-
nomadic barbarian society, spread over the steppe and
along the frontiers of the more settled communities in

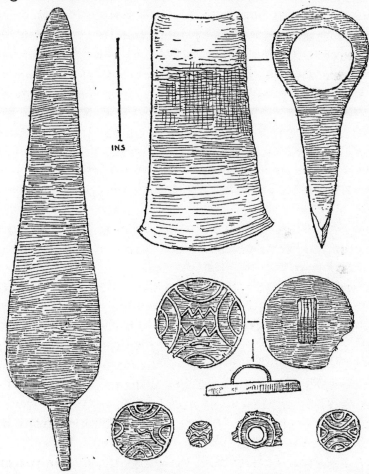

FIG. 26. Copper spear, shaft-hole axe, and compartmented
stamp-seals, Shahi-tump Cemetery

Mesopotamia or Persia, such types, ultimately originated by Sumerian metal-smiths, would have a wide and often rapid distribution.

The copper stamp-seals from Shahi-tump, five of which were found, are even more explicit in their western relationships (Fig. 26). They are all of one distinctive type, and it is significant that the only other example from Baluchistan comes from the final phase of the Sohr Damb at Nal, and is perhaps to be associated with its destruction by burning. They are all circular, with a simple pattern on their faces built up in compartments by projecting strips of metal, and seals of generally similar type have been found in Hissar II*b* and III*b*, in Anau III and at Susa, in a context which suggests a date about 2000 B.C. or a little later. And, as we shall see shortly, at least one similar seal is known from Sind, where it is later than the Harappā period. The evidence is therefore strongly in favour of regarding these metal objects in the Shahi-tump cemetery as indicating a date after 2000 B.C., and associated with movements from the west.

Do these objects represent trade or migration? To anticipate the further evidence discussed below, the latter seems the more likely, and, since the pottery represents a local tradition, it seems likely too that migration was one of persons travelling light, bringing with them only the portable property of seals, spears, and battle-axes. Can these be war-bands, enslaving or marrying the local women, who would make the pots, and is the Shahi-tump cemetery in some way related to the sacking of the Baluchistan villages? Skulls are slender evidence and deductions from their measurements must be used with caution, but the anatomist who examined the skull of the Shahi-tump man buried with the spear and axe reported that it showed 'traces of mixed origin and in certain respects tends to approximate to the Caspian or Nordic type of skull'. Unfortunate though the second adjective is in a modern context, it does at least seem probable that the Shahi-tump cemetery was that of newcomers to the region, rather than that of the old population, with a few novel types of seals and weapons acquired by trade.

And in this connexion I would draw attention to the evidence mentioned in the last chapter; as we have seen, in the final phases of Mohenjo-daro there was a sudden strengthening of contact between the Harappā Culture and that of Kulli, and pottery and stone vessels of South Baluchistan types appeared in the later levels of the city's occupation. Can this be wholly unconnected with the evidence for disturbed conditions in Baluchistan, and the establishment in the south of that region of newcomers from the west, suspect at least of being more than peaceful immigrant farmers? Were there refugees streaming down the passes of the Bolan, Lak Phusi and the Gaj Valley into the Indus plain, seeking shelter in the towns with which they long had traded? If this were indeed so, it is to be feared that they did not escape for long, for from Sind comes clear evidence that the mountains made no more than a temporary halting-place for the men from the west. Once over the Kirthar Range they could look down, upon prosperous communities, ripe for plunder, beside which the Baluchi villages were as nothing; they were on the frontier of civilization, but it was a kingdom unskilled in defence and unprepared for attack. Archaeology has shown something of the end of the Harappā towns at Chanhu-daro, Jhukar, and Lohumjo-daro in Sind, at each of which the invaders settled where they had plundered.

The site of Jhukar has given its name to this characteristic intrusive culture in Sind, which appears at all three sites stratified above and in the ruins of deserted Harappā settlements, but it is at Chanhu-daro that the largest body of evidence occurs. In the ensuing description, therefore, attention will be directed mainly to that site, with amplification where necessary from the other finds. The stratification at

Chanhu-daro can be expressed as follows, following normal practice in these matters:

Chanhu-daro I*a*	
Chanhu-daro I*b*	Harappā Culture
Chanhu-daro I*c*	
Chanhu-daro II	Jhukar Culture
Chanhu-daro III	Jhangar Culture

The final phase of occupation of this site will be described later, and for the present we are concerned with the Chanhu-daro II phase, a settlement of people of the Jhukar Culture.

This settlement was one of 'squatters' among the Harappā ruins of the I*c* phase, and, while there seems to have been some rough rebuilding of house walls with brickbats robbed from other parts of the site, other huts seem to have been made of some perishable walling, such as matting, roughly set round a rectangular brick floor, which in one instance was some 17 by 8 feet overall. These brick floors might also be interpreted as stances for tents, and at all events they suggest rather squalid and not very permanent settlement on the site. Fireplaces are an interesting innovation, sometimes roughly built into doorways or niches of ruinous house walls or made of small rectangular or curved settings of bricks on edge.

The material culture represented among these primitive habitations includes abundant and characteristic pottery; stamp-seals; amulets; beads; metal tools and pins; bone awls and a pottery head-rest (Fig. 27). It is altogether a curious and distinctive assemblage, contrasting strongly with that of the Harappā Culture it supplants, and yet not without clear contact with it. The pottery is a buff ware, with a varied repertoire of ornament painted on it in black and red. The forms include small-footed jars and bottles of types which have general parallels in Baluchistan, but the offering-stands and saucers with a looped pattern on the edge must derive either from Harappā or from the Kulli Culture in its Harappā-influenced phase. The range of ornament is quite varied, and employs geometric and stylized plant forms which in general have a strong resemblance to the trees on Kulli ware. Other simple geometric patterns accompanied with broad horizontal bands of plum red recall the Amri style; close-set chevrons in black and bright red can be paralleled precisely on a sherd from Zayak in South Baluchistan, where other patterns too can be matched – the multiple loops and ball-and-stem motifs of Jhukar, for instance, occur at Sar-Parom and Jai-damb. And one of the two animal representations at Chanhu-daro is really not unlike one from Periano-ghundai in North Baluchistan.

In general, then, the Jhukar pottery from the Sind sites seems to combine a variety of elements, in which Kulli and probably Harappā motifs predominate, with an underlying Amri strain. It is, in fact, just what might be expected from a native, non-Harappā substratum in the local population, with a certain infusion of novel strains from South Baluchistan. Isolated motifs could be traced farther west – for example the plant form with double-spirals occurs in Sialk III and in Hissar I*b*, but it then turns up again in the late cemetery of Jiwanri in the Makran referred to below. On the whole there seems no reason to regard Jhukar pottery as anything but a native product arising out of the disturbed conditions and folk-movements after the fall of the Harappā empire, when refugee tribes were leaving Baluchistan and settling in Sind.

A most interesting contrast and comparison with Harappā is afforded by the Jhukar seals and allied amulets found abundantly in Chanhu-daro II (Fig. 27). The seals are made of pottery, faience, stone, and metal, and are totally different in their ornamental motifs from the well-known Harappā series; they also lack any inscriptions. But they are stamp-seals (usually circular, exceptionally square) within the great Western Asiatic family of such objects, and certain parallels can be noted. One of the faience seals has a pattern precisely comparable with that on the copper seals from the Shahi-tump cemetery; the treatment of animals on two

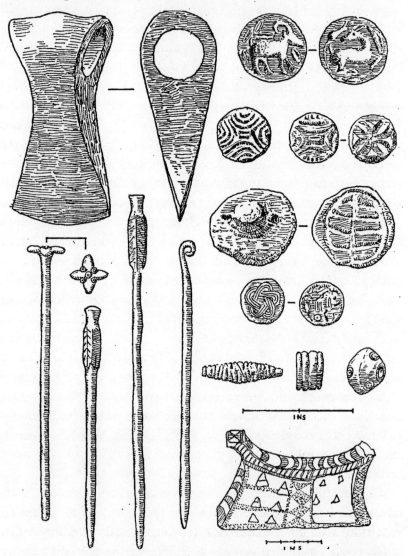

FIG. 27. Copper shaft-hole axe and pins, stone and faience stamp-seals and beads, and pottery head-rest, Jhukar Culture (after Mackay and Majumdar)

others recalls Sumer and Elam rather than anything Indian; an interlaced coil pattern on another seal is best paralleled in Hittite contexts in Asia Minor, and this region produces many other less precise parallels for the types of seals and double-sided amulets in Chanhu-daro II. Whatever may be said of the pottery, the Jhukar seals are foreign to India, and imply newcomers from the west, not unconnected with those who buried their dead at Shahi-tump.

The beads point in the same direction. One ornamented stone bead from Lohumjo-daro is paralleled at Hissar IIIc and Anau III, and the long, barrel-shaped faience beads from Chanhu-daro II, roughly ornamented to imitate segmented forms, recall similar segmented barrel-beads in Jemdet Nasr and Early Dynastic contexts in Sumer. The very large segmented beads from the same site are less easy to parallel, though in Egypt at least such clumsy forms come very late in the bead sequence. Again, we may infer the introduction of new types from the west, from the fringes of the kingdom of Sumer and Akkad.

A copper shaft-hole axe provides another link with the Shahi-tump cemetery, and the series of pins offers a contrast to the Harappā customs of dress, which did not include garments held with this type of fastening (Fig. 27). There are seven pins with the head rolled over in a manner known in Sumer since Early Dynastic times at least, but this type significantly makes its appearance first in the IIIb phase of Hissar. Of the other types of pins, it is difficult to say much except that one is vaguely reminiscent of a type found in Sialk IV.

The numerous bone awls were also an innovation, since none was found in the Harappā levels; Mackay suggested that they had been used for mat-weaving. These unsophisticated tools stress the barbaric character of the Jhukar Culture, which is already suggested by the hovels built among the ruins of the deserted town. The gaily-decorated pottery head-rest is a remarkable find, and it is difficult to suggest parallels, but once more the contrast with anything we know of the Harappā or the Baluchi Cultures is emphasized.

The picture given by the Jhukar material is not dissimilar from that of the less abundant relics from the Shahi-tump cemetery. In both cultures the pottery appears to represent a more or less indigenous type in a late stage of evolution or devolution, but the smaller portable objects, such as seals, beads, metal implements, and weapons, and habits of dress implied by the use of pins, all suggest the arrival of new blood in the region. At Chanhu-daro one of the most interesting features is the use of faience by the Jhukar people, and it can hardly be explained in any way except by the supposition that the invaders conscripted, or at least were prepared to acquire the products of, local craftsmen skilled in this technique who survived the Harappā disasters and were set to work imitating as best they could the type of beads demanded by their new rulers. Although the newcomers may have known faience by sight, they are unlikely to have brought with them craftsmen who could make it, though as we have seen, some faience beads may have been imported into India from the Eastern Mediterranean region. At these three sites in Sind where the Jhukar Culture has been found, we can feel only that we are witnessing the arrival of barbarians, either as the destroyers of the Harappā civilization or following hard in the wake of the first raiders. It is their portable objects that are significant and which give the clue to their origins: here for once we can relegate pottery to a secondary place in estimating the content of these allied cultures.

It is convenient here to say a few words about the Jhangar Culture, which at Chanhu-daro III appears as a final occupation of the site after the Jhukar settlement. Little enough is known of the culture, recognized only here and at the type-site, and also in Sind, except that it marks a break with the old painted pottery traditions, and has instead a grey or black ware with incised ornament. The pottery looks primitive, but its date is wholly unknown, and it may represent a purely local culture restricted to a small tribe or two, and may be not earlier than the first few centuries B.C. At Jhangar itself, apparently associated with the primitive ware, were sherds which look suspiciously like pottery of Sunga date, about the second or third century B.C.

When we turn to Mohenjo-daro, the evidence for the final phases of the city's history is less abundant than at Chanhudaro, and there does not seem to have been any actual settlement made on the ruins after the collapse of the Harappā Culture – at least, not in the areas excavated. But there are nevertheless several significant pointers to a disturbed state of affairs followed by disruption and decay, at this site as at others. I have already drawn attention to the hoards of jewellery and other precious objects found in the latest strata at Mohenjo-daro, and pointed out that the hiding of such hoards is a typical feature of disturbed and insecure conditions – there is a good early Indian parallel from the town of Rairh in Jaipur state, where numerous hoards of coins could be attributed to the troubled times following the collapse of the Mauryan dynasty early in the second century B.C. Many of the largest hoards of copper tools at Mohenjo-daro, too, belong to the later phases of the city, and emphasize the feeling of insecurity that must have been in people's minds.

The actual buildings and their construction show a falling-off in these latter-day levels as well: street frontages are not so strictly observed, brickwork may be shoddy, and large houses are divided up into smaller rooms to take more persons with a lowered standard of amenity. Pottery kilns are allowed to be built within the city boundaries in the DK area, one even in the middle of a street – a shocking piece of decadence which could never have been condoned by the

City Fathers of an earlier generation. Insecurity, the threat
of raids, the big houses split up into flats, the slackening of
civic pride and the decline of residential areas of the city
into industrial slums, are all familiar enough signs of decadence and impending collapse. And that raids, if nothing
more, were taking place at this time is shown by the hud-
dled skeletons of persons murdered in the street or on a
staircase – murdered under circumstances where no one was
concerned with giving them burial, but rather anxious to
save his own life by flight.

There are a few pieces of significant archaeological evidence which can be related to this 'time of troubles' at

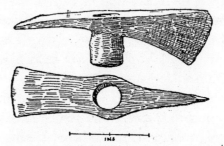

FIG. 28. Copper shaft-hole axe-adze, Mohenjo-daro
(after Mackay)

Mohenjo-daro. A copper axe-adze with a shaft-tube for
hafting was found in a late stratum, and is a completely exotic object among the metal types of the Harappā Culture
(Fig. 28). But it is characteristic of a number of sites in
North Persia – Hissar III, Shah Tepe, Turang Tepe – likely
to be approximately contemporary with the Akkadian
period in Mesopotamia, and surviving in other sites (e.g. at
Assur and in the B cemetery at Sialk) probably as late as the
ninth century B.C. It is an import from the west, and a
weapon of war, likely on the whole to date from the second
millennium B.C., and to be taken into consideration with the
shaft-hole axes from Shahi-tump and Chanhu-daro II.
There is also a group of what can only be called swords, up

to $1\frac{1}{2}$ feet long and with a strengthening mid-rib in a manner foreign to the Harappā tradition, found again in the later strata only, and which present something of a problem when 'one comes to look for parallels. The swords or daggers nearest in type to those from Mohenjo-daro, with a tang and rivets to hold the handle, come from Palestine and date between 1800 and 1500, where they are often associated with the Hyksos period, but Palestine is remote enough from India, and one would expect intermediate examples to have been recorded. However, they certainly seem intrusive at Mohenjo-daro, and likely to have been brought by invaders from somewhere outside the western frontiers of the Harappā kingdom.

There is one burial at Mohenjo-daro, made in the ruins of a deserted courtyard of a house in the HR area, which seems to belong to the invaders rather than the invaded. Among a confused mass of fragments of a large pot, and other objects, such as small vases, beads, a shell spoon, etc., were a few bones and a human skull. One pot found with this group (the only one published) is of a type which we shall find recurring at Harappā in a cemetery on that site which is demonstrably later than the main Harappā occupation of the city, though its ornament rather recalls Kulli or Jhukar motifs. Surprisingly enough, the skull from this burial is that which clearly belongs to the Mongolian group – closely comparable, for instance, to the modern Naga type. If this is really a burial of one of the attackers of the Harappā civilization in its last days, it suggests a very mixed invading force, possibly including mercenaries. Can he have been a Gurkha?

It had already been noted by Vats in his excavations at Harappā that the superficial deposits of the mound, which represent the ruins of the Citadel, contained sherds of pottery of a distinctive type, dissimilar from that of the Harappā occupation of the city, but identical with that which he found in an important cemetery lying beyond the limits of the city on the south – the 'cemetery H', demonstrably subsequent to the Harappā period. Stone has noted that Wheeler's excavations produced several segmented faience beads of types closely comparable to that equated with the Minoan faience bead of *c.* 1600 B.C., in these superficial layers of the citadel. The summit of the Citadel Mound is much disturbed by brick-robbing, and Vats did not establish an occupation layer to which this pottery could be assigned, but Wheeler in 1946 was able to show that his fourth (and final) period of construction at the West Gate and its associated terraces was in fact characterized by just this peculiar pottery. This last phase 'followed an interval during which the structures relating to the terraces had fallen into decay and had been covered by debris. It is represented by fragments of poorly constructed buildings, presumably dwellings, with walls sometimes only one brick in thickness'.

It seems likely that some of the structural remains found in the earlier excavations on the Citadel Mound in the uppermost strata belong partly to a decadent version of the Harappā occupation, with some mingling of the intrusive cemetery H elements. The typical cemetery H pot from Stratum II, recorded by Vats, would suggest that to this phase should be attributed the badly-built walls, made of re-used brick-bats, which he notes as characteristic of this stratum. Among these structures may be noted a circular bin or granary, still standing 6 feet high and 4 feet in diameter, and areas of brick paving, roughly square, which recall those of the Jhukar Culture in Chanhu-daro II. The similar pavements associated with the charred remains of pine and bamboo in what is alleged to be a Harappā stratum elsewhere on the Citadel Mound are suspiciously suggestive of the huts of barbarian squatters rather than of any structures likely to be within the Citadel walls in the days of its splendour, but the excavation records do not contain enough evidence for us to express a definite opinion. It should be noted in passing that what appears to be a 'fractional' burial was found in this same area, and was assigned to the Harappā Culture. If it is not a more or less modern grave, it is much more likely to be subsequent to the Harappā occupation than contemporary with it; the brachycephalic skulls of Alpine type with high-bridged noses in the grave at all events imply an intrusive ethnic element, and may conceivably be connected with invaders in the last phase of the site's prehistory.

Unquestionable evidence of the arrival of newcomers at Harappā after the main phase of occupation of the city is, however, afforded by the large cemetery H, itself of two periods, both of which have been shown by the recent excavations to be later than the R 37 cemetery, of Harappā age. This latter cemetery was situated in a natural hollow, which, at some time after the disuse of the cemetery, was filled up level with debris which contained a mass of Harappā potsherds, and it was into this debris, at a point some 120 yards to the north-east of cemetery R 37, that the graves of cemetery H were dug. It is characteristic of the conservatism of the Harappā Culture that no significant change in the types of pottery could be detected between the layers underlying the R 37 cemetery, the cemetery itself, or either of the two debris-layers overlying it. But with cemetery H the change is abrupt and decisive.

The earlier burials in cemetery H (Stratum II) are extended inhumations, normally lying north-east and south-west, with the legs slightly flexed, and at an average depth of six feet beneath the present surface. About twenty-four such burials were found in the area excavated: some were claimed as dismembered or fractional, but it is not clear whether these were not sometimes the result of ancient disturbance. The burials are sometimes accompanied by the remains of food-offerings – in one grave an entire dismembered goat had been laid with the dead man – and large numbers of pottery vessels were always present. In only two graves were any other objects found: a woman with a gold bangle on her wrist, and the three remaining teeth in the skull of another looped round with gold wire – 'for security or decoration', as Wheeler rather sardonically remarks.

The later burials in cemetery H (Stratum I) were only some two to three feet below the present surface, and consisted of true fractional burials in large pots, without any accompanying grave-goods or offerings. The bones in many instances showed that the bodies must have been exposed after death for some time before burial, when only the skull and a few long bones were selected for deposition in the cemetery. About 140 such burials were found, and a dozen of these were of babies, buried whole and crouched up in the funeral jars. These jars were closed at the mouth by lids of broken pots. The pottery from both strata of the cemetery is dissimilar from that of the Harappā Culture, and although certain characteristic forms are confined to the upper and lower strata respectively, this distinction is functional rather than cultural, and the technique of ware and painting is essentially the same in both phases of the cemetery. We can then regard it as a whole, and as the product of one culture despite the change in burial customs.

Before proceeding to discuss this pottery, however, it will be convenient to summarize the very scanty knowledge available of the human types represented. No adequate report has yet appeared, but the dominant skull-form in the earlier phase seems to have been the proto-Australoid type, and there is at least one such skull among the second phase burials. But in these burials there can be traced a 'small, low-headed race, such as is seen among the present aboriginal population of India', and probably (though not certainly) from the second phase of the cemetery are two skulls considered by Friederichs and Muller to be Armenoid. On the whole, however, there seems little to suggest an intrusive ethnic type which could plausibly be connected with migration from the west.

The pottery from both strata is very well made, with a hard red fabric and a brilliant red slip, and the frequent ornament painted on in black has often the same 'running' at the edges already commented on in the otherwise totally dissimilar ware from Shahi-tump. Apart from Harappā, this ware is known only from two sites in Bahawalpur State, 150 miles away to the south, on the other side of the Sutlej River. Although its technique in detail is not that of Harappā ware, the use of a black-on-red decorative scheme may imply some sort of relationship, at least within the Red-ware province as a whole, while one of the characteristic forms of the earlier phase of the cemetery is a squat 'offer-ing-dish', which itself might be compared with the higher Harappā types. But the decoration takes us into a world entirely removed from that of Harappā.

The technique of painting is as assured and sophisticated as the forms of the vessels, and implies the use of a kiln at least as advanced as those known from the late period of Mohenjo-daro. Characteristic motifs are stars of various kinds, stylized plant forms, ring-and-dot patterns, groupings of straight and crinkled lines, and short lengths of zig-zag lines used to fill up backgrounds. And in addition to these more formal elements of design, there occur frequent re-presentations of cattle, goats, peacocks and fishes, treated in a brilliantly decorative convention; sometimes in con-tinuous scenes which encircle the vase and sometimes in panels or in the roundels afforded by the circular undersides of pot-covers (Fig. 29). These representations are not naturalistic, but are instinct with symbolism – a series of peacocks, between groups of star or sun motifs, have within themselves a circle containing the tiny figure of a man; on another vessel peacocks alternate with a sort of centaur with the horns of a goat or deer. One remarkable vase from the upper stratum has a continuous frieze of design beginning with two peacocks and followed by a group in which a man with wild, flying hair holds two cows, behind one of which is a dog. Then comes a band of pattern, to be followed by an extraordinary version of a

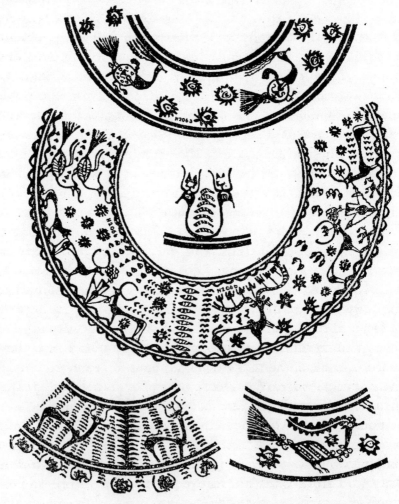

FIG. 29. Designs on pots from Cemetery H, Harappā
(black on red). (After Vats)

humped bull whose enormous horns bear seven enigmatic objects like little standards, and then another man between two cows (or bulls), each with a single standard between its horns, for all the world recalling a Minoan bull with double-axe. The whole scene is filled in with stars, leaves, and zig-zags, and similar zig-zags crowd the background in another vessel, where humped cattle stand between stylized trees.

It is very difficult to suggest even partial analogues to this remarkable series of pottery. As a whole, it is quite without parallel in any of the known cultures of the Ancient Orient, and one can only say that the groupings of animals and trees does recall the 'animals and landscape' designs of Kulli ware in rather more than general terms and the star and bird motifs in association recall similar patterns on pots from the Giyan II cemetery of c. 1550–1200 B.C. The treatment of the animals and men is quite different from that known in any of the prehistoric wares of Baluchistan or India, but although remote in time and space, it is worth mentioning that the treatment of the human figures, and to some extent that of some of the animals is not altogether dis-similar to that on Samarra ware and its analogues in Persia. It is just possible that these similarities may represent at least an ancient Iranian or North Mesopotamian strain in the culture responsible for the burials in cemetery H. Beyond this, we can say nothing, though again the possible relation-ships with the Kulli style may point to Baluchistan elements as well. The cemetery H people are certainly newcomers to the Harappā world, but where they came from or what was their later history only further excavation can tell us.

There remain a few scattered pieces of information to be brought together, not directly connected with the Harappā civilization and its end, but not without importance. A stray find from Kurram, in the North-West Frontier Pro-vince, is a curious type of flat copper axe with lateral lugs – the so-called 'trunnion-celt', that has a wide distribution in

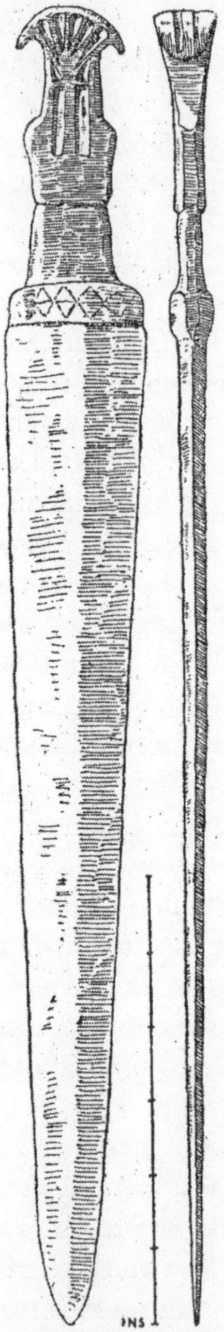

FIG. 30. Bronze Sword from Rajanpur, Punjab

time and space in Europe, but which in Western Asia appears to be represented only by a specimen from Turang Tepe in Northern Persia and that from Kurram The Turang Tepe axe would be contemporary with Hissar III–Anau III, probably early in the second millennium B.C., and the Kurram find may again imply arrivals from the west at a somewhat later date.

Another find suggesting western contacts of rather later date is that of a bronze sword from Rajanpur in the Punjab, a remarkable weapon with an elaborate hilt of a type well known in the Luristan graves of Persia, which are likely to be about 1400–1200 B.C., and similar to others from the Caucasus of approximately the same date (Fig. 30). This sword stands alone in India, though there are two hoards of swords of different types, one from Fathgarh in the Upper Ganges Valley and the other from Kullur in Hyderabad State, Deccan. The Fathgarh hoard contained no less than thirteen swords, said to be of copper, and with slight mid-ribs; all but one had characteristic hilts cast in one with the blade and spreading out into 'antennae,' and this was the type of the four swords from Kullur. Swords with hilts of the Rajanpur type occur in the Late Bronze Age Talish graves of the Caucasus, again about 1350–1200 B.C. and representing a school of metal-work closely in touch with that of Luristan. It is then just possible that all the swords in question may be related to Caucaso-Persian styles of the late second millennium B.C.

In the Ganges Basin and on the adjacent uplands to the south-east a number of finds of copper tools have been made, either singly or in hoards of up to 400 objects (as at Gungeria, Balaghat). The finds fall into two groups, one in the valleys of the Ganges and the Jumna rivers above their point of junction and the other centred round the Ranchi uplands, and the characteristic tool present throughout is the flat copper or bronze axe, of simple forms all similar in general terms to the flat axes of the Harappā Culture. But the very simplicity of the forms make close affiliation difficult, and we can turn with more confidence to another type recurring in these finds, the elongated axe or chisel which has been called a 'bar-celt'. Although precise parallels to these tools do not occur in the Harappā metal series, nevertheless at Chanhu-daro in particular very narrow, elongated axes appear, which could well be ancestral, and in the important series of copper tools from the Nal cemetery in Baluchistan a small version of the 'bar-celt' does in fact occur. As we have seen, the date of the Nal cemetery is likely to be approximately contemporary with the Harappā Culture, but it may in part survive later. It is a long way from Nal to the nearest 'bar-celt' find (Rajpur on the Upper Ganges), but in general the whole Gangetic axe and 'bar-celt' series is unlikely to be a separate and independent evolution from that of Harappā metallurgy.

Associated with these axe types in several hoards, confined to the valleys of the Jumna and Ganges, is a remarkable series of copper harpoons, which can be arranged in a typological series evolving from primitive types which clearly copy prototypes in bone or horn. These harpoons must represent a local development among river-side communities whose economy centred round fish-spearing and whose primitive equipment was transformed into metal when the knowledge of metallurgy spread among them. The implied existence of harpoons of forms similar to those known in many mesolithic cultures of Europe and Western Asia is of some interest, and has been commented on in Chapter II.

The date of these hoards of axes and harpoons cannot be fixed precisely. The axes and 'bar-celts' probably owe their origin to types within the Harappā or allied cultures in Western India, unless we assume an independent invention of metallurgy in another centre or centres of prehistoric India, and one's instinct is therefore to date the finds within the period of that culture or in one shortly after its end. The concentration round Ranchi suggests the exploitation of the local copper deposits there, and the distribution of the finds westwards to Rajpur, 300 miles east of Harappā, does strengthen the idea that there was a spread of metallurgical techniques, and of the people responsible for them, from the confines of the Harappā kingdom eastwards. It would be tempting to associate this movement with something more than trade, and to see in it the colonization of the Ganges Basin by refugees and displaced persons from the Punjab and the Indus Valley during the time of the break-up of the Harappā empire and the coming of the raiders from the west. The deposition of hoards itself suggests a time of in-security and economic instability, and may mean that the refugees were not left undisturbed for long, as the invasions gathered momentum and pressed on, beyond the old fron-tiers of the Harappā kingdom and down into the Ganges Valley. But here we leave archaeology for the ambiguous hints of legend and tradition.

In sum, however, the evidence from Baluchistan and from Sind and the Punjab is reasonably consistent in implying that at some period likely to have been before 1500 B.C. (to use a convenient round figure) the long-established cultural traditions of North-Western India were rudely and ruth-

lessly interrupted by the arrival of new people from the west.
The burning of the Baluchi villages and the equipment of
the graves at Shahi-tump suggest that these new arrivals
were predominantly conquerors who travelled light, and
adopted the pottery traditions of the regions in which they
established themselves. In Sind, at Chanhu-daro, a barbarian settlement appears in the deserted ruins of the Harappā town, and here some local craftsmen may have remained to work for alien masters, while the pottery suggests
a resurgence of local, non-Harappā elements. At Mohenjo-
daro it seems clear that the civilization that had survived so
long was already effete and on the wane when the raiders
came, and at Harappā we know from the evidence of the rebuilding of the Citadel walls that the inhabitants were on the
defensive in the last days of the city, though these pre-
cautionary measures did not suffice to keep away the in-
truders, wherever they came from, who afterwards settled on
the ruins and buried their dead in cemetery H for generations. From the Ganges Valley comes evidence suggestive of
a spread of techniques and peoples eastward from the old
Harappā kingdom as danger threatened from the west.

This movement of peoples, this sack of the ancient cities
by the outer barbarians, is something not confined to India in
the centuries immediately after 2000 B.C. In Mesopotamia
the kingdom of Sargon of Akkad rapidly disintegrated after
the death of his son Naram-sin, when the Guti and other
tribes broke in upon the land. Though there was recovery
and considerable prosperity, especially in the south, the barbarian attacks were renewed a couple of centuries later, when
the contemptuous if frightened scribe wrote in a year-date
of the Third Dynasty of Ur of the Amurru, 'a host whose
onslaught was like a hurricane, a people who had never
known a city'. It is the period that sees the rise of the Hittite
Empire in Asia Minor, while archaeological evidence of
folk-movements is clear in Syria and again in North Persia,

where in the Hissar III phase the elements alien to the old painted pottery cultures, already beginning to show themselves in Hissar II, dominate the town. In this phase, as in the contemporary sites at Turang Tepe and Shah Tepe, we see the appearance of novel types of tools and weapons and ornaments based on those of Early Dynastic and Akkadian times in Mesopotamia, and now for the first time spreading extensively among the barbarian tribes who had broken down the frontiers of the civilized communities, carrying off loot, a knowledge of new techniques, and doubtless actual craftsmen to their own chieftains' courts.

From the Caspian this movement of war-bands and migrating people can be traced as far eastwards as Anau in Russian Turkestan, where the third phase of the site's occupation shows clear traces of contact both with Hissar III and, less strongly, with Harappā. It is in this context of folk migrations around 2000 B.C., and the subsequent few centuries, that we can set the end of the Baluchi villages and the Harappā cities, but there is evidence that a second wave of conquest or colonization from the west left traces in Baluchistan nearly a thousand years later.

At both Giyan and Sialk the latest settlements and cemeteries on the sites represent a semi-barbarian culture that numbered amongst its achievements, however, the domestication of the horse for riding and probably chariotry as well. Typical pottery and bronze arrowheads from the tell of Nad-i-Ali in Afghan Sistan show that these people had reached the borders of India, and at Moghul-ghundai in North Baluchistan a small cemetery of cairn-burials produced a whole array of bronze objects – rings, bracelets, horse-bells, a bangle, and a tripod jar – typical of the B cemetery at Sialk. In South Baluchistan the cemeteries of Jiwanri and Zangian have pots of distinctive shapes related to those from the same Persian cemetery, and from Londo not far from Nal come painted sherds in a provincial version of the Sialk B

style with animal ornament, including a frieze of horses. The
Sialk B cemetery probably dates from about 1250–1100 B.C.,
so that a date around 1100–1000 B.C. would be likely for the
Baluchistan cemeteries just described.

All these migrations of peoples come at a time when there
is a breaking-up of the ancient Western Asiatic civilizations
and the introduction into the old strongholds of civility, of
new blood, new ideas, and even perhaps new techniques,
such as the use of the horse-drawn chariot in warfare. From
the mixture of old and new civilizations of an altered texture and fabric were in many places to arise, with the dis-
sonant characteristics toned down in a mutual blending over
generations. The barbarians imperceptibly assimilated the
traditions of the civilization they had despised yet prized;
they had conquered only to be themselves conquered at last
by its persuasive and subtle power. The attempt in a Dark
Age to re-create what the age itself has destroyed is not confined to early medieval Europe.

This chapter has been restricted to the evidence of prehistoric archaeology for the movements affecting India in
the middle of the second millennium B.C. But there is another part of the story to be told, based on the evidence of
philology and on scraps of literary evidence: dangerous
ground, full of quicksands and pitfalls which have too often
trapped the unwary, and not infrequently the would-be
wary too. The question of the dispersal of the speakers of
languages within the Indo-European group, and of the
arrival of the Aryan immigrants in Northern India, must be
considered in connexion with the archaeological evidence.

Notes to Chapter VI

The Rana-ghundai sequence is described in *Journ. Near Eastern
Studies* v (1946), 284–316, the burning of the Nal settlement
by Hargreaves, *Excavations in Baluchistan 1925* (1929), and that of
Dabar Kot by Stein in *Arch. Tour in Waziristan and North Baluchistan*

(1929), 57. The Shahi-tump cemetery is also described by Stein, *Arch. Tour in Gedrosia*, 88–105, and that of Khurab (Bampur) in *Arch. Reconnaissances* 106–110. I discussed the Shahi-tump stamp seals in *Antiquity* XVII (1943), 179–181; the skull from the cemetery was described by Sewell in *Arch. Tour in Gedrosia*, 191–200.

The Jhukar Culture occupation at Chanhu-daro is described by Mackay, *Chanhu-daro Excavations* (1943); for the pins, see my note in *Ancient India*, no. 3, 145. Jhukar and Lohumjo-daro were described by Majumdar in *Explorations in Sind* (1934), where Janghar is also published, though the late-looking pottery (in the Central Asian Museum) is not commented on. The late phases of Mohenjo-daro and Harappā are described in the relevant excavation reports quoted in Chapter V, and the final occupation of the Harappā citadel by Wheeler in *Ancient India*, no. 3, 59–130. In the same paper (pp. 84–86) the H cemetery is discussed, supplementing the original report by Vats in *Excavations at Harappa*.

The copper and bronze implements from the Ganges Basin are discussed by me in *Antiquity* XVIII (1944), 173–182, where the Kurram axe is wrongly assigned to the Ranchi district instead of to the N.W.F.P. The Rajanpur sword is in the National Museum of Antiquities, Edinburgh. For the Moghul-ghundai cairns see Gordon in *Man in India* XXVII (1947), 234; the Londo site was discovered by Miss B. de Cardi (see p. 131, above).

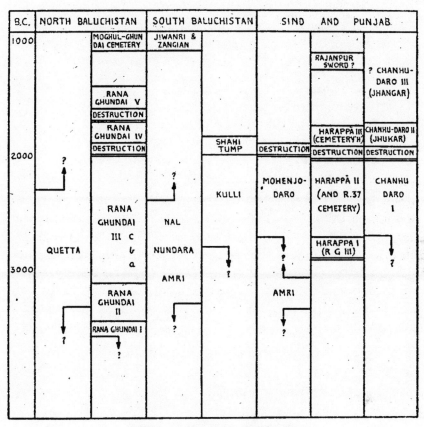

Chronological Table II

CHAPTER VII

Conquerors from the West – The Aryans and the Rigveda

The warrior's look is like a thunderous rain-cloud,
    when armed with mail, he seeks the lap of battle:
Be thou victorious with unwounded body; so let the
    thickness of thy mail protect thee ...
Whoso would kill us, whether he be a strange foe or
    one of us,
May all the Gods discomfit him. My nearest, closest
    mail is prayer.

Rigveda, VI, 75.*

TOWARDS the end of the eighteenth century two Europeans resident in India, a French missionary and an English administrator, made (apparently independently) an outstanding linguistic discovery. Cœurdoux in 1767 and Sir William Jones in 1786 published the conclusions they had been led to by a study of Sanskrit, the ancient Indian liturgical language (represented for instance in the *Rigveda*), which they both perceived to have the most remarkable affinities with the Latin and Greek tongues in vocabulary and grammar. It seemed to them that such striking similarities could be accounted for only by supposing that these languages had a common origin in some extinct tongue and that there had been a dispersal of peoples to east and west. This supposition

* The translations from the *Rigveda* are those of Griffiths (1896), but in a few instances, in consultation with Professor Dillon, I have ventured to substitute alternative words for his sometimes rather banal phraseology. While my interpretation of the *Rigveda* has been based on translations only, I feel that some attempt must be made by archaeologists who are not Sanskrit scholars to obtain at least the broad outlines of its significance.

was put on a sound footing by the later work of such grammarians as Bopp, and by 1813 someone had suggested the word 'Indo-European' as a convenient term for the group of allied languages and their presumed original. The name has been retained in modern studies, which have thrown much new light on the problems involved, and vindicated the ideas of Cœurdoux and Jones.

Today we can recognize the Indo-European group of languages as a relatively junior member of the Old World linguistic family, evolving at a time when such languages as Sumerian and those in the Hamitic and Semitic groups were of respectable antiquity. The original ancestral language from which its known variants developed and spread seems to have been mixed from the start and to have incorporated two main elements, one Uralic and the other probably related to the Caucasian group, and this mixture, with the emergence of a distinctive language group, is likely to have taken place somewhere on the outer boundaries of the kingdom of Sumer and Akkad, between South Russia and Turkestan. If there ever was an original Indo-European unity, in language at least, internal division into dialects and variants must soon have taken place. Early divisions in the main linguistic group can be traced, probably partly a result of an actual spread of populations west and east from the area of origin.

One such subdivision can be distinguished by the variant forms of the 'k' palatal, conveniently typified by the word for 'one hundred', in the one group represented by the Latin *centum*, in the other by the Sanskrit *satem*. The *centum* languages have on the whole a western distribution, and include the Celtic, Italic, Germanic, and Greek dialects among living tongues, Illyrian and perhaps Ligurian among those now extinct. The exception is also a dead language, Tocharian, known from manuscripts of the first few centuries A.D. found by Stein in Sinkiang, and the only *centum* language in the Orient. The *satem* group includes the Baltic and Slavic languages, Armenian, Iranian, and Sanskrit and its later Indian derivatives. Related to the *centum* group is the Nashili dialect of Hittite in the second millennium B.C., which many linguistic scholars would bring into close relationship with the Italo-Celtic group.Less importance is attached to this *centum-satem* division by contemporary philologists than by those of the past, and another grouping based on the passive and deponent in *-r* has been distinguished, which includes Hittite, Tocharian, Phrygian, Italic and Celtic.

But cutting across these divisions such close linguistic parallels can be traced within the whole known Indo-European group that it has been possible to reconstruct, with some conviction, the essentials of the original parent language and its cultural background. Verbal equations can be made through six or eight languages, representing ideas or objects which are fundamental to a society and not dictated by changes of environment; for instance, relationship within the family represented by the words for 'father' – Sanskrit *pitár-*, Greek πατήρ, Latin *pater*, Irish *athir*, Germanic *fadar*, Tocharian *pātār*, Armenian *hair* – or a characteristic domesticated animal such as 'horse' – Sanskrit *áśva*, Greek ἵππος, Latin *equus*, Celtic *ech*, Anglo-Saxon *ehu*, Lithuanian *aszwà*, Tocharian *yakwe*. Based on such equations as these, a hypothetical Indo-European community has been reconstructed, of agriculturalists who had also domesticated the horse, patrilineal in social structure, users of copper and bronze but not of iron, and worshippers of a pantheon of anthropomorphic gods with a certain ritual. The method has its dangers – the great Sanskrit scholar A. B. Keith once remarked that by taking the linguistic evidence too literally one could conclude that the original Indo-European speakers knew butter, but not milk; snow and feet, but not rain and hands! But nevertheless the broad outlines are certain enough, and the structure of the society as worked out from the linguistic evidence is convincing enough when it is tested against our knowledge of second-millennium archaeology in Western Asia and Eastern Europe.

There is one other point of some importance. There has been a growing appreciation among linguists of the concept of the geographical distribution of languages and language-groups in their relationship one to another, with a realization of a distinction between central language areas, where innovation is common and rapid, and peripheral regions, where ancient linguistic traditions survive more or less unchanged. In this context, equations may with some confidence be made between areas geographically remote, if these are within the peripheral zone, as they may contain the same survivals, lost in the central area of rapid development. Grammatical peculiarities in Tocharian, for instance, recur in the Italo-Celtic group, and Hittite and Old Irish both preserve archaic survivals lost elsewhere.

And it seems likely that this can be taken a step further, to include the ritual and mythology with which so much of the early languages were concerned, so that it is not by chance that elements of the curious and complicated ritual of the ancient Indian horse-sacrifice are found again among the Altai Turks of modern times, and survived until the twelfth century A.D. in Ireland. We shall see, indeed, that the whole structure of ancient Indian society, and the manner of its warfare, as reflected in the earliest Sanskrit texts, is often strikingly reminiscent of the Irish heroic tales' of the Celtic Iron Age, although so widely separated from them in time and space.

The location of a possible Indo-European homeland, and the identification of the culture implied by the linguistic evidence with a comparable archaeological phenomenon, has been a matter of debate since the idea was first formulated in the last century. Nationalistic feeling has sometimes vitiated the quest in Europe, as when the German school headed

by Kossina placed the original home of the Indo-Europeans
in the North European plain, peopled with blond Nor-
dics, while in India a love of the miraculous has led to such
fantasies as a derivation of the Aryans from the North Pole
six thousand years B.C. But responsible linguists and archaeologists have agreed in regarding the possible region of origin as relatively limited, and lying somewhere between the
Danube and the Oxus. Giles, on linguistic grounds, looked
to the Hungarian plains as a possible area for the evolution
of the earliest Indo-European speech, while others have suggested Central Asia. Much play has been made of the significance of certain words (such as that for a beech-tree) in
limiting down the possible area by reason of its natural features, but the careless use of names of plants and animals
among various peoples even today (the 'robin' in England
and America are, after all, two totally different birds!)
warns us of the danger of attaching too great an importance
to such arguments.

The most reasonable hypothesis, and one which seems
best to satisfy the demands of philology and archaeology, is
that originally put forward by Professor J. L. Myres and the
late Harold Peake, and developed by Professor Childe,
which sees the Indo-European languages evolving among
the earliest agriculturalists of the South Russian steppes
and the lands eastwards to the Caspian Sea. On linguistic
evidence this area had been favoured by such scholars
as Schrader in the last century, and the archaeology as we
now know it seems to provide the most satisfactory background of material culture in accordance with the hints
given by the language itself. In this South Russian area
the basic culture in the late third and early second millennium B.C. was that of agriculturalists, perhaps partly
nomadic but sufficiently sedentary for small cemeteries
to be formed, presumably close to relatively stable settlements. They domesticated sheep and cattle, and the

horse was certainly tamed in the latter phases of the culture, if not at the beginning; burials in separate graves, sometimes under a mound or barrow and often accompanied by a stone (exceptionally a copper) battle-axe, emphasize the presence of a stratum of warriors and chieftains in the social structure.

There are certain great tombs, such as that of Maikop in South Russia and others, of more than petty chieftains, and in these much of the metal-work can be seen to be of types derived from Early Dynastic or Akkadian tools, weapons and wrought silver or gold. Such metal-work can be traced farther eastwards, to such sites as Tepe Hissar and Turang Tepe at the south-east corner of the Caspian Sea, and again into Anatolia in the richly furnished tombs of Alaca Hüyük and, rather later, in those of Trialeti in the Caucasus. It is significant that the Indo-European words for an axe (Sanskrit *paraśu*, Greek πέλεκυς, presupposing an original **peleku*) and that for copper (**roudhos*) appear to be of Mesopotamian derivation (Assyrian *pilakku*, Sumerian *urud*) and there may be similar connexions with the words for an ox and a star. The adoption of the metal shaft-hole axe of Sumerian type by the barbarians on the northern fringes of the kingdom of Sumer and Akkad has been commented on in Chapter V — indeed, the Shahi-tump axe has its best parallels in the Maikop tomb.

It seems likely, therefore, that by about 2000 B.C. there was at least a loose confederacy of tribes, stretching from South Russia to Turkestan, who shared certain elements of culture, including a dependence on the higher centres of civilization for their metal-working techniques, and who spoke closely related dialects within the Indo-European framework. The evidence of historical documents from the literate urban cultures of Asia Minor and Mesopotamia supports this view, for the Nashili dialect of Hittite, a member of the Indo-European family, is recognizable soon after the

beginning of the second millennium B.C. in the extant inscriptions and documents of the Hittite empire.

About the beginning of the sixteenth century B.C. Mesopotamia suffered once again from the inroads of the moun-
taineers from the north on the break-up of the First Dynasty
of Babylon, which had been brought to its climax by the
great Hammurabi, and a new dynasty was set up under the
Kassites, whose monarchs bear Indo-European names. They
must have come from the north or north-east, and indicate
the beginning of the great dispersal of Indo-European speakers eastwards. Little is known of the dynasty, which, however, endured for over five hundred years; but during this
time we have the first intimations of another Indo-European
group on the north-west frontier of the Kassite kingdom, the
Mitanni, who occupied the district round the headwaters of
the Khabur River, and exercised authority over a considerable portion of Northern Syria.

In the fourteenth and fifteenth century B.C. Indo-European names are frequent among the Mitannian rulers, and
appear in the diplomatic correspondence from El Amarna
in Egypt and Boghaz Keui, the Hittite capital in Asia Minor,
in documents written in modified cuneiform script on clay
tablets. But the most exciting document is a treaty between
the Hittite king Subiluliuma and the Mitannian Mattiuaza,
son of Dusratta, in about 1380, in which the latter invokes
his gods as witness, in the formula *ilani Mi-it-tra-as-si-il ilani
U-ru-w-na-as-si-il ilu In-da-ra ilani Na-sa-at-ti-ia-an-na.* These
can only be the gods Mitra, Varuna, and Indra of the
ancient Indian pantheon as recorded in the earliest Sanskrit
religious texts (such as the *Rigveda*) described later, and the
last deity is likely to be the Nāsatyas, an alternative name
for the heavenly twins, the Asvins, in the same literature.
This Hittite treaty does not, of course, mean that there were
Indians in the Mitannian kingdom at this time, but it does
point to just that common stock of mythology among the

Indo-European peoples that the linguistic equations would suggest – the gods of the Mitanni were also the gods of the eastern branch of the great Indo-European family.

And there is additional evidence which, though not conclusive, points in the same direction to a common cultural heritage. Among the Boghaz Keui documents of about the same date there is a fragmentary handbook on chariot-racing, written by a Mitannian named Kikkuli, and among the technical terms used for so many 'turnings' round the course he employs forms which are very near to Sanskrit – *aikavartanna, teravartanna, panzavartanna, shattavartanna* – for one, three, five or seven laps of the race (Sanskrit *vartanam*, a turning). A class of military nobility, the *mariannu*, is mentioned in the same text, and might be equated with the Sanskrit *marya*, a young hero. Here again one must be dealing with common interests and sports – chariot-racing, as we shall see, was eagerly indulged in by the earliest Indo-European speakers in India – and a terminology which shows that Sanskrit and Mitannian could hardly have diverged much in vocabulary by the early fourteenth century B.C.

Archaeologically and linguistically, this is the nearest one can bring Indo-European speakers towards India in the second millennium B.C. When we turn from the Mitannian kingdom to Persia and beyond, we leave literate societies and enter a world in which direct archaeological evidence is lacking and where an oral tradition has handed down the early Indo-European literature in such a way that the date of its composition can be arrived at only by more or less approximate computation, in the complete absence of epigraphic or palaeographical evidence to provide a check. In Persia the *Avesta* and in India the *Rigveda* constitute two Indo-European religious texts which linguistically should belong to the period under discussion, but we are entirely dependent on internal evidence for this attribution. Our

concern here is with the *Rigveda*, and with the evidence
which can be extracted from it to contribute to our knowledge of the material culture of its composers, which in its
turn can be assessed against the archaeological evidence. To
anticipate, there is no reasonable doubt that it does represent a text going back in its essentials to the middle of the
second millennium B.C., and, in the light of our knowledge
of the archaeology of contemporary Western Asia, it takes
its place naturally as a characteristically Indo-European
document of that time.

After the extinction of the Harappā civilization, there are
no inscriptions or manuscripts known in India until the
middle of the third century B.C. To this date belong the
famous inscriptions cut at the command of Aśoka on surfaces
of natural rocks or on pillars to propagate Buddhism, in the
Brāhmī script, which itself appears to be of Semitic origin,
and thereafter one has a more or less regular series of epigraphic monuments. The climate of India is most unfavourable to the preservation of documents written on such
perishable materials as parchment, bark or leaves, and probably the earliest Indian manuscript is the fragmentary Buddhist religious text written on birch-bark in the late fifth
century A.D. and found in the Jaulian monastery at Taxila.
The Bakhshali manuscript, of the same material, seems the
next claimant for high antiquity, though this is only of the
twelfth century. Direct information on the earliest manuscripts in India is, incidentally, extraordinarily difficult to
come by. Paper was introduced by the Moslems into India
in the thirteenth century, but most of the early manuscripts
on this or similar substances have long ago decayed or been
devoured by white ants.

Although certain Hindu religious texts were written down
in the Indian Middle Ages and later, the whole tradition of
the Brahmans vehemently opposed this desecration of the
holy word by committing it to the written form. Essentially,

the tradition was, and very largely still is, that of oral transmission from teacher to pupil, both of whom may be formally illiterate but have their powers of memorizing preter-
naturally sharpened by their very lack of contact with the
techniques of reading and writing. Not long ago in Benares
an illiterate Hindu priest appeared who dictated a very long
religious work in verse, until then unknown and unrecorded,
which on internal evidence of style and language belonged
at least to the Middle Ages, since when it had been passed
on orally through a certain line of priests.

The writing down of the early Hindu religious literature
was in fact achieved only in the late eighteenth and early
nineteenth century at the instance of such British scholars as
Sir William Jones, with what was regarded as the highly
treasonable collaboration of certain Brahman priests. It is
therefore clear that we cannot use the principles of textual
criticism or of palaeography in studying this literature, since
we have only a single standard text handed down in a single
unvarying recension. Max Müller, after examining all the
available texts of the *Rigveda* in the last century, concluded
that 'no use can be derived from them as manuscripts, because all of them are but transcripts, more or less carefully
executed, of one and the same text'. But despite this extraordinary gap in time between the composition and the
eventual writing down of these works, we can place great
reliance on the purity of text. The exact preservation of
every syllable and accent was thought to be of vital importance – the very sounds had a magical significance that could
be varied only at the peril of the individual reciter. There is
a story in a late religious work that stresses this danger,
relating how the demon Tvaṣṭṛ recited a fatal magic spell
against the god Indra, but, making a single slip in an accent,
was himself killed by the spell recoiling against him.

This oral tradition in literature is, of course, by no means
uncommon among illiterate peoples, and within the Indo-

European group one can aptly cite the Celtic practice as
recorded by Caesar in Gaul of the first century B.C. 'It is
against the principles of the Druids,' he writes, 'to commit
their doctrines to writing ... During their novitiate it is said
that they learn by heart innumerable verses.' In the two
illiterate peripheries of the Indo-European dispersal, in west
and east, one sees the same technique of the oral transmission
of sacred lore: a technique unnecessary, and so lost, in regions where writing had been acquired at an early stage.

With these preliminaries we can turn to the ancient religious books of Hinduism and their chronology. They are
written in the Indo-European language Sanskrit and, as a
whole, they fall into four or five main divisions, among
which the poetical corpus known as the *Rigveda* stands alone
in that all the other works presuppose its existence and in
large part consist of commentaries based upon it. It must
therefore be placed first in any attempted sequence, and
nearly related to it must be a group of three other Vedic
books, the *Sāmaveda* (instructions for the tunes to which the
Rigveda hymns should be chanted), the *Yajurveda* (prose
prayers and spells based on the *Rigveda* and sometimes
merely paraphrasing it), and the *Atharvaveda* (verse incanta-
tions with occasional prose passages). Then there come the
Brāhmaṇas, which, as their name implies, are works of priestly liturgical exegesis based on the Vedic books, and the
Upanishads,* 'secret teachings' of metaphysics. In addition,
there are the *Sūtras*, which are much condensed manuals of
rites accompanying the Vedic prayers.

The position of the *Rigveda* as the archetype within this
series has already been pointed out, and internal evidence
makes it clear that the *Sūtras* are later than the *Brāhmaṇas*
and the *Upanishads*, so that a rough relationship of the various works seems established. But when we come to find a

---

* This word is so well established in this form in English that to use
the 's' modified by a diacritical would be pedantic.

chronological framework against which this sequence can be set, we have very little to go on. The one certain fact seems to be that the doctrine preached by Buddha is essentially based on and develops out of the philosophical concepts contained in the *Upanishads*, and there is a reasonable consensus of evidence to place the date of Buddha's death as within a decade or so of 500 B.C. The *Upanishads*, therefore, must have been in existence in the sixth century B.C.

Beyond that date we have to depend on a sort of philosophical dead-reckoning, invented by Max Müller and still generally accepted, by which the *Brāhmanas* are assigned to the seventh and eighth centuries B.C., the later *Vedas* to the ninth and tenth, and the older elements of the *Rigveda* to the eleventh or twelfth centuries. These dates Müller later insisted were minimum dates only, and latterly there has been a sort of tacit agreement (influenced no doubt by the discovery of the Mitannian document of about 1380 with the names of *Rigveda* gods) to date the composition of the *Rigveda* somewhere about 1400–1500 B.C., but without any absolutely conclusive evidence.

Yet, tested against the background of archaeology and the movements of peoples in Western Asia in the middle of the second millennium B.C. as we can now begin to discern them, this date has much to recommend it. In the last chapter we have seen that there is good archaeological evidence for the arrival in North-West India of invaders from the west in the centuries following 2000 B.C.: these need not be Indo-Europeans, but their arrival is likely to be connected with the general movements from the west about this time in which the Indo-Europeans were involved. The establishment of the Kassite and the Mitannian kingdoms is a significant pointer to warrior bands pressing eastward at least to the Persian frontiers, and the appearance of new cultures, if not actual ethnic types, in such North Persian sites as Hissar III and Sialk, may again not be unconnected with folk-movements spread over the first half of the second millennium, while the pottery from Anau III in Turkestan and Nad-i-Ali in Afghan Sistan, as well as the Moghul-ghundai and Jiwanri cemeteries, shows that colonies of these same people were established farther east at a later date, around 1100–1000 B.C.

We shall see that an examination of the material culture of the composers of the *Rigveda*, as extracted from the allusions in the text, is entirely compatible with what we know of conditions at this time from archaeological evidence from other regions of early Indo-European colonization around the edges of the old city civilizations in Asia and the Aegean. I think we are justified in accepting the *Rigveda*, on archaeological grounds, as a genuine document of the period, preserved intact by the constant fear of the consequences if the magic word were altered by a hairsbreadth. An epic can be altered, brought up to date, recast and adapted to suit the changing tastes in heroic literature – the Indian epics, the *Mahābhārata* and the *Rāmāyaṇa*, are notable examples of this, their extant forms going back no further than the first few centuries A.D. In a religious text there is no need to delete an anachronism or explain an act whose significance is forgotten. Meaning is of less account than the precise sequence of words and phrases. We do not ourselves worry unduly about the meaning of archaic phrases in the Book of Psalms or even in Hymns Ancient and Modern.

The *Rigveda* is a curious document. In length, it is approximately equal to the *Iliad* and the *Odyssey* together, and consists of over a thousand poems, or 'hymns'. These vary from more or less epic chants, hymns of praise, and prayers to the gods, to magic spells and fragments of popular songs, all of very varying standard – 'sometimes true, genuine, and even sublime, but frequently childish, vulgar and obscure', as Max Müller remarked. The language is elaborate and self-consciously literary, and the metrical composition, based on syllabic verse-forms, is often extremely complicated. In a word, however barbarous and archaic may be the life and thought reflected in the *Rigveda*, it is a laborious and sophisticated anthology, put together with conscious artifice by professional hymnologists at a relatively late stage of the culture of those people who in it are called the Aryans (*Ārya*) and who figure as conquerors in a newly-won land.

As a source-book it is full of limitations and difficulties. The archaic Sanskrit in which it is written soon lost its precise significance, and by the Indian Middle Ages elaborate commentaries had to be devised to 'explain' the ancient text – which often meant forcing elaborately metaphorical interpretations on the misunderstood original. For the student of Aryan religion it gives only a partial picture, since it is concerned almost wholly with a limited group of ceremonies and gods, and many aspects of belief and ritual must be wholly unrepresented. In its interpretation the later works based on it can hardly be disregarded, as, however late their composition, they may often contain ancient elements dating back to the earliest phase, and in any discussion of Aryan religion the *Rigveda* cannot be isolated from its related books such as the *Atharvaveda* and the others.

This method of interpretation, however, is one which grew up at a time when the Harappā civilization was still undiscovered and when it was assumed that the Aryan invaders of India encountered only a rabble of aboriginal savages who could have contributed little save a few primitive animistic beliefs to Vedic thought, nothing to the structure of later Indo-Aryan society. With such an assumption it was safe to regard the whole Vedic corpus as representing in the main an Aryan evolution owing practically nothing to the older vanquished people of the Punjab. But as the preceding chapters of this book have shown, the Aryan advent in India was, in fact, the arrival of barbarians into a region already highly organized into an empire based on a long-established tradition of literate urban culture. The situation is, in fact, almost reversed, for the conquerors are seen to be less civilized than the conquered. In the *Rigveda* we see (or rather accidentally glimpse) this conquest from the Aryan point of view alone: they are the heroes, and scant tribute is paid to their contemptible opponents, more skilled in the arts of peace than in those of warfare. But, as we shall see, the Harappā tradition is very unlikely to have been suddenly and totally wiped out.

With this knowledge, it is clear that it would be danger-ous, in trying to work out the material culture of the first Aryan communities in North-West India, to use evidence from works compiled at a time when Harappā elements may have permeated Aryan society. In the ensuing sections of this chapter, therefore, I have used only the *Rigveda*, which does seem likely to represent faithfully the entrance phase of Aryan conquest, before the Indo-European tradition had become mixed with Harappā elements, while occasionally making reference to the later texts.

Even with these limitations, however, we still encounter considerable difficulties in using the text of the *Rigveda* as a source for information on material culture. In the hymns the transition from the more or less literal to the wholly meta-phorical is often sudden, and frequently almost impercept-ible. The physical war-chariot of an Aryan chieftain turns, with bewildering rapidity, into the noon-day sun; the roister-ing young cattle-raiders are suddenly the four winds of heaven. And the accident of survival of words descriptive of aspects of material culture is really dependent on their adaptability to religious metaphor and their appropriate-ness to the warrior aristocracy for whom the hymns were composed; chariots are described in such detail that a mod-ern coach-builder could probably turn out a passable replica of Indra's vehicle, but we hardly know what the Aryan house looked like.

But there is much that we can recover and interpret in the light of archaeological knowledge. We are building up a picture of Aryan communities presumably settled in some area of North-West India, or westwards in Afghanistan, at a time when their conquests had not extended farther east than the Ambala region of the Punjab: some scholars are inclined to think that the *Rigveda* was composed in this particular district. Such description of landscape as is contained in the hymns implies a knowledge of snow-capped mountains, fairly certainly the Himalayas, and a land of great rivers; while the rainfall seems to have been plentiful enough to suggest that the westward extension of the monsoon region, which we have seen is likely to have influenced the climate during the hey-day of the Harappā Culture, still affected the Punjab. In modern India Lucknow is usually taken as representing the approximate boundary between the wheat-growing areas to the west and the rice lands to the east, and the *Rigveda* knows nothing of rice, nor of the tropical animals such as the tiger, both of which are mentioned in the *Atharvaveda*, which implies that by the time of its composition Aryan territory had been extended eastwards down the Ganges, though as we have seen the tiger is depicted on the Harappā seals.

The *Rigveda* hymns reflect the aspirations and life of members of the upper classes of a society which, in common with other Indo-European communities, was formally divided into a threefold grading of warriors, priests, and artisans – *Kṣatriyas*, *Brahmans*, and *Vaiśyas*, comparable with the *milites*, *flamines*, and *quirites* of Roman society or the *equites*, *druides*, and *plebes* of the Celts of Gaul as recorded by Caesar in the first century B.C. But it is important to realize that the concept of *caste*, as known in later literature, is quite unknown in the *Rigveda*. The tripartite arrangement is perhaps an obvious enough division of responsibilities within a community, but its formal recognition is characteristically

Indo-European. The hymns are composed by the priests on
their own behalf and on that of the warriors, their patrons,
and are addressed mainly to a group of anthropomorphic
deities, or to the deified sacrificial liquid, *soma*, round the
cult of which the whole group of hymns is really centred.

In several of the gods we can see the Aryans themselves
magnified to heroic proportions. The greatest god of the
Rigveda is Indra, to whom about one-quarter of the hymns
are addressed, and he is the apotheosis of the Aryan battle-
leader; strong-armed, colossal, tawny-bearded, and pot-
bellied from drinking, he wields the thunderbolt in his more
god-like moments, but fights like a hero with bow-and-
arrows from his chariot. 'He is strong, young, immortal, and
ancient', as Keith puts it; his appetite is enormous and he
devours prodigious quantities of beef, porridge, and cakes,
swilling them down with the intoxicating *soma* or with mead,
and both his drunkenness and its after-effects are described
with convincing fidelity. He is a cattle-raider, and above all
he is the destroyer of the strongholds of the enemy, the victorious leader of the Aryans in their conquest of the hated
ancient empire in the Punjab. With him fight the young
warrior-band, the Maruts, who seem to be commanded by
Rudra, rival to Indra and yet in some ways his counterpart,
'unassailable, rapid, young, unaging, ruler of the world' and
with the malevolent characteristics which develop in later
Hinduism in the person of Śiva.

The portraits carry conviction in their artless barbarism,
so curiously transmitted in the sophisticated Sanskrit verse.
The atmosphere is that of the Irish tales that reflect the conditions of the Celtic Iron Age of the first century B.C. in Ul-
ster and North Britain; Indra is often reminiscent of the
grotesque Dagda with his insatiable appetite, Rudra and the
Maruts make one think of Finn and the *fianna*, the young
band of heroes, and the cattle-raiding is as familiar. But the
Aryan reivings are carried out on the plains of the Punjab,

and Indra and his followers fight against foes who, if not
feared as opponents on the battle-field, are regarded with
the superstitious dread of the simple soldier for the subtle
townsman.

These opponents of the Aryan onslaught, the despicable
enemy who dares deny Indra's supremacy in heaven and on
earth, are referred to as the *dasyus* or *dāsas*. They have black
complexions, no noses to speak of (*anāsa*), they are 'of un-
intelligible speech' and above all they are infidels. They
have no 'rites', they are 'indifferent to the gods', they 'follow strange ordinances', they do not perform the Aryan
sacrifices, and they probably worship the phallus. But they
are wealthy, with great stores of gold, they are formed into
groups or states, and they live in fortified strongholds. Their
names may refer to their eventual fate in Aryan eyes, and be
related to the root of *das*, to lay waste: the dwellers in the
waste land after conquest.

Our knowledge that the Harappā civilization was flourishing in Northern and Western India at the beginning of the
second millennium B.C., centred on cities with strongly fortified citadels and containing among its population a large
proportion of proto-Australoids with dark skin and flat
noses, and that these cities came to a sudden and violent end,
makes the identification of the *dasyus* and *dāsas* with the inhabitants of Harappā and Mohenjo-daro something near to
a certainty. Indra's exploits as a destroyer of forts, recently
discussed by Wheeler in connexion with the defences of the
Harappā citadel, go to confirm this view.

> With all-outstripping chariot-wheel, O Indra, thou
>   far-famed, hast overthrown the twice ten kings of men
> With sixty thousand nine and ninety followers ...
> Thou goest on from fight to fight intrepidly,
>   ,destroying castle after castle here with strength.

Thus a hymn in the first book of the *Rigveda* (1, 53). The
forts destroyed by Indra are said to be of stone, or with the

CONQUERORS FROM THE WEST

epithet *āmā*, which may refer to unbaked ('raw') brick walls; some are 'autumnal', which may mean that they were protected from the river floods after the rains. Indra is *puramdara*, the fort destroyer: 'Thou smitest foemen down, and many a citadel', 'thou breakest down the seven citadels' say the bards in his praise. He 'rends forts as age consumes a garment'.

The attack seems to have included setting fire to the buildings:

> ... in kindled fire he burnt up all their weapons,
> And made him rich with kine and carts and horses (ii, 15)

says another hymn of one of those favoured by the war-god. And it is possible that one can trace references to the destruction of the 'bunds' built to protect the Harappā cities from flood, so that the waters turned against them; it is difficult to be sure of this, because of the possibility of a sudden transition to the metaphorical usage of words describing Indra in his celestial character of Jupiter Pluvius releasing the rains and swelling the rivers, but the association of flood and conquest is significantly brought together in the same hymn from which the last quotation is taken:

> The mighty roaring flood he stayed from flowing, and carried
> those who swam not safely over,
> They having crossed the stream attained to riches ...
> He slaughtered Vala, and burst apart the defences of the
> mountain ...
> He tore away their deftly-built defences ...
> There the staff-bearer found the golden treasure ... (ii, 15).

And again, 'he sets free the rivers' paths', and 'all banks of rivers yielded to his manly might' (II. 13).

In the past, these 'forts' of the *dasyas* and the *dāsus* were considered to be either mythological or at best the primitive earthworks and palisades of the supposed aborigines of Northern India at the time of the Aryan conquest. But now, as Wheeler has said, 'the recent excavation of Harappā may be thought to have changed the picture. Here we have a highly-evolved civilization of essentially non-Aryan type, now known to have employed massive fortifications, and known also to have dominated the river-system of north-western India at a time not distant from the likely period of the earlier Aryan invasions of that region ... On circumstantial evidence, Indra stands accused.'

The archaeological evidence given in detail in Chapter V fits so well with the tale of conquest in the *Rigveda* that it is difficult to come to any other conclusion. The forts of the *dasyus* are the citadels of the Harappā civilization, wrecked and plundered by the war-bands who invoked Indra, Lord of Hosts, as they slaughtered those who would not accept his supremacy.

Like the Amurru in Mesopotamia, the Aryans were 'people who had never known a city'. Their way of life is clearly presented in the *Rigveda*, and is far from being that of the complicated urban organization traditional to the ancient centres of oriental civilization since the beginning of the third millennium. It belongs to the simple pattern of agricultural communities known throughout the prehistoric world of Europe and Asia up till and after the Roman Empire – more barbarous than the Homeric world and nearer to that of Beowulf. Its background is an agricultural economy which includes the growing of a grain crop, but in which herds of cattle and flocks of sheep and goats are of prime importance; wealth is reckoned in cattle, following the Indo-European tradition which gives the equation *pecus = pecunia* in Latin, a war-band is described as 'the horde seeking cows', and the root of the verb 'to protect' simply implies 'to guard cows'.

As in all simple pastoral societies, the Aryan vocabulary is rich in names for every aspect of the herd, with special words for 'a cow with a strange calf', 'a cow barren after calving', 'a three-year-old ox', and so on – one may compare the infinity of Arab words for camels. Red, black, dappled, and light-coloured cows are mentioned, and herds were differentiated by distinctive nicks cut in the ears, following a well-known custom which survived in Wales, for instance, to the last century. Milk evidently formed an important item of diet, either fresh or as curds or butter, but there is no direct evidence of cheese-making, nor of the use of fermented mare's milk (*koumiss*) in the ancient steppe tradition. The cows were milked three times a day, and castration was practised, oxen being used for the normal purposes of farm transport, and beef was freely eaten as the main meat dish. 'Slaying cows for guests' was an attribute of highest praise to an Aryan squire, and Indra was a champion beef-eater: the present-day Hindu doctrine of *ahimsa*, and the ritual prohibition of flesh food, is connected with the later (post-*Brāhmaṇa*) ideas of transmigration, which are entirely foreign to the earlier Aryan beliefs.

The Aryan feasts recall those of the Celts: there is the bronze cauldron (Sanskrit *caru*, Irish *coire*) slung over the fire by pot-hooks, with the guests waiting for the Champion's Portion –

> The trial-fork of the flesh-cooking cauldron, the vessels out of which the broth is poured,
> The warming-pots, the covers of the dishes, hooks, carving-boards ... (1, 162)

as one hymn lovingly enumerates. Meat was also roasted on spits, and mutton and goat-flesh were eaten, in addition to beef. Leather was used for many purposes, such as slings, bow-strings, chariot-traces, reins, and whips, and some sort of a tanning process and the wetting of the hide preparatory to stretching it are implied by references in the *Rigveda*.

The grain grown seems likely to have been barley, known, as we have seen, from Tell Halaf times in Northern Meso-

potamia and with its wild ancestors growing in Asia Minor,
Turkestan, Transcaucasia, and Northern Persia. Fields were
tilled by an ox-drawn plough, which was presumably fairly
large and heavy, since ox-teams of some size were in use at
least in immediately post-*Rigveda* times, but a yoke does not
seem to have been used, as it is nowhere mentioned in the
Rigveda in this connexion. This is significant in view of the
representations of ox-drawn ploughs in Early Dynastic
Sumer and early (Third Dynasty) Egypt, in which no yoke
is used, but the plough-traces are shown tied to the beasts'
horns. A similar representation of Kassite origin in Mesopotamia shows the same technique, and the oxen employed
seem to have the characteristic hump of the Indian breed
known from the earliest pottery-paintings at Rana-ghuṇḍai
and throughout the duration of the Harappā Culture. Whatever the significance of this feature, it is interesting to see the
Kassites, presumably members of the Indo-European linguistic group in the fifteenth century B.C., using the same
method of plough traction as can be inferred for the Aryans
in India.

The ripe ears of barley were cut with a knife or sickle,
bound into sheaves or bundles, strewn on a threshing-floor,
and eventually winnowed or sifted to separate the grain
from the chaff. Some form of container or measure was used,
for which the word *ūrdara* is used – Indra is filled with drink
as one fills an *ūrdara* with grain – and one may recall the circular structure interpreted by Vats as a grain-bin in the
final (post-Harappā) occupation on the deserted citadel of
the type-site in this connexion. Some artificial water-supply
is implied by a reference to 'waters produced by digging' in
one hymn, suggesting wells rather than any more ambitious
scheme of irrigation.

Dogs were used for guarding houses and for boar-hunting,
and they got driven away from the sacrifices, but there is no
direct evidence of their use in herding, which seems to have

been carried out by a herdsman armed with an ox-goad. The flocks included both sheep and goats, kept for their wool as much as their flesh. The Sanskrit word for a sheep is used by transference for wool, and no doubt sheep's wool was mainly used, but there is evidence that goat's wool was also used, presumably from such long-haired animals as those of Kashmir, already mentioned in Chapter V. The wool when spun was woven, probably by women, on a loom of which the names of warp, woof, and shuttle are preserved.

But, apart from cattle, the really characteristic domesticated animal of the Aryans was the horse. From the descriptions of the colouring of horses in the *Rigveda*, Ridgeway concluded that they had chestnut heads and backs, shading off into dun on the lower parts of the body, in the manner of the wild horse of the steppes known as Przewalski's horse, and that they were of Mongolian or Upper Asiatic stock. They seem to have been kept in stalls on occasion at least, and were hobbled when put out to graze. Stallions were sometimes gelded, but mares were especially used as draught animals in war-chariots, and riding seems to have been very exceptional and never formed a technique of warfare. This may well have been partly due to the fact that the invention of stirrups seems to come unaccountably late in the development of horse-harness, and that a secure seat for a fighting man could hardly be attained without them. Military cavalry was known to the Assyrians and the Achaemenids, and the invention of stirrups must be an ancient oriental contribution to horsemanship. In India stirrup-loops appear on carvings of the second century B.C. at Sanchi in the Deccan and on an engraved copper vessel of rather later date from North India, but in any case their adoption must have been long after the early Aryan phase.

The Aryan horses seem to have been used essentially as chariot-animals, whether in warfare, as described later on, or for chariot-racing, which was a favourite sport. It seems to have been indulged in purely for amusement and for prizes (except on a few formal religious occasions, such as the royal consecration), and the race took place along a course to a mark round which the chariots turned and came back again – the *aikavartana* and so forth of the Mitannian Guide to the Turf mentioned above. Such a race-course is presumably the ancestor of the Roman *circus* and the Greek στάδιον such as that at Olympia, where a race with ridden horses was first introduced as a novelty in the middle of the seventh century B.C., though chariot-racing still remained popular. One is reminded too of the ancient Celtic horse-races at the Fair of Carman and the other assemblies in Dark-Age Ireland.

. The horse appears to have been domesticated in South Russia by Middle Kuban times (between 2000 and 1500 B.C.), and representations of Przewalski's horse appear on a silver bowl from the rather earlier Maikop tomb. But the evidence from Anau and Sialk shows that an apparently domesticated horse was known in Persia and Turkestan in very early times, and it again appears in Baluchistan in Rana-ghundai I and, though rarely, in the Harappā Culture. One cannot, therefore, hold that the Aryans were the first people to domesticate the horse in India or on its western border-lands, but they were certainly among the first to introduce the idea of rapid transport made possible by its use. For their farm work, ox-drawn four-wheeled carts seem to have been used, and horses bred solely for use with the light two-wheeled chariot for sport or warfare.

Practically nothing can be gleaned of the appearance or lay-out of an Aryan settlement, or of the houses, but we are clearly dealing with nothing larger than farmsteads and villages. Such mundane affairs did not lend themselves to metaphor in hymns to the war-gods, though the goddess of Dawn does make a homely, rustic appearance in her ox-drawn cart, reminding us of Demeter and of the Teutonic

goddess Nertha described by Tacitus, whose image was similarly transported, and of the actual ritual carts carrying a
deity's throne known in Europe from Italy, Alsace, and
Denmark, and dating from the fifth century B.C. onwards.
All the Aryan buildings, however, appear to have been of
wood, and the house seems to have been rectangular, with a
thatched roof, divided into more than one room or com-
partment; possibly some phrases may be construed to imply
that the cattle and sheep, as well as the household, were
under a single roof. If the linguistic equation of the Sanskrit
word for a doorway, ātā (always used metaphorically for the
doors of the sky) with the Latin antae is to be taken literally,
it should have the meaning of a porch formed between the
projecting end-walls of the building. This architectural device is characteristic of the *megaron* house, known in the
Troad and Eastern Europe at least as early as the beginning
of the third millennium B.C., and certainly associated with
the early speakers of Indo-European languages in Greece,
but it is dangerous to force the analogy.

As in the *megaron*, so in the Aryan house, the central
hearth has a position of peculiar importance, and is the
focus of the household religious rites. The use of roasting-
spits and bronze cauldrons, with flesh-forks to impale the
savoury gobbets of boiled beef, has already been mentioned,
and presumably among the household gear must be reckoned saddle-querns for grinding, or pestles and mortars for
pounding the corn into flour: the former are probably, the
latter certainly, referred to in the *Rigveda*. Pottery vessels are
again mentioned, and the drink available at feasts included
mead, the name of which runs convincingly through the
Indo-European vocabularies to suggest that it was an early
invention common to all branches (Sanskrit *mádhu*, Greek
μέθυ, Celtic *mid*, Old High German *metu*, Old Slavonic,
medu). Another intoxicating drink was *sura*, which was probably a kind of beer brewed from grain. The mystic liquid

soma, extracted from the stems of some now unknown plant, seems likely to have been used almost entirely for religious ritual; its preparation and drinking is fully described in the various hymns dedicated to this aspect of Aryan religious practice.

Little, again, can be gathered of clothing, except that it was mainly of woollen cloth. Clothes that were either embroidered or woven in ornamental patterns were worn by women, and a cloak or mantle was worn, probably by both sexes. We are reminded of the garment dyed red and purple and the cloak of brown wool found in one of the tombs contemporary with that of Maikop, at Tsarskaya in South Russia. It is interesting that the use of a turban (surely derived from the Harappā Culture) is mentioned only in texts from the *Brāhmaṇas* onwards. Men wear ear-ornaments in the *Rigveda*, and there is mention of an ornamental headdress for women, which the etymology suggests stood up like a 'horn', while gold was used for anklets and rings, neck-ornaments and others worn on the breast. Shaving is mentioned, and there are references to moustaches and beards – Indra is famous for his tawny beard.

Specialized crafts within the community include that of the metal-smith, who may make metal vessels as well as tools or be an armourer. No direct mention of a potter occurs, but the carpenter has an important and honoured trade, working with an axe or adze, and making fine carved work for chariots or to enrich the door-posts of a house. His equipment presumably included the bow-drill, the use of which is implied in the fire-making appliance with which the sacred (and presumably the ordinary) fire was kindled. Bronze seems to have been the only metal worked; it follows that copper must also have been used, although the word for this metal occurs only later than the *Rigveda*, as does that for tin.

The community had periodic assemblies in what appears

to have been a regular club-house or meeting-hall, from
which women were excluded and in which not only the business of the clan was discussed, but ordinary farmers' gossip
was retailed. There too the men gambled at a game of
chance played with nuts and usually rendered 'dicing',
though it cannot have been played according to the methods
usual with marked dice (such as those known in the Harappā
Culture, for instance). The nuts were thrown towards a hole
or depression in the ground, and bets were laid according to
some complicated system: I once watched what must have
been a similar game, also played with nuts thrown towards a
hollow in the ground, in a village of the Kangra district in
the Himalayan foothills. The stakes were evidently often
high – one of the hymns of the *Rigveda* (x, 34) is a rueful
Gambler's Lament, in which he prays for better luck next
time. He has gambled away even his wife, or at least her
affections – in the old days

> She never vexed me nor was angry with me, but to my
> friends and me was ever gracious

yet now 'my wife holds me aloof, her mother hates me'. Still
the game calls him –

> The gamester seeks the gambling-den, and wonders, his
> body all afire, Shall I be lucky?

and all he can do is to warn the others by his fate –

> Play not with dice; no, cultivate thy corn-land. Enjoy the
> gain, and deem that wealth sufficient.
> There are thy cattle, there thy wife, O gambler!

There is some interesting evidence for Aryan music. Cym-
bals were used to accompany dancing, and in addition to
this and the drum there were reed flutes or pipes, a stringed
instrument of the lute class, and a harp or lyre, which is
mentioned as having seven tones or notes. This last piece of
information is important for our knowledge of ancient

music. Galpin has shown that instruments possessing fixed scales, such as harps, lyres, and flutes, are known from Western Asia from very early times (a bow-shaped harp was used in Jemdet Nasr times, and other more elaborate types were, as is well known, found in the Early Dynastic Royal Tombs at Ur). There is good evidence that these instruments were constructed according to the heptatonic scale (seven notes, with the eighth completing the octave, as with all European instrumental music of the present day). This heptatonic scale is the basis of modern Hindu music, where it exists (as in other regions of the world) side by side with another, more primitive, scale, that of five notes, or the pentatonic, based on quintal harmony and primitive vocal traditions. It is our normal musical scale with the third and seventh, the semitone intervals, missing. Curwen has recently taken this question of the two musical scales a stage further and related it to our archaeological knowledge, and he makes it clear that the spread of the heptatonic scale is intimately associated with instrumental music originating in the ancient urban civilizations of Western Asia, but dispersed beyond its original home by Indo-European peoples in the second millennium B.C. and later. He traces an early dispersal to India and even to China, and a later diffusion westwards with the Celtic peoples, with Britain as perhaps its last place of arrival in the middle of the first millennium B.C., so that the Hebridean folk-songs still retain the ancient, pre-Indo-European mode of the pentatonic scale today. (Incidentally the pentatonic idiom, derived from West Africa, plays its part in modern jazz music.)

Among the *Rigveda* hymns there is one (IX, 112) which can hardly be other than a secular lyric – scarcely less out of place than the Song of Songs in the Hebrew religious collection – which has been made a little more appropriate by the insertion of a refrain, 'Flow, Indu, flow for Indra's sake', after each couplet. Omitting these pious asides, we are left with an almost colloquial poem (it uses the Sanskrit equivalents for 'Dad' and 'Mum' rather than 'Father' and 'Mother', for instance), which gives a surprisingly natural and fresh picture of the Aryan scene in the Punjab of the middle of the second millennium B.C. (The syllabic metre is that of the original.)

> We all have various hopes and plans
>   and many are the ways of men:
> The craftsman seeks for jobs to do,
>   the priest his flock, the leech the sick.
>
> The arrow-smith with hard dry reeds
>   and feathers from the airy birds,
> Bronze for the tips, and glowing coals,
>   seeks out the man who'll pay him best.
>
> I am a poet, dad's a leech,
>   and mother grinds corn on the quern:
> As cows go following, one on one,
>   we all seek wealth in different ways.
>
> The horse likes a light-laden cart,
>   gay hosts attract the laugh and jest:
> Man longs for woman, natural as
>   the parched frogs longing for the rains.

Perhaps this could be claimed as the earliest known Indo-European pastoral poem: at all events it gives a glimpse of lost secular poetry in Sanskrit of the early phase, describing the everyday life of the people, that we would do much to recover. But the main purpose behind the *Rigveda* is the sterner stuff of war, and to this we must now turn.

Even though the composition of the hymns is likely to be later, the conditions they reflect are those of victorious conquerors in the first flush of success. The warrior aristocracy, the *Kṣatriyas*, are the heroes, and the great gods are made in their image; Indra is the tutelary god of the soldier, and his exploits are those of the barbarian chieftain leading his followers to victory. We do not then see Aryan warfare from the point of view of the soldier in the ranks – the war-bands included 'hand-to-hand fighters', who are presumably infantry – but from that of the aristocratic warriors who drove to battle in their chariots, and constituted the mobile, light-armoured force.

The fact that Aryan warfare was based on the use of swift, horse-drawn battle-chariots, carrying a warrior armed with a bow and driven by a charioteer, is in itself of very great archaeological importance. Later we shall see that the *Rigveda* descriptions are so detailed that we can form a very good idea of the construction and to a large extent of the appearance of the chariots of the Aryan invaders of India in the middle of the second millennium B.C.; the chariot suits itself to the metaphors of Oriental religions, and such familiar lines as 'His chariots of wrath the deep thunder-clouds form' might come from the *Rigveda* itself. The Harappā civilization, while fully cognizant of wheeled vehicles, does not seem to have made use of them in warfare – indeed, as we have seen, evidence for any military organization for defence or offence within the Harappā empire is strangely lacking – and the Aryan chariots clearly owe nothing to native Indian traditions. They appear as startling innovations, and to trace their ancestry we must look to the west.

Some scholars have claimed that in Western Asia the earliest representation of a wheeled vehicle, that might be a form of chariot, is depicted on a Tell Halaf painted pot, where a human figure stands by a circular object divided by cross-lines in such a manner as to suggest an eight-spoked wheel. If this interpretation is correct, it implies that the accomplished carpentry and wheelwright's craft necessary to produce such a wheel had been evolved on the Khabur River at an extremely early date, which is surely unlikely. The production of a spoked wheel demands good metal tools of a

standard certainly not attained by the hesitant, experi-
mental metallurgy of Tell Halaf times, and I find it difficult
to accept this representation as that of a wheeled vehicle at
all.

But by the beginnings of Early Dynastic times in Sumer
we are on firm ground. 'Scarlet Ware' vessels of E.D.I date
show light two-wheeled chariots with high fronts carrying
one or two people and drawn either by asses or by oxen; the
wheels are represented (very schematically) as solid. And in
the slightly later Early Dynastic reliefs from Ur and Kafajah,
and on the famous inlaid 'Standard' from the Royal Tombs
of Ur, similar ass-drawn chariots are shown in great detail,
with solid wheels made of two half-discs dowelled together
against the hub. (On the 'Standard' the chariots at first
sight appear to be four-wheeled, but, as Sidney Smith has
pointed out, this is the result of a curious Picasso-like technique of representing frontal and lateral views of the same
object in one convention!) Though these chariots doubtless
creaked and rumbled on their clumsy wheels, yet when the
pair of asses was at full speed, as in the final scenes on the
'Standard', they must have been a notable added terror to
the enemies of Sumer when first encountered.

Early in the second millennium similar chariots were in
use in Asia Minor, but with two important modifications:
they have light, spoked wheels and are drawn by a pair of
horses. Such chariots also make their first appearance in the
Aegean countries, significantly associated with Indo-European speakers, soon after this time: in Mainland Greece
before 1500 (to survive, of course, to the Homeric period) and
in Crete about 1450 B.C. A century or so later there is some
evidence to suggest that young Achaean princes were on
occasion sent to the Hittite capital to be trained in chariotry.
In Egypt the earliest representation of such a chariot is of
the time of Amenhotep I, about 1550, at the beginning of
the campaigns of the Eighteenth Dynasty rulers against the

Levant, whence chariot-warfare seems to have been introduced into the Egyptian army. By the end of the fifteenth
century B.C. chariots were being exported to Egypt by the
Mitanni themselves (Fig. 31).

In Central and Northern Europe the appearance of the
chariot among the Indo-European Celts is not attested before the fifth century B.C., in the Middle Rhine and the
Marne (ultimately presumably derived from Western Asia),

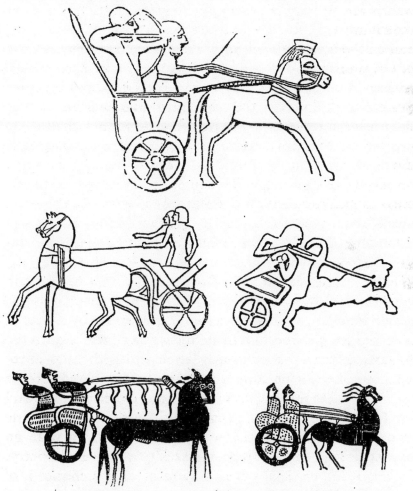

FIG. 31. Representations of chariots, 15th to 13th centuries
B.C., from Zincirli, Egypt, Mycenae and Cyprus

and thereafter we have considerable evidence for its structural features, which confirm its general relationship with
the earlier series from the ancient Orient now under discussion. Sir Cyril Fox's recent brilliant interpretation of the
Celtic evidence has given a lead which may be followed in
examining the oriental material.

It looks, therefore, as if the battle-car was an invention of
Early Dynastic Sumer and that its use was adopted, with
other technological devices, such as metallurgy and the
shaft-hole axe (and probably the heptatonic scale in instrumental music), by the Indo-Europeans on the northerly
fringes of the kingdom of Sumer and Akkad soon after 2000
B.C., given added speed and lightness by the use of horses and
the invention of the spoked wheel, and spread by them in
their expansion to east and west. It remained, of course, an
essential weapon of the armies of Babylonia and Assyria until
well into the first millennium B.C., as a vehicle to carry a
bowman.

The Aryan chariot, as it appears in the *Rigveda*, has a
name (*ratha*) which is an Indo-European 'wheel' word,
represented by the Latin *rota*, Celtic *roth*, Old High German
rad, and Lithuanian *ratas*, and similarly common to the
whole language group are the words for wheel, axle, nave,
and yoke. The body of the chariot is denoted by a word
which is also used for a bucket (*kośa*), and implies a more or
less closed vehicle, unlike the Celtic Iron Age version, open
back and front, but agreeing with the Western Asiatic, Mycenaean, and Egyptian chariots, which (as Sir Cyril Fox has
remarked) are all built on the principle of a modern milk-
float. The material of which this body was built is unknown,
but by analogy it is likely to have been of wicker-work
(Aegean and Celtic chariots), or perhaps leather (as in
Egypt) on a light wooden framework.

To the wooden floor of the chariot was attached the axle,
apparently by leather straps: it would project free of the

chariot body on each side and carried the wheels, secured by lynch-pins on their outer faces – their stability against the fast-spinning wheel is made use of in effective metaphor. On analogy, again, one would expect this axle to be fixed centrally to the chariot floor, as in those of Mycenaean and in the earlier (fourteenth century) reliefs from Malatya in Asia Minor (and, incidentally, in Iron Age Europe); later Assyrian coach-builders' practice moved the axle to the back of the body. The use of lynch-pins is common to the Celtic and the Egyptian chariots and is likely to have been universal, providing as it does a flexible mode of attachment giving stability over rough country, which ensured its retention in English farm carts up to the present time.

The wheels of the Aryan chariot have spokes, though the number is nowhere mentioned. There seems to have been a tendency to increase the number from four (Mycenaean, Egyptian, early Hittite examples) to six or eight (Homeric chariots have eight spokes; Celtic examples with from four to ten or twelve are known: so, too, later Hittite and Assyrian vehicles with six or eight). The importance of the hole of the nave-hub being 'sweetly-running' [on] the axle was recognized and is mentioned. An extremely interesting point with regard to the construction of the wheels, however, is the references to the felloe being bent into shape:

I bend with song, as bends a wright his felloe of solid wood

(VII, 32)

runs the simile, and this must surely imply that the felloe was single-piece, and bent into the circular shape, just as the Celtic chariot-wheels were made. The Egyptian chariot-wheels and probably (to judge by the representations) the Mycenaean examples were not made thus, nor do the later Hittite or Assyrian reliefs suggest this primitive, but extremely strong and light, form of wheel-construction. It presumably needs a fairly large number of spokes to make it function effectively, and might be a pointer to the Aryan wheels having more than four. Its occurrence in the two peripheral areas of Indo-European culture, so remote in time and space, is fascinating, and it still survives in Turkestan. The wheels were shod with metal tyres, as were the Homeric chariots and those of the Iron Age Celts just mentioned.

The horses were harnessed to a single central pole, which, on analogy with known representations, probably rose in a curve from the bottom of the chariot and then continued straight, to meet the yoke almost horizontally. This use of a yoke, a form of harness appropriate to oxen but very unsuitable to a horse (with it, as Contenau put it, 'the capacity of the horse's effort is only equal to its resistance to strangulation'!) is, however, characteristic of the whole ancient world, and the beginnings of the modern type of harnessing and horse-collar is not seen until Roman Imperial times in Europe at the earliest. The yoke is used universally with the chariot, whether in Eighteenth Dynasty Egypt or in Celtic Britain of the first century B.C., and from the *Rigveda* descriptions we can see that in all respects its fastening to the pole is equally typical of Indo-European practice. The problem was to provide a strong yet slightly flexible junction between pole and yoke, to allow for unequal stress whether the animals were pulling or checking, and this was done by providing a stout pin or bolt through the chariot-pole near its far end, against which the wooden yoke was lashed with thongs –

As with the leather thong they bind the chariot yoke to hold
    it fast (x, 60)

and (crossing a river)

So let your wave bear up the pins, and ye, O Waters, spare
    the thongs (III, 33)

as the verses run. It recalls the extant Egyptian example and the description of the yoking of Priam's waggon in the *Iliad* –

The yoke they set firmly on the polished pole, on the rest at the end thereof, and slipped the ring over the upright pin, which with three turns of the strap they lashed to the knob, and then belayed it close round the pole, and turned the tongue thereunder.

There is some evidence for the use of traces on the outer sides, and one word (*vānī*) might have the significance of a swingle-tree or splinter-bar to which these were fastened. Two horses were usually employed, but an additional one or two animals could on occasion be harnessed outside – one is seen, indeed, in such a position on one of the 'Scarlet Ware' scenes mentioned above from Sumer, and the practice was also known in Homeric times.

The chariot held two people, the warrior and his driver. The warrior was on the left, and seems to have been provided with a seat, which he could use at least when he was not actively engaged in warfare. His weapon was a bow and sometimes a spear, but he did not use a sword, at least at the time of the first Aryan advent in India, though a word used for 'knife' in the *Rigveda* takes on the significance of a weapon which might be a sword or a dagger in the *Atharvaveda* and the Epics. The charioteer had no seat provided – one of his titles, *sthātr*, he who stands, emphasizes the distinction between him and the bowman, but his calling was one of honour, and he might be the noble warrior's kinsman, as in Homeric Greece and Iron Age Ireland.

The dimensions of certain parts of the chariot are given, in a rather late text, the *Śulba Sūtra*, in terms of *anguli*, or 'finger's-breadths'. The lengths given are for the pole, the axle, and the yoke, and if these are calculated on the assumption that 16 *anguli* equalled 1 foot (the value usually assumed for the *angula*) it produces a pole nearly 12 feet long, an axle of some 6 feet 6 inches, and a yoke of 5 feet 4 inches, all of which seem strangely large. Now it is possible to estimate certain dimensions of ancient West Asiatic chariots fairly

accurately from a large number of representations, and the
pole length, constantly seen in profile, is always somewhere
between 6 feet and 7 feet 6 inches long. This agrees with the
extant Egyptian chariots (6 feet) and those of Iron Age
Europe (6 feet 6 inches to 7 feet). If we adopt a value for the
angula of $\frac{1}{2}$ inch, we obtain a pole length of about 7 feet 10
inches, and since a word (*praüga*) exists which suggests that
the Aryan pole had a significant projection forward of the

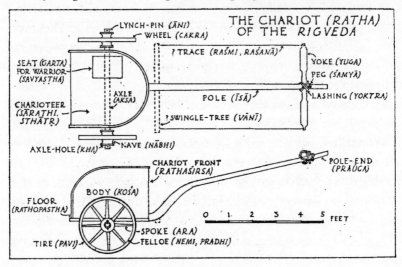

FIG. 32

yoke, this would be very reasonable. Our confidence in it is
increased when we calculate the other dimensions on this
value, and arrive at an axle-length of about 4 feet 6 inches,
and a yoke-width of about 3 feet 6 inches. It is true that the
Egyptian chariot has a wide wheel-base of 6 feet 5 inches,
but the European Iron Age vehicles had what is today the
'standard' gauge of carts in Britain, 4 feet 6 inches to 4 feet
8 inches, and one known in the Mediterranean at least in
the first millennium B.C. Yoke-widths (one Egyptian, two
European Iron Age) vary between 2 feet 8$\frac{1}{2}$ inches and
3 feet 10$\frac{1}{2}$ inches, so one feels strongly that the *Śulba Sūtra*
measurements are in the correct ratio, and that they must be

interpreted on the assumption that, for this purpose at least, the *angula* has a value of about ½ inch, and that the Aryan chariot had the same proportions as those known from material evidence.

The wheel diameter, not given in the Sanskrit text cited, is on analogy likely to have been from 2 feet 6 inches to 3 feet, and the body of the chariot would have risen a similar amount above the axle. Przewalski's horse is a small animal, not more than 12 to 13 hands high, and the extant representations show similarly small horses drawing the Western Asiatic chariots. In Europe the Iron Age horses were as small as 11½ hands at the withers (3 feet 10 inches). These conclusions are embodied in a drawing (Fig. 32) of the likely appearance of the Aryan war-chariot of the middle of the second millennium B.C.

The sum of our enquiries, therefore, is as follows. It has proved possible, by a correlation of the Vedic texts with the evidence of archaeology, to show that the war-chariot of the Aryans in India was essentially the same vehicle as that known from other areas of Indo-European colonization, whether in Mycenaean and Homeric Greece or in Celtic Britain. The chariots from Iron Age Europe and Britain have a slight but significant modification in the open body, which was otherwise built on a U-shaped plan, but in all other features the resemblance is extremely close and often (as in the single-piece felloe, the yoke and its fastening, and perhaps the wheel-base) identical in the two peripheral areas of Britain and India. Coach-builders' and wheel-wrights' practice over the whole intervening area seems to have been substantially the same over a period of something like a thousand years.

Chariot warfare in Aryan India shared with that of most of the Orient the use of the bow as the essential weapon of attack; in Homeric Greece the spear and in Iron Age Europe the long sword became the chosen weapons of the warrior. We know from the *Rigveda* that the bow was kept relaxed until needed, and then strung; the bow-string was a cow-hide thong and it was pulled back to the ear (not, as in Homeric Greece, to the breast). The arrows were tipped with metal, and may have been barbed, and the left wrist was protected from the recoil of the bow-string by a wrist-guard or bracer. But we cannot find decisive evidence of the type of bow – whether in fact it was simple or composite.

The distribution of bow-types among modern primitives and what we know of its early history suggest that there are two main families – simple bows of wood with a mainly African centre of distribution and perhaps origin, and composite bows in which horn and sinew are used to build up a shorter, stiffer bow, which is known on the steppes and Siberia, in Turkey, Persia, and India, and among the North American Eskimo. There is a Danish example dating from the Mesolithic period. The evidence from Crete suggests the adoption of the composite horn-bow by the Minoans at the same time as they acquired the use of the war-chariot, and composite bows in ancient Egypt are confined to one in the Nineteenth Dynasty (the time of the wars with Syria and the adoption of the chariot) and the other as late as the sixth or seventh century B.C. and presumably of Scythian origin.

Representations in Assyria of first millennium date show that bowmen in chariots used a composite bow: its shorter form would be an advantage over the longer simple bow. It is on the whole likely that composite bows of horn and sinew were invented in the Asiatic steppe and may have formed part of the early Indo-European armoury. Such bows may, in fact, have been used by the Aryans in India. Whatever the type, it was a well-loved weapon, with the twang of the bow-string sounding in the warrior's ear like a woman's endearments –

With Bow let us win kine, with Bow in battle, with
  Bow be victory in our hot encounters,
The Bow brings grief and sorrow to the foeman: armed
  with the Bow may we subdue all regions.
Close to his ear, as fain to speak, she presses, holding
  her well-loved friend in her embraces.
Strained on the bow, she whispers like a woman – this
  Bow-string that preserves us in the combat (VI, 75)

The religious beliefs of the Aryans have been the subject
of a literature of their own, and this complex study lies
beyond the scope of this book. We have noted in passing the
anthropomorphic gods Indra, Rudra, the Aşvins, and the
Maruts; the Indo-European sky god, *Dyaus-pitar*, holds a
less important place in the *Rigveda*, as do Mitra and Varuna.
The sun-god Surya and the dawn-goddess Uśas are personi-
fications of natural phenomena, just as Agni is that of fire,
or Soma, the deified intoxicating juice of the unknown
plant on which the gods carouse and on which so much of
Vedic ritual centres. The relationship of the Aryan peoples
to their gods is that of a frank expectation of favours if the
right sacrifices are performed and the correct words chanted,
and Keith rather cynically pictures the priests saying, un-
ashamed, to Indra, 'We have our wishes; you have gifts;
here are we with our songs' and expecting 'that the god will
see that the exchange is fair'.

Ritual is mainly domestic, and centred on the hearth, but
there are various hymns appropriate for ploughing or for
driving cattle to and from pasture, for marriages and for
funerals. There is no evidence that any temples were built,
and the altar is nothing more elaborate than a pile of turf,
but in the animal sacrifices that played an important part in
Vedic ritual the post to which the beast was tied for sacrifice
was set up with considerable ceremony, and there are references in one hymn (III, 8) to what seem to be smaller poles or
stakes set up in lines. The sacrificial post (*yupa*) is addressed –

> Ye whom religious men have firmly planted; thou Forest ·
> Sovran whom the axe has fashioned,
> Let those Stakes divine which here are standing be fain to .
> grant us wealth with store of children.
> O men, who lift the ladles up, these hewed and planted in
> the ground   .
> Bringing a blessing to the field, shall bear our precious gift to
> the gods ...
> Like swans that flee in lengthened line, the Pillars have come
> to us arrayed in bright colours ...
> Those stakes upon the earth with rings that deck them ...

One can only comment, in passing, that the setting up of
sacred posts in lines and circles is a ritual well attested in
Bronze Age Europe among those whose traditions are connected with the battle-axe folk of the South Russian steppes,
and there may be some underlying religious continuity between the two areas within the Indo-European language
groups; and there is another possible point of contact with
regard to burial rites.

The *Rigveda* evidence for burial traditions is almost confined to a single funeral hymn (x, 18). There is reason to
believe that in the early Aryan phase inhumation and cremation were alternative rites existing side by side, though
the latter was soon to become dominant. The hymn describes
an inhumation ceremony in which the warrior's bow is taken
from his hand as he lies in the grave, and he is committed to
Mother Earth with the moving lines —

> Betake thee to the lap of Earth the Mother, of Earth far-
> spreading, very kind and gracious.
> Young Dame, wool-soft unto the guerdon-giver, may she
> preserve thee from destruction's bosom.
> Heave thyself, Earth, nor press thee downward heavily:
> afford him easy access, gently tending him,
> Cover him, as a mother wraps her skirt about her child, O
> Earth.

There is then reference to a standing post erected in connexion with the ceremonies, and earlier there is an enigmatic phrase, 'Here I erect this barrier for the living',
which has been taken by the commentators to imply some
sort of fence around the grave or its covering mound.

The evidence is very slight, but it does imply inhumation
under a mound, with some sort of 'barrier' set between dead
and living. I have, following the views of Peake and others,
suggested that this may be connected not only with the
known practice of setting up ritual timber post-circles round
tumuli in Bronze Age Europe, but also with the monuments
known as *stupas* which suddenly appear in Mauryan and
Sungan times in India (third and second centuries B.C.) as a
part of the Buddhist cult. Many of these have elaborate
stone versions of wooden fences surrounding them, the copying of carpenters' techniques in masonry being so slavish as
to imply that the wooden prototypes were no very distant
memory. It seems generally agreed that the idea of the
stupa, which in its ritual form enshrines a relic, is based on a
burial mound originally covering an interment, and in some
instances at least surrounded by a wooden post-and-rail
fence, and that such prototypes would not be out of place in
what we know of Aryan burial customs. At present we have
no archaeological evidence of such burial mounds (the structures at Lauriya Nandigarh, sometimes claimed as such,
were found to be in fact stupas themselves), and their identification remains among the challenges to Indian archaeology
of future years.

While tangible archaeological evidence of the Aryan conquest of India consists of nothing but the ruins of the cities
they wrecked, with a few flimsy huts that may have been
made by camp-followers after the battle had moved on,
nevertheless we have, I think, been able to piece together a
reasonably coherent picture of some aspects of their material
culture from the *Rigveda*. There remains one outstanding

problem to be discussed – what was the relation between victors and vanquished after the entrance phase of the invasion? Have we any evidence to suggest that the impression so sedulously propagated by the Aryans themselves in their literature, that they conquered utterly the wretched *dasyas* and that all that follows after is the glorious tale of Indra's darlings going on from strength to strength, may be tinged with partisan feeling, to say the least? On the face of it, such extermination is surely improbable. The people the Aryans attacked were not barbarous forest tribes or simple hill-men, but members of an ancient and elaborate civilization that, however unprepared it might be for its violent end, could hardly have vanished away without tingeing profoundly the thoughts and literature of the conquerors. It is unlikely that the Mycenaean bards had much good to say of the Minoans, but we know enough of ancient history to realize that the Indo-European strain is not the only one that combined to form the eventual pattern of Greek life and thought.

Since the discovery of the Harappā Culture it has been recognized that many elements in medieval and modern Hinduism which cannot be traced to an Aryan source are, in fact, foreshadowed in what we know, by inference, of the religious cults of the older civilization. There is no need to elaborate this point, which has been demonstrated in detail and has won general acceptance. Clearly, after the first drastic 'Aryanization' of the Punjab, some sort of *modus vivendi* was arrived at; if not there, eastwards in the Ganges Basin as the frontier receded eastwards, and Harappā ideas permeated the religious thought of the Brahmans. If we are right in thinking that the Harappā civilization, like most of its contemporaries in Western Asia, was largely priest-ruled, the growth in power of the Brahmans over the Kṣatriyas, which is a commonplace of Vedic evolution, might fall naturally into its place as a phenomenon arising from a blending of the two cultural traditions. In the *Rigveda* the

priests, though important, do not seem to hold a very dominating position in society. And if we accept (as we must) the
Harappā influence on religious thought, can we not expect
to see a similar mixture in other realms of human activity?

The Dark Ages of India in the second half of the first millennium B.C. are suddenly illuminated, round about 300
B.C., by light from the West. Megasthenes, a Greek at the
court of the first of the great sovereigns of the Mauryan
dynasty, Chandragupta Maurya, wrote an objective account
of the civilization in which he found himself, which has survived in fragments. He presents a picture of a regime which
had established control over a large part of Northern India
at least: fully literate, urban, highly organized, and ruling
from an impressive citadel within a great walled town at
Pataliputra on the Ganges. The state is held together by a
powerful army, with a war office divided into six departments, dealing respectively with cavalry, infantry, light mobile armour (chariots), heavy armour (elephants), quartermaster's stores and maintenance of war engines, and finally
liaison with the naval forces. No less elaborately organized is
the civil service, which has a ministry of agriculture and
public works controlling road construction, irrigation canals,
mines, forests, land taxes, and big-game hunting. The city
council, subdivided like the war office into six departments,
deals with industry, weights and measures, registration of
births and deaths, control of state shops, collection of sales
tax, and the supervision of the affairs of foreign visitors.
The king, who succeeds by patrilineal right, leads the army,
which includes infantry equipped with 6-foot bows and
others with slashing swords; there are some Buddhists, but
essentially the picture is one of a Hindu society.

There is surely something very familiar in this startling
picture of an authoritarian regime, with its power over so
large a tract of India: the control of manufactures, and of
weights and measures; the elaborate city civilization, with

its centralized government – the picture we can reconstruct from the evidence of the Harappā civilization is, after all, not so dissimilar. The Mauryan empire may be the result of indigenous evolution of the Aryan tradition, from the humble beginnings in the log cabins of the West to this sophisticated bureaucratic state a thousand years later, but can we ignore altogether the other, more ancient, urban tradition of India which the Aryans found? Chandragupta Maurya was not a foreigner, no invader such as Harṣa or Babur, coming in from the north-west to impose his will on the Indian people, but a product of a long tradition within India itself; he must have based his rule on long-established custom, in which was blended the ancient civic tradition of Harappā, with its bureaucracy and mercantile organization, and the more barbarous but invigorating Aryan warrior-caste which could make the state strong against its enemies and implant something to offset the fatal tendency to stagnation and decay that had been Harappā's downfall.

Perhaps it would be too much to say that Chandragupta Maurya and his dynasty were the ghosts of the Harappā Empire sitting crowned on the ruins thereof, or to claim, in Toynbee's phrase, that the Harappā kingdom was 'apparented' to that of the Mauryas. But to the complex pattern of the Indian Middle Ages the ancient urban civilization of the Punjab and the Indus surely contributed not a little. And this was a contribution not only in the sphere of religious speculation or in traditions of ritual and ceremonial observances: the whole character of medieval Hindu society and the structure of its polity and government seem inevitably a reflection of the Bronze Age civilization of Sind and the Punjab.

Notes to Chapter VII

The literature on the Aryans is enormous, but the best general accounts are in *Cambridge History of India*, Vol. 1; V. G. Childe,

The Aryans (1926); Masson-Oursel, etc., *Ancient India and Indian Civilization* (trans. Dobie, 1934); L. de la Vallée Poussin, *Indo-européens et Indo-iraniens* ... (1936); C. S. Coon, *Races of Europe* (1939). My basis for the *Rigveda* evidence has been A. A. Macdonell and A. B. Keith, *Vedic Index of Names and Subjects* (two vols., 1912) supplemented by R. T. H. Griffith's translation, *Hymns of the Rigveda* (1896); for the religious aspect, A. B. Keith, *Religion and Philosophy of the Veda* (Harvard Oriental Series, Vols. 31–32, 1925). The Indo-European tradition is discussed by Myles Dillon in *Trans. Philolog. Soc.*, 1947, 15–24; *Proc. Brit. Acad.* xxxiii (1947) (Rhys Memorial Lecture).

For Maikop and the South Russian cultures, see V. G. Childe, *The Dawn of European Civilization* (1939); and C. Schaeffer, *Stratigraphie Comparée* (1948); the evidence for the Aryan destruction of Harappā is discussed by R. E. M. Wheeler, *Ancient India*, no. 3 (1947), 82. For ploughs in Western Asia, C. W. Bishop in *Antiquity* x (1936), 261; horses, W. Ridgeway, *Origin and Influence of the Thoroughbred Horse* (1905); carts, *Reallexikon der Vorgeschichte*, s.v. Wagen, Djebjerg, Ohnenheim; Tacitus, *Germania* xl. The heptatonic scale is discussed by F. W. Galpin, *The Music of the Sumerians* (1937) and by E. C. Curwen, *Antiquity* xiv (1940), 347. The basic lines on which the study of the chariots must proceed are given by Sir Cyril Fox, *A Find of the Early Iron Age from Llyn Cerrig Bach* (1947) (European Iron Age evidence); for early Mesopotamian representations, V. G. Childe, *New Light on the Most Ancient East* (1934); for the Orient and the Aegean, Sir Arthur Evans, *Palace of Minos*, iv, 809; for Egypt and Homeric evidence, W. Ridgeway, *op. cit.*, and assistance from Miss Lorimer acknowledged in the preface. Bows are commented on by Evans, *Palace of Minos* ii, 48; iv, 832; *Reallexikon*, s.v. Bogen; *Journ. Anthrop. Inst.*, xix (1890), 220; xxiv (1895), 51; xxvi (1897), 210.

I have discussed the antecedents of the stupa in *Antiquity* xvii (1943), 1. The account of Megasthenes is conveniently accessible in McCrindle, *Ancient India* (1877), 86, and the remains of Mauryan Pataliputra are described and illustrated in *Ancient India* no. 4, 95–103.

INDEX

Philip Glasier

THE AUTHOR

Stuart Piggott was born in 1910 and is the holder of the Abercromby Chair of Prehistoric Archaeology in the University of Edinburgh. Until 1942 his original work had been confined to research and excavations in Europe and Britain. In the intervals of Military Intelligence duties during the war, however, he had the opportunity of making a first-hand detailed study of the archaeology of prehistoric India in museums and in the field. He has continued work on certain aspects of Oriental prehistory since, though European studies now claim most of his attention.

In addition to numerous papers in archaeological journals, his publications include *British Prehistory* and *William Stukeley: an 18th-Century Antiquary.*